GATHERED BY LOVE

GATHERED BY LOVE

Worship Resources for Year C

L AVON B AYLER

United Church Press
Cleveland, Ohio

United Church Press, Cleveland, Ohio 44115

© 1994 by United Church Press

Printed in the United States of America on acid-free paper

99 98   5 4 3 2

Library of Congress Cataloging-in-Publication Data

Bayler, Lavon, 1933–
    Gathered by love : worship resources for year C / Lavon Bayler.
        p.   cm.
    Includes indexes.
    ISBN 0-8298-1008-0
    1. Church year.   2. Worship programs.   I. Title.
BV30.B38   1994
264—dc20
                                          94-35081
                                          CIP

TO SARAH ELIZABETH,
DAUGHTER OF DAVID
AND JENNIFER,
WHO IS TEACHING US
NEW WAYS TO LOVE.

C o n t e n t s

Introduction ix

W O R S H I P R E S O U R C E S

The Advent Season 3
The Christmas Season 13
Epiphany and the Season Following 29
The Lenten Season 53
The Easter Season 83
Pentecost and the Season Following 103
Special Days 163

R E L A T E D H Y M N S

The Advent Season 169
The Christmas Season 179
Epiphany and the Season Following 195
The Lenten Season 221
The Easter Season 249
Pentecost and the Season Following 265
Special Days 303

I N D E X E S

Alphabetical Index of Hymns 308
Topical Index of Hymns 310
Index of Scripture Readings 327
Index of Themes and Key Words 333

About the Author 346

Introduction

Every Sunday (or Sabbath day), we are gathered by love to sit at the feet of Jesus. John's gospel asserts that God is love, and Luke brings that loving spirit into sharp focus through the parables and healing acts of Jesus that he reports. The Gospel of Luke is central to year C of the *Revised Common Lectionary*. As we journey with him through the life of Jesus, we are reminded of our call to be a loving, healing force in the world.

During the first half of the year, Advent through the Easter season, the first suggested reading is usually from one of the Old Testament prophets. It is intended to illuminate the gospel text. The psalm is chosen to be a congregational response to or meditation on this first reading. Increasingly, churches are recovering the ancient practice of singing the psalm. For the second selection, a number of New Testament epistles are visited, including semicontinuous readings from 1 Corinthians and Revelation.

After Pentecost, the revised lectionary presents us with new options. Either we follow a somewhat chronological reading from the prophets, highlighting Jeremiah, or we choose the traditional Roman pattern of paired readings from throughout the Jewish Scriptures, chosen for their close relationship to the gospel. In this book, we list all suggested scriptures, but our main focus is on the first option. Please note that each pattern has its own consistency, so worship planners using the lectionary should decide to follow one track or the other. To shift back and forth will bring repetition or omission of important texts over the three-year cycle. The last half of the church year C also features semicontinuous readings from Galatians, Colossians, 1 and 2 Timothy, and 2 Thessalonians.

For each occasion in year C, this book provides a call to worship, invocation, call to confession, prayer of confession, assurance of forgiveness, collect, offertory invitation, offertory prayer, commission and blessing, and at least one new hymn text related to one or more of the day's scriptural readings. It is suggested that persons preparing for worship employ these writings in their daily devotions as they read and meditate on the Scriptures. If some of the prayers or responsive readings are chosen for the public liturgy, permission for reprinting is granted on the copyright page at the front of the book. Your own creativity is encouraged.

Just as more material is provided for each week than can be used, there are worship resources for more weeks than will occur in any given year. Part of the Epiphany season and/or the season after Pentecost will be omitted every year, depending on the date of Easter. A late Easter lengthens Epiphany and shortens the Pentecost season. An early Easter means that Lent begins earlier, thus reducing the number of Epiphany Sundays.

The indexes—the part of the book most time-consuming to prepare—will make the resources of this volume readily accessible to those who prefer to do thematic worship planning rather than follow the lectionary. Of special assistance are the topical index of hymns and the index of themes and key words.

Having been gathered by love, we are sent back to our everyday world to share love, not as a sentimental feeling but in caring actions. Whether through caring listening, tough decision making, or creative confrontation of problems, we seek to be faithful followers of the one who embodied God's love all the way to the cross. May the words of worship inspire deeds of discipleship.

Worship Resources

THE ADVENT SEASON

Jeremiah 33:14–16   Luke 21:25–36
Psalm 25:1–10   I Thessalonians 3:9–13

CALL TO WORSHIP

The days are surely coming, says our God,
when justice and righteousness will appear.
> **God's promises will be made known to us,**
> **and we will declare God's goodness and salvation.**

Lift up your souls in trust and praise;
open your hearts and minds to God's teaching.
> **God's ways will be demonstrated to us,**
> **and we will seek to walk in them all our days.**

Render thanksgiving to God for all life's benefits.
Watch and pray, in holiness and abiding faith.
> **God's mercy and steadfast love will surround us,**
> **and we will abound in love for one another.**

INVOCATION

In obedience and trust, we approach you, God of the covenant. Day by day, your promises are fulfilled among us. Our redemption is drawing near. Help us to prepare ourselves and our communities for Christ's coming. Equip us now to worship you with all the saints, past and present, nearby and far away. Amen.

CALL TO CONFESSION

A new church year is dawning. An air of anticipation challenges us to fresh beginnings. Are we weighed down by the cares of life? Are we deceptive and untrustworthy? Do we project on others our own destructive habits? This is a time to rid ourselves of old ways and embrace the newness God offers.

PRAYER OF CONFESSION

God of promises and possibilities, we admit that we color the world according to our own limited vision. We are often unjust in our judgments and faithless in our relationships. We are haunted by sins we have not confessed. Hear us as we entrust them to your forgiving care. Help us to let go of our transgressions, to renew our covenant with you, and to live constructively with one another. In the spirit of Jesus Christ, whose coming among us we await with great expectation. Amen.

Assurance of Forgiveness

The mercy of God is new every day. We are free to accept the difference it can make in us. God's steadfast love is waiting to embrace us as whole people, to instruct us and to lead us in the paths of truth. Put your trust in God, for that is our only security.

Collect

Direct our attention, O God, above the turmoil of our times, beyond the distress of human greed. We look for signs that your realm is near, that your Word rules the world. Free us from the weight of heavy cares to bear your joyous truth into our relationships. Join us together in a spirit of thanksgiving and earnest prayer. Amen.

Offertory Invitation

As our love for one another increases and abounds, so does our generosity. The circle of our concern widens. Our passion for justice expands. Our desire to join in Christ's redeeming work extends to the whole human family. What a privilege to have so much to share!

Offertory Prayer

Thank you, God, for this family of faith, which enriches our lives and enables us to share. Thank you for making us aware that some faint with fear and others dwell in hopelessness. We are grateful that you show us ways to lift the burdens of our sisters and brothers. May our offerings further this ministry among us and beyond our community. Amen.

Commission and Blessing

Watch and pray, seeking the strength Christ offers.
Live as thankful stewards of all God's gifts.
> *Our souls are lifted up to trust in God;*
> *our spirits rejoice to learn God's ways.*
Those who are humble will discern new paths.
For God is teaching us, day by day.
> *Secure in God's love, we venture with confidence.*
> *We are willing to try a new way of being.*
God's steadfast love never fails;
God will keep covenant and lead us in all truth.
> *We will look for signs that God's realm is near;*
> *we will rely on God's Word to guide us.*
Amen. **Amen.**

(See hymns 1, 2.)

Malachi 3:1–4   Philippians 1:3–11
Luke 1:68–79   Luke 3:1–6

CALL TO WORSHIP

Listen! Listen for a messenger from God.
The way is being prepared for Christ's coming.
> *We are here to listen for a word from God.*
> *We have gathered to prepare for Christ's advent.*
Come with your joys and sorrows, laughter and tears.
There is a place for you in the company of seekers.
> *We thank God for our acceptance in the church.*
> *We rejoice to offer the love of Christ to others.*
We are partners in the gospel of Jesus Christ.
Claim anew today this opportunity and responsibility.
> *We are glad God is doing great things among us.*
> *We want to rejoin ourselves to God's work in the world.*

INVOCATION

How good it is to gather where garments of sorrow and affliction are removed.
Here, we are wrapped in the beauty of God's glory and welcomed to life at its
fullest. Surely you restore us to our best, mighty God, and equip us for productive
living. Make a difference within and among us today so we can work for a better
tomorrow. Amen.

CALL TO CONFESSION

We come before the refiner's fire, that all falseness and impurities may be burned
away. Beneath all the pretense and brokenness of our lives, God helps us to
discover pure silver and gold. We are highly valued by our Maker. Let us be fully
open to God's forgiving spirit.

PRAYER OF CONFESSION

O God, we have tried to cover up our sins, yet you know the disorder we have
caused in our lives. You have witnessed our poor choices and our destructive
habits. We have denied our baptism and ignored the responsibilities of discipleship.
The good we do is often self-serving, while we avoid the full claims of gospel
partnership. Hear our cries of repentance and turn our lives around, that we may
know the wonder of your forgiveness. Amen.

ASSURANCE OF FORGIVENESS

Good news! God has done great things for us. We are loved; we are forgiven; we are claimed by God's grace. The Holy One has begun a good work in us. Even now, the love of God is expanding our knowledge, sharpening our discernment, and equipping us for excellence. Go and bear fruit.

COLLECT

God of the prophets, whose salvation is freely offered to all flesh, open our imagination to participate in these moments in the study of your truth. May ancient words hold for us a fresh message that engages our best efforts. Straighten the crooked ways and smooth out the rough places in our lives that we may be about the same ministry in the world. Amen.

OFFERTORY INVITATION

What is a fitting offering that is pleasing to God? When we sense the wonder of God's majesty and realize the amazing extent of God's concern for us, we can only respond with all that we have and all we are. What we place on the altar is a small measure of our gratitude.

OFFERTORY PRAYER

How good you have been to us, gracious God! How meagerly we have responded. You have restored our fortunes when we felt all was lost. You have filled our mouths with laughter and our tongues with shouts of joy. We give thanks, not only with a portion of our income, but also through renewed commitment to righteous living. By your grace, we share in the work Christ came to accomplish among us. May love abound in and through us. Amen.

COMMISSION AND BLESSING

Remember those messengers of the faith you have known;
rejoice and give thanks for their witness.
> *We, too, will prepare the way of Christ;*
> *we will help to level the hills and valleys.*
Hold one another in your hearts day by day;
pray that love may rule all your relationships.
> *We will weep with those who weep.*
> *We will rejoice with those who rejoice.*
God will be with you wherever you go;
the good work begun in you will be brought to completion.
> *All flesh will see the salvation of our God;*
> *we will live in covenant with our Creator.*
Amen. **Amen.**

(See hymns 3, 6.)

Zephaniah 3:14–20   Philippians 4:4–7
Isaiah 12:2–6   Luke 3:7–18

CALL TO WORSHIP

Rejoice, give thanks; call on God's name;
the Holy One is in our midst.
> *How good it is to come home to God's house!*
> *How good it is to gather in Christ's presence!*

Sing aloud! Exult with all your heart;
the Sovereign One has done glorious things.
> *We offer up our anxieties, seeking God's peace.*
> *We face our plenty, eager to share.*

Shout your praise! Express your joy!
The God of our salvation welcomes us.
> *God's love is renewing us in these moments;*
> *God's strength is becoming our song!*

INVOCATION

God of our baptism, renew in us today the gifts of your Holy Spirit and fire. We have come together, eager for good news. We are here for instructions, ready to do the work you call us to do in the world. Equip us in this time of worship to draw deeply from the waters of salvation. Fill us with your love that we may pass it on. Recall us to truth and excellence and justice in all we say and do. Amen.

CALL TO CONFESSION

Every tree that fails to bear good fruit is cut down and thrown in the fire. We cannot flee from our unfaithfulness. But we can reclaim our baptism and seek once more to bear fruits that befit repentance.

PRAYER OF CONFESSION

What shall we do, O God? We can never do enough to deserve your love. We confess that we are not always truthful. We have defaced the purity of your love for us. We have embraced ugliness and oppression rather than loveliness and grace. We have distorted your cries for justice in order to benefit ourselves. We have given less than our best to others and to you. Forgive us, we pray. Amen.

Assurance of Forgiveness

God has taken away the judgments against us. The evil we have feared cannot triumph. The enemies we have harbored in our own souls will no longer oppress us. Disasters we have experienced are not the last word. God restores us to the family, welcomes us with open arms, and strengthens us for each day's challenges. Praise God, give thanks, and let the world know of God's marvelous deeds.

Collect

God of life and love, whose good news often comes in strange packages, open our eyes and ears to see and hear your message. Open our hearts to embrace one another in our caring. Help us to share generously and to receive graciously the gifts we have received from your hand. Guide us to honest, peaceful, joyous relationships, that your will may be done among us. Amen.

Offertory Invitation

Whether we face plenty or hunger, abundance or want, we are in debt to God for all we have and all we are. In these moments of thankfulness, we remember how God has blessed us. We give with joy because we trust the God of our salvation.

Offertory Prayer

We rejoice, O God of peace, in the privilege of giving without fear. You come to us daily with blessings too numerous to count. You are the Holy One whose presence relieves our anxieties, feeds our hungers, and stirs our compassion. Through our offerings, we express our gratitude. As we give of ourselves, we respond to your call to bear fruit and to make your name known among the nations. Thank you for accepting all we offer. Amen.

Commission and Blessing

The whole universe is God's dwelling place.
Find your home with God wherever you go.
> *Surely God is our salvation;*
> *we will trust and not be afraid.*

Rejoice, for Christ has come and is coming,
whose presence brings peace to our hearts and minds.
> *We can do all things in Christ, who strengthens us.*
> *We have much to share with the world.*

God, who has blessed you, commissions you for service.
Shout and sing for joy; praise God in all you do.
> *God has renewed and refreshed us this day.*
> *God's strength will be our song wherever we go.*

Amen. **Amen.**

(See hymns 4, 5, 6.)

Micah 5:2–5a   Hebrews 10:5–10
Psalm 80:1–7   Luke 1:39–55

CALL TO WORSHIP

Before the majesty of God, we gather to worship;
in quiet expectation, we come to hear God's promises.
> *This is where we belong; here we are warmly greeted.*
> *Surely God will feed our deepest hunger.*

Before God's strength and power, we bow down;
in hesitant anticipation, we listen for God's judgment.
> *This is our home, where our lives are redirected.*
> *Surely God will show us new ways to live.*

Before the mercy of God, we lift our hearts;
in humble imagination, we welcome a new visitation.
> *This day God is present with us; we feel it.*
> *Surely God is preparing for us a time of joy.*

INVOCATION

Let your face shine on us, mighty God. Break through the obstacles that keep us
from seeing your way. Melt down the barriers that keep us from knowing the
embrace of your love. Remove from us the low self-esteem that keeps us from
valuing the overwhelming gift of life that you entrust to us. Speak to us here in
life-changing accents. Amen.

CALL TO CONFESSION

We do not like to think that God might be angry with us. Yet, we know the
emptiness of our prayers, the greed of our consumption, the limits of our compassion. God understands more profoundly than we our failure to become the people
we are intended to be. In silent reflection, be open to the wisdom and forgiveness
of the Creator.

PRAYER OF CONFESSION

Merciful God, when we sense who you are, we are ashamed. How do you tolerate
our pettiness? The abundance you have given us has made us proud more than
thankful. We act as if our accomplishments were all our own doing. We seldom
acknowledge your generosity or let you rule our lives. We go through the forms of
worship, but we try to keep you at a safe distance. We fill our lives with status-
producing activity that blocks out your call and limits our response. O God, we
need to change. Will you help us? Amen.

ASSURANCE OF FORGIVENESS

Those who allow themselves to know God are already in touch with God's mercy. It is newly experienced every day. It is available to the least of us and the greatest. All whose spirits hunger for God discover how richly they have been fed. God has been doing great things for us. Let us commit the bodies God has given us to doing God's will. May our spirits rejoice as we magnify our God together.

COLLECT

Holy God, whose coming to us in Jesus Christ we celebrate with joy and whose mercy is from generation to generation, visit us today to restore our memory of all your goodness to us. Trample our vanities and lift up our crushed and timid spirits so we all can participate fully and equally in the inheritance we have received from your hand. Amen.

OFFERTORY INVITATION

In this season, we remember the greatest offering of all time, God's gift of salvation in Jesus Christ. The only appropriate response is our giving of ourselves. What we place on the altar today symbolizes the depth of our commitment. May we show how thankful we are.

OFFERTORY PRAYER

Thank you, God, for your mercy and protection, for feeding us physically and spiritually, for caring for us like a shepherd. We present our offerings as an act of gratitude. What we can never repay we pause to appreciate. In the name of generosity we cannot match, we seek to be generous toward others. May these offerings do far more than support our church. We dedicate ourselves and these gifts to honor Christ through ministry in the world. Amen.

COMMISSION AND BLESSING

Depart from this place to do God's will.
Carry your discipleship and service into the world.
> *Our spirits rejoice in God's saving grace.*
> *Our lives have been equipped to meet the world.*
Greet strangers as you have been greeted here.
Feed them as you have been fed by a living God.
> *Our estrangement has been overcome.*
> *We want to welcome neighbors into God's family.*
God's mercy continues from generation to generation.
You are accepted and loved and sent forth.
> *In gratitude and joy we accept our commission.*
> *Our spirits rejoice to share good news.*
Amen. **Amen.**

(See hymns 7, 8.)

THE CHRISTMAS SEASON

CHRISTMAS EVE/DAY
(PROPER I)—A, B, C

Isaiah 9:2–7   Titus 2:11–14
Psalm 96   Luke 2:1–14, (15–20)

CALL TO WORSHIP

Let the heavens be glad, and let the earth rejoice.
The grace of God has come to save us.
> *For our sakes, God sent the child of Bethlehem.*
> *For our salvation, Jesus came to live among us.*

Let all people sing for joy and give thanks.
Tell the world what God has done in our midst.
> *God has called and chosen us to hear good news.*
> *God's marvelous works are new every morning.*

Glory to God in the highest.
Peace on earth to all who please God.
> *We seek to honor God in this time of worship.*
> *We want to see for ourselves what God has done.*

INVOCATION

Out of deep shadows, we are attracted to your brightness, Glorious God. From the trauma of life's battles, we are drawn to the peace you alone can provide. Away from our irreligion and worldly passions, you invite us to center our lives in you. Come, Holy One, to reign among us. Bring the joy we cannot know apart from you. Lead us in the ways of justice and righteousness that you intend. Establish among us your marvelous works that we might declare them to a waiting world. Amen.

CALL TO CONFESSION

The arrival of a baby recalls to us the preciousness of life. We stand in awe before one who is helpless and dependent and thereby realize once more our own vulnerability. Before the purity of the child, our sins are exposed. At the manger, we are driven to our knees.

PRAYER OF CONFESSION

God of the commonplace, we confess that we have been impressed by power and authority. We do not expect to meet you in the poor of the land, in cold barns, or on lonely duty watches. We are slow to hear the angels or to embrace the "good news of great joy." We hesitate to leave our chosen tasks to share in your larger purposes. We settle for idols of material security even as you thrust us into the battles of life, where we have nothing on which to rely other than our faith in you. Forgive our lack of trust. Renew us in the Holy Spirit, we pray. Amen.

ASSURANCE OF FORGIVENESS

The grace of God has appeared for the salvation of all. Do not be afraid. This is a day for good news of great joy. The Savior is born anew in our midst. Glory to God in the highest! Praise God for all we are seeing and hearing, as love is made known among us.

COLLECT

God of mangers and palaces, of shepherds and kings, reveal yourself to us here in the mystery and magic of the season. Free us to see the signs of your promise and hear the whispers of good news. May we join the songs of joy that proclaim to the world your presence among us. We would glorify and praise you in ways that might convince the world of your grace and transform us all according to your love. Amen.

OFFERTORY INVITATION

We are a people chosen for good deeds. Together we can accomplish much as we bring our offerings into God's courts. Through our sharing, God brings a new day to many. Let our offerings be an expression of thanksgiving for the incarnation, for the peace God gives, for the joy that is ours today.

OFFERTORY PRAYER

Thank you, God, for coming to us in a human life so expressive of love that two thousand years have not extinguished the flame. May that love burn so brightly in our lives that its fires will spread. Use our offerings to ignite in the world such caring and compassion that all your children may know joy and peace, in Jesus' name. Amen.

COMMISSION AND BLESSING

Walk no more in gloom and shadows.
The light of Christ will shine within and among us.
We will look to that light on life's journey.
The one called Wonderful Counselor walks with us.
Lift one another's burdens and sing together for joy.
The grace of God has appeared to save us.
We will center our lives on Jesus Christ.
God calls us to faithfulness and good deeds.
Carry the peace of Christ into the world.
Glorify and praise God in all you do.
We will tell of what we have seen and heard.
The good news of great joy is for all people.
Amen. **Amen.**

(See hymns 9, 10, 11.)

Isaiah 62:6–12   Titus 3:4–7
Psalm 97   Luke 2:(1–7), 8–20

CALL TO WORSHIP

Enter God's holy courts rejoicing and singing.
The goodness and loving kindness of God have appeared.
Good news of great joy has come to all people.
To us is born this day a Savior, Christ the sovereign.
We are a holy people, redeemed by God.
We are a sought-after community, called into service.
God reigns in our midst, in justice and righteousness.
God is lighting the way for us to learn and give care.
We are heirs of hope, justified by God's grace.
Eternal life has become a living reality here and now.
Glory to God in the highest; all glory to God's name.
May God be pleased with us and grant us peace!

INVOCATION

Thank you, God, for calling us back to remember the heritage of faith in which our lives have found meaning. We praise you for calling us out of the world to rediscover the values that give purpose to our everyday lives. Restore us to our spiritual foundations in this time of worship. When we consider who you are, we tremble before your majesty. How dare we ignore you here or when we depart from this place? Find us here, we pray, that we may discover anew our own true center. Amen.

CALL TO CONFESSION

God loves those who hate evil. But we have become so complacent about evil that we do not recognize it in ourselves or in the structures of our society. Our tolerance for idolatry has multiplied, to drown out the voice of our Creator. Let us examine ourselves before the God of the universe.

PRAYER OF CONFESSION

Let your glory shine on us, loving God, so we can see ourselves as we really are. We pursue dubious pleasures that tear down and destroy the best that we know. We worship the gods of technology, consuming far more than our share of the world's resources. Our individualism flies in the face of long-term commitments and genuine community. We need radical regeneration, but we are not sure that we really want it. O God, save us from ourselves. Amen.

ASSURANCE OF FORGIVENESS (TITUS 3:4–7)

When the goodness and loving kindness of God, our Savior, appeared, we were saved; not because of any works of righteousness that we have done, but according to God's own mercy, through the washing of rebirth and renewal by the Holy Spirit. This Spirit God poured out on us richly through Jesus Christ our Savior, so that having been justified by God's grace, we might become heirs according to the hope of eternal life.

COLLECT

God of glory, you have met us all in unexpected places, just as you encountered the shepherds in the fields where they worked. Reveal yourself to us in this time of worship and attune us to your appearing so we will not miss your communication with us in the midst of our daily activities. May the prompting of your spirit move us to glorify and praise you in ways that attract our friends to the new life you offer. Amen.

OFFERTORY INVITATION

The gift in the manger—unexpected, vulnerable, dependent—prompts our giving. What shall we offer in thanksgiving for our lives? What is a worthy offering of gratitude for the new life in Christ that is entrusted to us? Let us respond to the goodness and loving kindness of our God.

OFFERTORY PRAYER

Here, O God, is a portion of the riches you entrust to our management. At best, it is the first fruits of our labors, set aside to support your mission through and beyond our church. You have asked us to clear the highways of stones so our brothers and sisters can find their way to your side. In providing a way for them, we, too, see your pathways more clearly. Help us to walk in your paths as we dedicate ourselves with our offerings. Amen.

COMMISSION AND BLESSING

Go back to all your circles of work, play, and home.
Praise and glorify God for all you have received.
> *Thanks be to God for rescuing us from our enemies.*
> *Praise God for saving us from ourselves.*
Build concern for other people into your daily ministry.
Take time for yourself to meet God in prayer.
> *Let all the earth rejoice in God's love and care.*
> *Let the redeemed of God respond each day to God's call.*
Good news of great joy is yours to enjoy and share.
Light dawns and joy abounds for the upright of heart.
> *Glory to God in the highest, and peace on earth.*
> *We will pass on to others what we have seen and heard.*
Amen. **Amen.**

(See hymns 12, 13.)

Isaiah 52:7–10   Hebrews 1:1–4, (5–12)
Psalm 98   John 1:1–14

CALL TO WORSHIP

Break forth into singing, all God's people.
Hear the good tidings of salvation and peace!
> **God has done marvelous things among us.**
> **Let us make a joyful noise together.**

There is a new song in the air.
The whole universe responds to the child in our midst.
> **The winds lift up the songs of angels.**
> **Flames of fire proclaim the spirit's presence.**

A light shines amid our gloom.
The Word comes to make a difference in our lives.
> **As children of God, we bear witness to the light.**
> **As followers of Christ, we proclaim the wonder of rebirth.**

INVOCATION

God of the prophets, we hear you speaking again in the word made flesh. Help us to listen with awe and wonder and to look with seeing eyes for your presence right here, right now. We praise you with horn and lyre and trumpet. We lift our voices in joyous response to your message of peace. Enlighten us in ways that change us and transform our world, for we want to live as your faithful children. Grant us your peace, that we may be peacemakers. Amen.

CALL TO CONFESSION

God comes to judge the world with righteousness and equity. The light God brings reveals the shadows in which we live. Before the purity of the word made flesh, our sins are exposed. We want to be rid of them. Let us pray for forgiveness.

PRAYER OF CONFESSION

O God, you reign over all creation, yet we have tried to reduce you to the limits of our understanding. You have come to enlighten us, and we have shielded ourselves from the brightness of your revelation. You have a plan for us, but we have altered and defaced the blueprints. Only in Jesus Christ do we see what you have intended for us. Forgive us and help us to sing a new song. Amen.

ASSURANCE OF FORGIVENESS

Victory and vindication! God has done marvelous things. With steadfast love and faithfulness, God reigns among us, opening to each of us exciting possibilities for fulfillment and joy. Let the floods clap their hands and the hills sing together. The whole universe witnesses to the Word that is light and life. May the grace and truth of Jesus Christ transform us and make us whole.

COLLECT

Word of God, shine among us, live within us, enlighten the world through the witness you empower us to make. We who believe proclaim your sovereignty and accept your reign. May your rule so discipline our decisions and our actions that your presence and power will be manifest in our lives. Amen.

OFFERTORY INVITATION

Our world is meant to be the place of God's dominion. God chooses us as partners in establishing the reign of righteousness and peace. Who will receive the Word because of what we share today for the work of our church in the world? Who will know God's love and faithfulness tomorrow because we live close to them as children of light?

OFFERTORY PRAYER

No offering is adequate to express our thanks, loving God, but what we give, we bring with joy. May the good tidings of salvation live in these gifts and in our lives. May the ends of the earth know the steadfast love of God. Grant comfort to those who mourn, peace to those who face the world's turmoil, and joy to all who serve in Christ's name. Amen.

COMMISSION AND BLESSING

In many and various ways, God speaks to us.
Listen for the Word as this day of blessing continues.
> *Eye to eye and ear to ear, we will be alert*
> *to see and hear the good tidings from God.*
Share what you observe and give voice to your joy.
Sing praises to God who reigns among us.
> *We will clap our hands and raise our voices,*
> *for we are heirs with Christ to all good things.*
Bear witness to the light that is God's gift.
Live as children of God; this is your heritage.
> *We will welcome the Word in our homes,*
> *for God empowers new life in our families.*
Amen. **Amen.**

(See hymns 14, 15.)

I Samuel 2:18–20, 26   Colossians 3:12–17
Psalm 148   Luke 2:41–52

CALL TO WORSHIP

Men and women, old and young, together:
Praise God and exalt the Author of Life.
> *Praise God in the highest heavens.*
> *Praise God, all dwellers on the earth.*

God commanded, and we were created.
God sustains us and enables us to grow.
> *Praise God, all who seek to live in faithfulness.*
> *Glorify God's name and join the loving community.*

Know that we are chosen by God, holy and beloved.
We are called into one body, the church of Jesus Christ.
> *Let us draw close to God and to one another.*
> *Let us join with all creation to worship God.*

INVOCATION

Height and breadth, length and depth, the whole universe proclaims your glory, faithful God. Your wisdom fills the universe with possibilities we have not tapped. Your Word comes to us filled with riches we have not mined. Within ourselves is the potential for greatness as yet unrealized. Confront us here with your eternal claim on us that we may become the kind, compassionate, and patient people you intend for us to be. Amen.

CALL TO CONFESSION

If God were dependent on our communication to know where we are or who we are, would God know us? We expect of God evidence and signs of caring. Does not God, who gave us life, have the right to expect to hear from us daily in prayer? How have we cut ourselves off from God?

PRAYER OF CONFESSION

Heavenly Parent, we have wandered away to pursue our own agenda. We have laid aside your expectation that we will forbear one another and forgive. We harbor grudges against people. There are some we neglect and some we disdain. We have viewed them neither as your beloved nor as our sisters and brothers. The peace of Christ does not rule in our hearts. Your truth is not what flows from our lips or finds expression in our actions. O God, turn us around, that what we do may be a genuine expression of your love, through Jesus Christ. Amen.

ASSURANCE OF FORGIVENESS

God has already forgiven us. When we are truly sorry and repent of our neglect and our wrongful thoughts and deeds, we are able to accept that forgiveness.

God offers healing for our brokenness. The scars of resentment against others are taken away so we can forgive them. The love of God enables us to love. Praise God from the earth. Draw close to the eternal and exalt the name of the one who rules all time and space.

COLLECT

All-knowing God, whose favor rested on Jesus of Nazareth and whose love is poured out for all of humankind, inspire us here to ask questions, to pursue understanding, and to share our faith. May we grow in wisdom, respond to your blessing, and reach out to minister to and with your children—our brothers and sisters. Send the peace of Christ to rule among us, uniting our hearts in thankfulness and praise. Amen.

OFFERTORY INVITATION

In the name of Jesus Christ, we respond to God's forgiveness and empowerment with thanksgiving and praise. As we have been blessed, so we share. May our offerings express compassion and kindness within our faith community and in our outreach to our immediate surroundings and to the world.

OFFERTORY PRAYER

We are thankful for the love that gave us life, for the mission that gives purpose to our days, and for the peace that Christ grants to us. Keep us from needless anxiety, that we may give without counting the cost. We give ourselves as well as our money, that your Word may spread where it is not known and take root where it has not been heeded. Amen.

COMMISSION AND BLESSING

Let the Word of Christ dwell in you richly.
Teach and admonish one another in all wisdom.
> **We will spend time in study and prayer.**
> **We will listen and speak as God inspires us.**

Put on—as God's chosen ones, holy and beloved—
compassion, kindness, meekness, and patience.
> **We will forgive as we have been forgiven.**
> **We will put on love that binds us in perfect harmony.**

The peace of Christ will rule in your hearts.
You will know God's favor day after day.
> **We will praise God's name in all we do.**
> **We will join with faithful people to give daily thanks.**

Amen. **Amen.**

(See hymns 16, 17.)

Ecclesiastes 3:1–13   Revelation 21:1–6a
Psalm 8   Matthew 25:31–46

CALL TO WORSHIP

A new year has dawned; the old is past and gone.
This is a time for beginnings, a time to encounter God.
>   *O God, how majestic is your name in all the earth!*
>   *You are the Alpha and the Omega, the beginning and the end.*
Look to the heavens and wonder at the magnitude of space.
Look around you at the amazing variety of creation.
>   *You have made everything suitable for its time.*
>   *You have made us and crowned us with glory and honor.*
Ponder the meaning of our days in the face of eternity.
Consider again what God has called us to do and to be.
>   *You have given us dominion over the works of your hands.*
>   *You have called us to minister to the least of your children.*

INVOCATION

God of creation and newness, we bring to you our past, that it may teach us. We bring our future, that it may be blessed with vision and hope. We bring this present moment, that you may fill it with your transforming presence. We want to be part of your new heaven and new earth. We seek to enjoy your creation without destroying it, to take pleasure in our toil while making of it a ministry, to learn to live together in peace, reaching out to assure that all are benefiting from your good gifts. Feed us, clothe us, welcome us, that we may do the same for others. Amen.

CALL TO CONFESSION

Jesus promised a time of judgment when our faithfulness to God and one another would be tested. How easily we put this off as a distant future event rather than a present reality! Yet every deed shapes our character and every neglect dulls our compassion. Let us seek forgiveness.

PRAYER OF CONFESSION

O God, what are we that you even notice us? How is it that you care about us? Why have you entrusted to us the stewardship of the earth? We confess that we have seen the hungry without giving food, the thirsty without digging wells to fill their cups, the homeless without standing beside them to build shelters from the cold. We count ourselves worthy of your blessing while we consider others undeserving. Forgive our misjudgments, our inaction, our lukewarm faith, we pray in Jesus' name. Amen.

ASSURANCE OF FORGIVENESS
God is making all things new. Our past does not prescribe our future. God will dwell with us to make us a new people, responsive to God's eternal design. God will open our eyes and our hearts to the sufferer and the stranger. In them, we can find and serve our God. In our service, we will discover a new way of being. We will find life and happiness.

COLLECT
Ruler of all worlds, whose love draws us into community and whose judgment separates us according to our empathy and stewardship, draw near to us now in those persons and events through which you long to speak to us. Keep us from missing your presence or neglecting to show hospitality. Help us to experience eternal life in the events of the here and now. Amen.

OFFERTORY INVITATION
As God wipes away tears and reframes our suffering into opportunities for growth, we are challenged to reach out to those who are suffering in our own community and in other lands. Some hurts do not show easily, but others are painfully obvious. We are called to see and listen and give, that the worth and dignity of all may be affirmed.

OFFERTORY PRAYER
Generous and loving God, receive our gifts; receive our lives made new by your blessing. May we plant seeds, heal wounds, and build up your world. May we love and seek and embrace your children. We dedicate these offerings and ourselves toward the realization of your realm in our midst. Multiply and prosper our ministries in Christ's name. Amen.

COMMISSION AND BLESSING
Face this new day, this new year, recreated and empowered.
You have inherited God's own realm; here God dwells with us.
We have been fed and clothed and welcomed.
We have been visited and comforted and blessed.
This is the season for discerning God's activity;
this is the time to toil with God for the sake of humanity.
We will give thanks for the gifts we receive;
We will give gifts and opportunity to those who are in need.
As we serve among the least of God's children, we are blessed.
As we humble ourselves before God, we are glorified.
Thanks be to God for dwelling with us!
Thanks be to God for equipping us to serve!
Amen. **Amen.**

(See hymns 18, 19, 20.)

CELEBRATION OF JESUS AND MARY
(JANUARY 1) — A, B, C

Numbers 6:22–27   Galatians 4:4–7
Psalm 8   Philippians 2:5–11 (alt.)
           Luke 2:15–21

CALL TO WORSHIP
God's face is shining on us in this new year.
God's majesty and glory fill the heavens.
> *How amazing are the works of God!*
> *Who are we that God should care for us?*

God calls us by name and promises to bless us.
God names us as children and heirs with Christ.
> *We can leave behind our slavery to things.*
> *We can aspire to spiritual fulfillment.*

The God who exalted Jesus calls us to discipleship.
We are being saved to do God's work in the world.
> *God is at work in us, doing great things.*
> *Our efforts are crowned with glory and honor.*

INVOCATION
In awe, we seek your presence, O God of all majesty and glory. You have created us to share your spirit. You have granted us stewardship over all you have made. The future of all living things—plants and creatures—is in our hands. We cannot create life; we can only protect and nurture your gift. We cannot make everything fit together; we can only seek to sustain and extend the relationships you have made possible. Draw us now into that partnership in which we are marked with your name and made heirs of your promises. Amen.

CALL TO CONFESSION
What are human beings, that God cares for us? We have misused the work of God's hands, squandering resources for our immediate pleasure, destroying the earth over which God gives us dominion. It is time for us to repent and seek salvation.

PRAYER OF CONFESSION
O God, we have reached for your power without accepting responsibility. We have exploited the resources entrusted to our stewardship. We have claimed to be Christian without following Christ. We profess to be people of faith without exploring what that means. We claim to praise and glorify you yet fail to proclaim to others the good news we have heard and seen. We are not ready to empty ourselves to serve in humble obedience. O God, silence the enemies within us, that we may respond to you. Send to us the spirit of your own child, that we may greet with joy the renewed opportunity to live as your children. Amen.

ASSURANCE OF FORGIVENESS

We have been made a little lower than God, crowned with glory and honor. We are redeemed at the manger of God's holy child. We are tested at the cross of Jesus Christ. Now the time has fully come for our wholehearted response. God is blessing us that we might become a blessing to others. Praise God and serve with joy!

COLLECT

When our highest moments pass, when the voices of angels are stilled, God of all majesty, come once more. O Holy One, whose glory fills the whole universe, visit us where we worship, where we live, where we work, where we play. Give us a story to tell and the courage to share it. May the love that shines from the heavens, that awakened the shepherds, that lodged in the heart of Mary, dwell among us, sparking our enthusiasm to embrace the mind of Christ. Amen.

OFFERTORY INVITATION

God's gift in Jesus Christ: who can understand it? God's love for us: who can comprehend? Perhaps, if we empty ourselves of the fears and pretensions that mark our lives, we can fully receive God's gifts. Then we will be free to share these blessings joyfully.

OFFERTORY PRAYER

For all we have inherited from your hand, for making us in your own image, for the gift of new life in Jesus Christ, we give you thanks, glorious God. Nothing we do can repay you. No service we render, no obligations we fulfill can discharge our debt to you. We can only pour out our gratitude and give our best, that this world may become a place where your reign is realized. Amen.

COMMISSION AND BLESSING

You are redeemed, adopted as God's own.
As children of God, go out to live obediently.
> **God has honored us with responsibility for the earth.**
> **God is equipping us daily for our service.**
God bless you and keep you every day!
God's face will shine on you and be gracious to you!
> **O God, how majestic is your name in all the earth!**
> **We will look to the heavens for help and inspiration.**
Receive once more the gift of Jesus Christ.
Rejoice that God sends us the peace of heaven.
> **Let us take on ourselves the mind of Christ.**
> **Let us glorify and praise God for all we have received.**
Amen. **Amen.**

(See hymns 19, 21.)

SECOND SUNDAY AFTER CHRISTMAS — A, B, C

Jeremiah 31:7–14
Psalm 147:12–20

Ephesians 1:3–14
John 1:(1–9), 10–18

CALL TO WORSHIP

True light is entering our world through Jesus Christ.
Sing for joy and praise God, all people.
> **God's Word makes the winds blow and water flow.**
> **Jesus Christ is God's Word to us and for us.**

Receive the Word, and believe the good news.
Know you are children of God, born of the Spirit.
> **The Word became flesh to dwell with humanity.**
> **Grace and forgiveness are lavished upon us.**

Be radiant in appreciation of God's goodness.
Hear the Word of God and declare it to others.
> **In Christ we have obtained an inheritance.**
> **Spiritual blessings are abundantly available to us.**

INVOCATION

From near and far, we come to worship. Amid our joys and sorrows, we come to praise. In our strength and in our weakness, we gather for refreshment and renewal. You have called us together like a shepherd keeps a flock. As a gardener waters growing plants, you care for us and provide for our growth. Praise be to you, O God, for your protecting love and freeing grace. Shine upon us here that we may know your truth and receive it into our lives. Amen.

CALL TO CONFESSION

God has set before us straight paths to follow, but we have stumbled along our own byways. God shows us the way of peace, but we choose the vanity of competition and strife. God gives us the day, but we flee into the deepest night. God is calling us now to repentance and new life.

PRAYER OF CONFESSION

Infinite God, look upon your finite creatures, broken and bereaved, with compassion and consolation. We view your world with unseeing eyes. We listen to the cries of your hurting people with ears that do not hear and hearts that do not feel their plight. The wind blows among us, but we do not discern your Spirit. You offer wisdom and insight, but we reject your counsel. You present to us the gospel of salvation, but we turn away from its saving grace. O God, help us change the direction of our lives so we may act like your children and reflect your love into the world. Amen.

ASSURANCE OF FORGIVENESS

The Word made flesh in Jesus is for us. God's gift of new life is ever available. God grants us power to change if that is our sincere desire. The Holy Spirit is at work in our midst. We are destined to live as children of God. Let us open our eyes, unstop our ears, and live with empathy for all. With faith, we can live our beliefs, praising God who has blessed us in Christ.

COLLECT

Light of the world, whose coming reordered human priorities, dwell with us here, that your Word may refresh us and your truth remold us. Reveal your will to us in ways we cannot escape or ignore. Deepen our respect for your law and our faithfulness to the truth we encounter in Jesus Christ. May your Word run swiftly through this assembly with life-changing power. Amen.

OFFERTORY INVITATION

In these moments, we are challenged, not just to reach for a contribution, but to reorder our lives. We look beyond pledges to productivity. Will we be enlightened by the gifts we dedicate here? Who will receive the Word because we are faithful? How will the world be changed by our investment in this community of faith?

OFFERTORY PRAYER

Your goodness, O God, has satisfied us with abundance beyond our deserving. The return on your investment in us is not adequate to express our thanks. Use our lives as channels of your grace. May our individual efforts and the combined outreach we can accomplish together turn mourning into joy and hopelessness into purposeful living. In Jesus' name. Amen.

COMMISSION AND BLESSING

Go out to fulfill your destiny as children of God.
Let your hope be in Christ and live as disciples.
> *We will live in the true light of Jesus Christ.*
> *We are listening for God's will for our lives.*
Bear witness to the light, that all might believe.
Share the grace and truth of Jesus Christ.
> *In Christ, we have inherited spiritual blessings.*
> *We seek to pass them on to sisters and brothers.*
You are marked by the Holy Spirit.
God's promises are being fulfilled in and through you.
> *Thanks be to God for goodness and mercy.*
> *Praise God for making us instruments of peace.*
Amen. **Amen.**

(See hymn 22.)

Epiphany and the Season Following

Isaiah 60:1–6
Psalm 72:1–7, 10–14

Ephesians 3:1–12
Matthew 2:1–12

CALL TO WORSHIP

Arise, shine; for your light has come.
The glory of God has risen among us.
We are awake; we are alive!
Praise God for deliverance and blessings.
Lift up your eyes to see all around you.
Let your hearts rejoice, and be radiant with hope.
May justice water the earth like a shower;
let righteousness and peace abound.
Receive again the promises of the gospel.
Participate in the mystery of Jesus Christ.
God's ways are being revealed to us today.
Our church proclaims the unsearchable riches of Christ.

INVOCATION

Eternal God, because your purposes become clear to us in Jesus Christ, we come with boldness to claim our relationship with you. We are grateful for pioneers in the faith whose stewardship has salvaged for us a way of life rooted in the gospel. The flames you ignited in them have not gone out, in spite of our faithlessness. Your wisdom is still proclaimed in the church, challenging centers of earthly power with the claims of heaven. Today our search for meaning has led us to this place of worship. You are here; we rejoice! Amen.

CALL TO CONFESSION

The Epiphany season celebrates God's inclusiveness. The mystery of Jesus Christ is revealed, not to an elite few, but to the whole world. Yet we continue to build barriers to protect our own interests and keep others at a distance. If loyalty to God calls for accepting and embracing all God's children in love, we have much to confess.

PRAYER OF CONFESSION

God of light, we admit our retreat into the shadows of pretension and exclusion. How often we choose to associate with people who are like us and then look down on others who differ from us. It is easier to discover their sins than to admit our own. We judge the poor and join their oppressors, while you call us to identify with those in need, that all may prosper together. We imagine that we alone are faithful stewards of your grace, while you welcome, as fellow saints with us, many whom we ignore. Save us from our earthbound judgments, that we may look up and be guided by the star that draws all people to yourself. Awed by your forgiving presence, we fall down to worship you. Amen.

Assurance of Forgiveness

Through faith in Jesus Christ, we can come to Almighty God in boldness and confidence, assured of the gift of grace and empowerment of the Spirit. Lift up your eyes to see the glory of God. Receive light and healing, for God has come to dwell in us and among us. Let your hearts rejoice and your faces be radiant as we share the abundance of God's love.

Collect

God of the stars, whose guidance is always available to those who look up and listen, speak to us now. We are troubled by many things. Break into our thoughts to reveal great joy at the heart of life, that we may worship wholeheartedly, offer you our best, and lead others to the discoveries of faith. Amen.

Offertory Invitation

We are stewards of God's grace, entrusted with the unsearchable riches of Christ, channels through which the wisdom of God is offered to the world. Our prosperity gives us the marvelous opportunity to share. What treasures will we offer today to honor Christ? What costly offerings will be given with joy and worshipful devotion?

Offertory Prayer

For the joy of giving, we offer the products of our labor for the ministry of this church, in outreach to the world. With concern for those who are poor, oppressed, and needy, we rededicate ourselves as helpers and advocates. Out of devotion to Christ, we commit our best, that the church may bear witness among the principalities and powers of this world. Help us all, O God, to be faithful stewards. Amen.

Commission and Blessing

God sends us on our way, a bold and confident people.
Look up, and be guided by the star of joy.
> *We will open our eyes to the presence of God.*
> *We will look for God's activity all around us.*
God's purposes in Christ are to be lived out by us.
We are called to invite others to share in God's grace.
> *We will witness to all we have seen and heard.*
> *By God's power, we will minister to others.*
The glory of God has risen among us.
We are blessed beyond all deserving.
> *What we have received, we pass on with joy.*
> *We offer to all the unsearchable riches of Christ.*
Amen. **Amen.**

(See hymns 23, 24.)

FIRST SUNDAY AFTER EPIPHANY
(BAPTISM OF JESUS)

Isaiah 43:1–7

Psalm 29

Acts 8:14–17

Luke 3:15–17, 21–22

CALL TO WORSHIP

Gather from East and West, from North and South.
God is calling us; listen, for God is naming you.
> *The voice of God thunders through our midst.*
> *The voice of God is powerful and full of majesty.*

Bow in awe before the one who created you.
God knows you completely, yet accepts you.
> *The voice of God commands our attention.*
> *The voice of God is like fire and tornado.*

God reaches out to strengthen, not condemn us.
God brings us through terror to a place of peace.
> *Ascribe to God glory and strength.*
> *Worship God in awe, wonder, and joy!*

INVOCATION

God of cleansing waters and purifying fires, touch our lives today to recall us to the power of our baptism and reconfirm our commitment to Jesus Christ. Name us again as your own people: precious, gifted, created to glorify you in fullness of life, in peace with ourselves and one another. Send your Holy Spirit once more to energize our worship and enliven our witness in the world. Hear us as we pray for one another and for your church in every place. Amen.

CALL TO CONFESSION

We are baptized, set apart to be a ministering people, called to be agents of change, created to give glory to God in word and deed. The Holy Spirit has claimed us to be praying, caring, giving disciples of Jesus Christ. In this time of confession, we acknowledge how far we are from what we were created to be.

PRAYER OF CONFESSION

O God, the waters of faithfulness run deep, and we have been afraid they will overwhelm us. The fires of your Spirit burn brightly, and we fear we may be consumed if we display too much enthusiasm. We retreat to safe places where we hope to avoid challenges, conflicts, and uncertainty. When we shrink from risks, we miss much that enriches life. We fail to notice your amazing activity among those who respond to your leading. Free us, we pray, for daring service. Amen.

Assurance of Forgiveness

God has redeemed us, claimed us, called us by name. We are precious in God's sight. Surely our God will strengthen us to face times of difficulty. There are no safe hiding places in life, only the assurance of a relationship with a God whom we can trust in life and in death. Our God forgives and empowers. God blesses us with a peace that is more powerful than any outward circumstance. The assurances of God are eternal.

Collect

God of gifts and blessings, who opened the heavens to the prayers of Jesus, send your Spirit among us that we, too, may learn to please you and live as your beloved children. Baptize us with the Holy Spirit and with fire so our lips may sing to your glory and our hands reach out to heal and bless your people, in Jesus' name. Amen.

Offertory Invitation

God has gathered us from East and West, from North and South, to offer our best in worship and praise. Now we bring the fruits of our labor as an offering of thanks. We invest in people and programs, near and far, to benefit God's scattered children who have missed the majesty. Let our generosity aspire to match the lavish gifts of God.

Offertory Prayer

For bringing us safely to this hour, we give you thanks, O God of wind and fire. May our offerings honor you. May our lives reflect your mercy. May our hands bestow on others the blessings we have received. May our prayers unite us with one another and with Christ, in whose name we celebrate the privilege of giving. Amen.

Commission and Blessing

Dare to face the world in joyous freedom.
You have been baptized with the Holy Spirit and with fire.
We pray for courage to do what is right.
We seek the strength to witness for peace.
We are God's beloved children.
Let us seek to live in ways that are pleasing to God.
God has created us for glory.
We will worship the God of power and strength.
Even now God's hand of blessing rests on us.
The dove of peace descends upon us.
We welcome the Spirit's presence among us.
We celebrate the Spirit's work within us. Praise God.
Amen. **Amen.**

(See hymn 25.)

First Sunday after Epiphany   33

Isaiah 62:1–5   I Corinthians 12:1–11
Psalm 36:5–10   John 2:1–11

CALL TO WORSHIP

With steadfast love, God calls our names.
Come to find refuge in the shelter of God's ways.
> *We long to be recognized and affirmed.*
> *We are eager for a place of shelter and security.*

Feast on the abundance of God's house.
Come to drink deeply from the fountain of life.
> *We are ready to hear the Word of God.*
> *We want to be guided by eternal truth.*

Reach out to claim the gifts God pours out on us.
The Spirit is eager to inspire and empower each one.
> *When God calls us, we cannot remain silent.*
> *When Christ is real to us, we accept our discipleship.*

INVOCATION

How awesome it is that you care for us, God of all life! Your delight in us brings out our best. When you rejoice in us, we come to believe in our capacity for goodness. When your light and salvation dawn in our lives, we want to share the joy. Remind us now of the gifts you so freely bestow. Help us to recognize them in ourselves and in one another, that we may use them to serve people in need and give glory to your name. Amen.

CALL TO CONFESSION

Despite our best intentions, there is much in life that separates us from God. We find ourselves living for things and being ruled by our appetites. Our possessions become for us dumb idols that keep us from taking risks and making sacrifices of faithfulness. Join me in confessing our sin.

PRAYER OF CONFESSION

God of the heathen and the righteous, we confess that we have moved away from our commitment to Christ. We have denied your gifts, ignored your inspiration, and wandered from your healing presence. Yet we cannot escape your claim on us, for wherever we go, you are there. How precious is your steadfast love that saves us from our selfish desires to live for higher values! Strengthen us to do as you tell us, as Christ demonstrated among us. Amen.

ASSURANCE OF FORGIVENESS

God does not treat us as heathens, forsaken and desolate. We are welcomed with rejoicing, enfolded by love, celebrated as persons of beauty in whose salvation God delights. Let your hearts be lifted up. We are not bound to our old ways but are freed for a new identity. God's benevolent gifts are apportioned to each of us in abundance.

COLLECT

Gracious God, whose miracles surround us day by day and whose revelation in Jesus Christ awakens our wonder, let this be an hour of powerful encounter with you in which our gifts are called forth for the sake of your church and for the transformation of your world. Work within us, among us, and through us, we pray, that believing minds may blossom into trusting hearts and helping hands, fully committed to your service. Amen.

OFFERTORY INVITATION

What will we give in gratitude for God's forgiveness and healing grace? Who can repay the many gifts we have received with the miracle of life? Let us rejoice in the mission God entrusts to us.

OFFERTORY PRAYER

God of our baptism, whose Holy Spirit fires our imagination and fills our lives with purpose, we rejoice to commit ourselves anew with our gifts. May what we share strengthen your children spiritually, inspiring each person to invest fully in the work you set before us. The varieties of gifts you entrust to us can be realized only if they are used. Thank you for granting us this joy. Amen.

COMMISSION AND BLESSING

Depart to serve, strengthened by the Holy Spirit.
Use the wisdom, faith, and knowledge you received.
> *We cannot rest in God's care or keep silent.*
> *The love of God must be lived and shared.*
Go forth with praise on your lips.
The steadfast love of God will light your paths.
> *We want to offer light and hope to others.*
> *Daily, we will seek inspiration for this joyous task.*
Reach out as listening, caring, healing people.
Your love will become a miracle for someone in need.
> *We pray that God will keep us open to further learning.*
> *May our humble witness attract others to Christ.*
Amen. **Amen.**

(See hymns 27 and 28. For a hymn based on the gospel reading, see "At a Marriage Feast," *Refreshing Rains of the Living Word*, p. 175.)

Nehemiah 8:1–3, 5–6, 8–10   I Corinthians 12:12–31a

Psalm 19   Luke 4:14–21

CALL TO WORSHIP

Let the ears of all people be attentive;
the heavens are telling the glory of God.
> *Everything around us proclaims God's handiwork.*
> *Let us bow down and worship our Creator.*

Day and night, God is at work among us.
We are drawn together into one body, the church.
> *As we commune with God, we know we need one other.*
> *Let us honor the good to be found in all people.*

Hear once again the laws and commandments.
Find them sure and right and true for all.
> *We weep and mourn our lack of faithfulness.*
> *We seek true community in which all are honored.*

INVOCATION

On this holy day, we come together to make sense of our lives. We look to your Word, O God, as a source of understanding. Revive our souls that our hearts may rejoice in your presence. Cleanse and enlighten us with your truth. Liberate us from self-imposed limitations. Let the words of our mouths and the meditations of our heart be acceptable in your sight, O God, our Rock and our Redeemer. Amen.

CALL TO CONFESSION

Who can discern their own errors? Are we innocent of great transgression? Are there hidden faults of which we are unaware? Do we seek to dissociate ourselves from part of the human race, our sisters and brothers? Let us examine ourselves that we may be open to the leading of the Spirit.

PRAYER OF CONFESSION

Sometimes, God, we do not know what to confess. We seek to keep your law, but the right course is not always clear. We want to follow your direction, but it is hard to discern what is true. Sometimes it is difficult to care about people whose values are different from ours. How can we be one with those who do not share our beliefs? At times, our own faith is shaken—our faith in ourselves and our faith in you. We need your help, God, so our sins will not have dominion over us. Amen.

ASSURANCE OF FORGIVENESS

Do not weep or mourn before the law of God. Rather, let the law revive your soul and enlighten your eyes. The Spirit of God is eager to teach, inspire, and strengthen you. Desire to know the purpose of God. Pursue understanding more than riches. God is your Rock and your Redeemer.

COLLECT

Spirit of God, who inspired the Scriptures and gave them fulfillment in Jesus Christ, open our eyes to the gifts you have entrusted to each one of us and show us how to work together to realize your purposes in our midst. We long to live in a world where mutual caring and support replace competition and violence. Help us to honor one another's gifts and strive for the greatest of all gifts, the embodiment of your love. Amen.

OFFERTORY INVITATION

We are part of the body of Christ which extends around the world. Together, we form a caring community, united in spite of many differences in appearance, understanding, and function. If others are suffering, we, too, will suffer. When we have the ability to help, it is a joy to do so. May our offerings preach good news, proclaim liberty, and recover among us all the ability to see and hear and respond.

OFFERTORY PRAYER

In the spirit of Christ, we give our best for the world. Your rule among us, O God, is more to be desired than riches. Therefore, we share what you have allowed us to use, giving thanks for the joy of helping others and entering into partnership with them. This is only the beginning of our offering, for we dedicate here our varied gifts as apostles, prophets, teachers, healers, helpers, administrators, speakers, workers. In all we do, we will seek to serve you by sharing your love. Amen.

COMMISSION AND BLESSING

May the words of our mouths proclaim God's love.
May the meditations of our hearts be acceptable to God.
We go forward as praying, witnessing people.
We greet this week with high anticipation.
The Spirit of God accompanies us on our journey.
We are anointed for the sharing of good news.
Our words and deeds will release captives.
What we do and say will change our world.
The joy of God is our strength.
The law of God revives us and makes us wise.
In purity of heart, we seek to serve.
In quiet confidence, we dare to change and grow.
Amen. **Amen.**

(See hymn 29.)

Third Sunday after Epiphany   37

Jeremiah 1:4–10   I Corinthians 13:1–13
Psalm 71:1–6   Luke 4:21–30

Call to Worship

Come, people of God, to the one in whom we trust.
Praise God who delivers and rescues us.
> **God is our rock of refuge, our strong fortress.**
> **God saves us amid wickedness and cruelty.**

Hope in God, who has created you.
Open yourself to the one who knows you well.
> **God accepts us, even when people do not.**
> **God affirms us, even when we fail.**

Our God gives us tasks to do and strength to do them.
God's Word of love is ours to proclaim.
> **We have come to embrace the mysteries of our faith.**
> **We are here to worship the God who empowers us.**

Invocation

God of love, in whose name we have been consecrated for discipleship and service, encounter us in this hour, that we may grow in knowledge and actions. Disturb our certainties so we will be open to new insights. Upset our priorities to make room for faith, hope, and love. Expand our horizons to encompass ideas we have not entertained before. Open our hearts to people we have failed to welcome into our midst. Perfect among us that childlike trust that allows change to transform us in the presence of your love. We pray in Jesus' name. Amen.

Call to Confession

How often we have been ruled by our fears rather than our faith! How often we have trusted in things rather than in God! How seldom do we utter praise to the one who touches our lives with great possibilities! Let us seek God's forgiveness, that we may know God's mercy.

Prayer of Confession

Merciful God, you know us better than we know ourselves, but we have not believed this. You care about us even when we do not love ourselves, but it has been hard for us to understand that this is true. We see so dimly and hear your Word so faintly that we doubt your truth. We dare not trust the prophets or risk the cost of discipleship. We are afraid to believe, hope, and endure when there is suffering all around us. O God, grant us courage to change, to follow Jesus in spite of ridicule and rejection. Yet keep us from insisting on our own way, which may not be your way. Amen.

ASSURANCE OF FORGIVENESS

God does not condemn us for our imperfection nor abandon us to our fears. The one who designed our being promises to be with us when we are challenged, to deliver us when it seems the whole world is against us, to love us at all times and in all circumstances. We are forgiven, healed, and empowered for our ministry.

COLLECT

Reassuring God, whose Word became flesh in Jesus, and whose healing touch empowered Christ the physician, look upon us with the compassion of a wise parent. Equip us to listen, to hear, to speak, to embody love that is patient and kind. May we bear, believe, hope, and endure, so that through us the world will hear good news, give up childish ways, and respond to the touch of your hand. Amen.

OFFERTORY INVITATION

God has called the church to be an agent of change. With prophetic voice and courageous work, we are to influence the world. Such a task requires our best: our continued growth in faith, our commitment to love, our giving of self and substance. The resources we dedicate here are a symbol of our whole life response.

OFFERTORY PRAYER

With awe and wonder before you, O God, we dare to enlist all our efforts toward the realization of your realm. Where there is injustice, we would champion those oppressed and misunderstood. When some feel rejected, we reach out to accept them in Christ's name. May these offerings preach and teach and heal. Amen.

COMMISSION AND BLESSING

Go forth with faith to move mountains.
Reach out with love that transforms the world.
> *Love is patient and kind, not jealous or boastful.*
> *Love rejoices in all that is right, not in wrong.*

Let the Scripture be fulfilled by your faithfulness.
Let the Word take flesh in all you do.
> *Love bears, believes, hopes, and endures.*
> *We participate in the love of God that never ends.*

God promises to be our rock and our refuge.
God is ever with us to deliver us.
> *God's Word will be in our mouths.*
> *God's love will warm our spirits.*

Amen. **Amen.**

(See hymns 31, 32, 33.)

Isaiah 6:1–8, (9–13)   1 Corinthians 15:1–11
Psalm 138   Luke 5:1–11

CALL TO WORSHIP

Holy, holy, holy is the God of hosts;
the whole earth is full of God's glory.
> *Our hearts are filled with thanks, O God.*
> *We bring before you our songs of praise.*

All rulers of the people are called to praise God.
All people of the earth are subject to God's rule.
> *The steadfast love of God surrounds us here.*
> *We have come to see and hear and understand.*

Let the thresholds shake with the power of God's voice.
Let all the people tremble before God's glory.
> *God's purposes endure and will be fulfilled.*
> *Our lives can be channels for God's grace.*

INVOCATION

O God, whose presence fills this place of gathering, we bow before your majesty in awe and wonder. When we consider the vast universe of your dominion, we are humbled by your attention to us. Your steadfast love and faithfulness amaze us. Your care for the lowly gives us a sense of our own dignity and worth. Send your gospel to teach us, to save us from ourselves, to lead us into all truth. Show us the tasks we can accomplish for you and grant us the courage to reach out in your name to do them. Amen.

CALL TO CONFESSION

The voice of God shakes the deficient foundations on which we have built our lives. We are summoned to account for our faithlessness. Called as disciples and apostles, we have not followed in the footsteps of Jesus or led others to the grace of God. Let us remind ourselves of God's sovereignty and confess our broken commitments.

PRAYER OF CONFESSION

Awesome God, we are afraid to admit the many ways we have failed you. We are sinful people who forget to thank you and who delay consulting with you about the decisions we must make. We prefer the safety of familiar programs, even when they are ineffective. We cling to our routines, even when they cause us to lose sight of your purposes. We are people of unclean lips, dwelling among people who deny your presence and power. O God, we fall down before you, seeking forgiveness. Amen.

Assurance of Forgiveness

Stand up, people of God. Our Creator reaches out to lift us up and deliver us from the troubles around us and the distress within. God touches our lips to cleanse us and take our sins away. By the grace of God, Christ comes to us, reclaiming us, showing us a new way, empowering us for effective service.

Collect

God, whose Word calls us to take risks and whose revelation in Jesus Christ gives us confidence to try again when we have failed, appear to us now as we listen to the Scriptures and lift our eyes to see your face. Grant that we may feel your presence and discern your will. Equip us to respond with confident faithfulness to the work you give us to do. We want to go where you send us and live up to what you expect of us. Open your people to live together as you intend. Amen.

Offertory Invitation

When we are genuinely thankful for the steadfast love and faithfulness of God, we are eager to share this bounty. When we truly discern the grace of God, we want others to experience it, too. Christ calls us to reach out to our sisters and brothers with the good news of God's reign. Our offerings help to take God's Word to the world.

Offertory Prayer

Your voice, O God, we have heard. Your presence has moved us to respond. Send us where you want us to go. Use the resources we dedicate here to empower others to witness to your love and care. Fill our lives with thanksgiving. Fill our days with purpose. We rededicate ourselves to work and worship that express our profound gratitude for life and all its opportunities. Amen.

Commission and Blessing

God has touched us amid our pain and fears.
We have been comforted and blessed.
> *We have felt a healing, restoring presence.*
> *God is leading us through troubled times.*

God has cleansed us from the sins that destroy us.
Our guilt is lifted from us and taken away.
> *We give thanks and sing praise to God.*
> *We have received blessings in abundance.*

Who will witness to the grace of God?
Who will go out to serve in Christ's name?
> *Here we are, ready to be sent into the world.*
> *We will go where God directs, to share good news.*

Amen. **Amen.**

(See hymns 34, 35.)

Fifth Sunday after Epiphany   41

Jeremiah 17:5–10   I Corinthians 15:12–20
Psalm I   Luke 6:17–26

CALL TO WORSHIP

Blessed are those who trust in God,
who delight to meditate on God's law.
We long to hear the Word of God
and let the Word shape our lives.
Blessed are all who seek the realm of God,
who hunger to find meaning in their lives.
We intend to give our best to our Creator,
bearing fruit in all we say and do.
Blessed are the ones who serve God with joy,
who risk all they have in faithfulness and hope.
We come now to worship and find new life,
to receive healing and empowerment for our journey.

INVOCATION

Come, Holy God, to search our minds and try our hearts. Grant us in this hour wise counsel and clear direction. Touch us, teach us; hear us, heal us. Send your Spirit to walk with us, as Christ walked with the disciples long ago, that your realm may become for us a present reality as well as a future hope. Grant us living water to quench our thirst and sound preaching to feed our hunger. Amen.

CALL TO CONFESSION

Come with your troubled spirits and confused values to seek forgiveness. Come from your misplaced trust and limited vision to open yourself to the transformation God offers. Come from the parched places where doubt and cynicism block God's revelation.

PRAYER OF CONFESSION

Sovereign God, we confess that we have chased after wealth and temporal security while neglecting matters of the spirit. We put our trust in things and in sinners' empty promises. We even deceive ourselves, shaping our words and actions to please the crowd. We have doubted the resurrection, surrendering to a sense of futility and skepticism. Turn us around, God, so we can learn to trust you and find strength in giving of ourselves. Amen.

ASSURANCE OF FORGIVENESS

The healing Jesus offered to disciples long ago is available to us. They were freed to love with generous abandon; so are we. They learned to care for others without first measuring the benefits to themselves; so have we. They were led to the mountain top to commune with God; so are we. They found hope and new life in Christ; this is also God's gift to us.

COLLECT

Powerful God, whose love poured out in Jesus Christ invests us with strength the world cannot offer, cleanse us from unclean spirits and troubled attitudes, that all who are poor, hungry, and grieving may find a new focus for their lives in the ministry we share. May we be righteous, true, and compassionate, that the world may be transformed. Amen.

OFFERTORY INVITATION

Quenched by living water, we are privileged to bear fruit. Contributing our material riches, we discover unanticipated spiritual rewards. The blessings we share are multiplied in the service of God. Let us give with joy.

OFFERTORY PRAYER

Thank you, God, for the consolation you offer, the hunger you satisfy, and the healing you produce in those who respond to your love. You have touched our lives in ways that make us rich. Now use what we have shared to provide fulfillment in other lives, among our neighbors, near and far. Enlist our best efforts in the extension of your realm, that our offering of ourselves may bear fruit daily. Amen.

COMMISSION AND BLESSING

Go forth into a parched and needy world
to share the water of life with others.
> *We go out with renewed faith and hope in Christ,*
> *for resurrection is a living possibility for us.*

Turn to God each day to delight in the Word
and meditate on God's law.
> *We will trust God to provide all we really need.*
> *We seek to bear fruit in all we say and do.*

Be assured that the realm of God is ours.
God knows us, loves us, blesses us in Christ.
> *Christ is the first fruits of those who have died.*
> *We shall rise with Christ to new life.*

Amen. **Amen.**

(See hymns 36, 37.)

Sixth Sunday after Epiphany   43

Genesis 45:3–1, 15
Psalm 37:1–11, 39–40

I Corinthians 15:35–38, 42–50
Luke 6:27–38

CALL TO WORSHIP

Come near to one another and to our God.
Be still before the one who fulfills our hearts' desires.
This is a time for meeting and greeting.
This is the hour for quieting life's stresses and worries.
Wait patiently, for God will be revealed to us.
God is our refuge in whom we trust.
We believe God is here and will be known by us.
Our faith nourishes us as we rest in God's care.
We are here to receive life in all its abundance.
God is providing for us and has a purpose for us.
God raises us up and sends us forth.
Surely God will help us wherever we go.

INVOCATION

Loving God, you bring light to our days and hope to our hearts. We draw near to you as survivors of another week, grateful for your care. You have provided for us, preserved our lives, and invited us once more to this time of prayer. Now we would be still before you, leaving behind our distress and anger, entrusting our weaknesses to your empowering spirit. Raise us up to embrace your way of love. Amen.

CALL TO CONFESSION

Are we envious because the wicked seem to prosper while righteous people struggle? Are we impatient with those whose ways disappoint us? Do we judge others by standards we ourselves cannot keep? Jesus invites us to examine ourselves, that we may be freed from the oppression of our own attitudes.

PRAYER OF CONFESSION

Kind God, we have sinned against you. We have judged and condemned those whose actions offend us. We hesitate to forgive our enemies or make allowances for the behavior of those less fortunate than ourselves. We confess that we do not pray regularly for our friends, much less for our enemies. Our giving is motivated by self-interest as much as by thankfulness and compassion. We admit our failures and ask once more for pardon and renewal, in Jesus' name. Amen.

Assurance of Forgiveness

God is merciful and calls on us to offer mercy to those who have wronged us. God forgives and bids us to forgive others. God's love is always available to us, and we are to pass it on. God provides for us; and out of that bounty, we minister to our sisters and brothers. Let us live as people who recognize and appreciate God's gifts.

Collect

Merciful and loving God, whose clear direction to us includes loving actions toward all people, we pray for the insight and will to treat others as we wish to be treated. Lift us above the physical limitations we have accepted for ourselves so the image of dust may be replaced by the image of heaven. Help us to embody lasting values in all our relationships and to become a part of your transforming plans for our world. Amen.

Offertory Invitation

Our prosperity in comparison with most of the world's people gives us the joyous opportunity to be generous. We can go beyond the expected tithes and offerings required of our spiritual ancestors. We are privileged to offer mercy and help that can transform the lives of others. Let us give with delight, that our brothers and sisters may live.

Offertory Prayer

Receive our joy, O God, along with our gifts. We reach out with this offering to do good in and through our church. May any who have harmed others be helped. Heal us of unjust anger, jealousy, and strife. Through our shared life in this community of faith, create in us the image of one who dwells in heaven. Let us share with the whole world the blessings we receive from your hand. Amen.

Commission and Blessing

Love your enemies and do good.
Lend to others, expecting nothing in return.
As we want people to treat us,
we commit ourselves to treat them.
Judge not, and you will not be judged.
Condemn not, and you will not be condemned.
We want to forgive as God forgives us.
We would be merciful as God is merciful.
God will raise you up to new life.
Be still before God and wait patiently each day.
God is our refuge and our salvation.
We recommit our ways to God.
Amen. **Amen.**

(See hymns 38, 39.)

Isaiah 55:10–13   I Corinthians 15:51–58
Psalm 92:1–4, 12–15   Luke 6:39–49

CALL TO WORSHIP

The Word goes forth from the mouth of God.
Mountains and plains break into singing.
> **It is good to give thanks to God.**
> **We will join in songs of gladness and praise.**

Rain and snow water the earth.
Life is renewed, and people are fed.
> **We rejoice in God's abiding faithfulness.**
> **Let all people declare God's steadfast love.**

Signs of God's presence are all around us.
God's purposes will be accomplished among us.
> **We will flourish like fruitful trees.**
> **Our work gains meaning as God strengthens us.**

INVOCATION

Before the mystery of your grace and the promise of immortality, we open
ourselves to your light and leading, O holy God. In your courts, we are renewed.
Our limitations are transcended. Our presumptions are modified. The foundations
of our lives are rebuilt. Meet us here, that your work may prosper among us and
through us. Fill our lives with the joy and peace that you alone can give. Amen.

CALL TO CONFESSION

We who are quick to notice the flaws in others often cannot see our own faults.
When we propose to remove the speck from another's eye, we may not see the log
in our own. This is a time to bow humbly before our Creator, that God may help
us to see ourselves as we are and to become the persons we are intended to be.

PRAYER OF CONFESSION

O God, we are sinners, existing in deadening routines. We are afraid of change,
reluctant to grow, distressed when our discipleship is challenged. We listen to your
Word but do not really hear. Your will is evident to us, but we do not live by it.
Our lives are filled with thorns and brambles that we allow to flourish. The good
in us cannot bear fruit because it is choked out by weeds. Hear us, O God; we
want to change. Amen.

ASSURANCE OF FORGIVENESS

We will be changed. That is God's promise. Even now, God is creating new life within us, adding good treasure to our hearts. Let us rejoice to receive God's gifts. Let us listen once more to the stories of Jesus. Let us dare to grow to be like our teacher.

COLLECT

Good teacher, whose purposes can be trusted and from whom we learn to distinguish good fruit from that which is rotten, take the logs out of our eyes so we may see clearly the work you would have us do. Remove the plugs from our ears and open our hearts so we may discern your directions. Help us to bear fruit that will feed others and bring them to you. Amen.

OFFERTORY INVITATION

Bread to eat and seeds to plant are among God's gifts, entrusted to us to accomplish God's purposes. All the treasures God loans to us are meant to produce good fruit among us. Today we give as we have been blessed.

OFFERTORY PRAYER

We give thanks, O God, that our wealth and our hands can support your work in the world. Your abundant gifts fill us with joy in sharing. Open our eyes to the opportunities around us to provide teaching, healing, and faithful service. When we see what you would have us do, help us make a faithful response. May this offering reach out to people in need of your love. Amen.

COMMISSION AND BLESSING

Go out to build on the solid rock.
Let God's love be the foundation of your life.
>*We want to focus on what is important.*
>*We seek to value the imperishable.*

Be steadfast, immovable, abounding in God's work.
Know that your labor is not in vain.
>*God will grant us victory in our struggles.*
>*God will teach us and equip us for service.*

Go forward in joy 'and peace.
God will accomplish many things through you.
>*We give thanks to God as we do our work.*
>*Our praise will be evident in all we say and do.*

Amen. **Amen.**

(See hymns 40, 41, 42.)

I Kings 8:22–23, 41–43   Galatians 1:1–12
Psalm 96:1–9   Luke 7:1–10

CALL TO WORSHIP

O sing to God a new song;
sing to God, all the earth.
> *We have come to raise our hands toward heaven.*
> *We are here to bring our worship and praise.*

Sing to God, bless God's name;
tell of God's salvation from day to day.
> *God offers us forgiveness and healing.*
> *We gather to receive God's priceless gifts.*

Great is our God and greatly to be praised.
God is to be revered above all gods.
> *There is no one like our God in heaven or earth.*
> *You keep covenant daily with your servants.*

INVOCATION

God of covenant promises and daily fulfillment, we are drawn to this house of
worship to marvel at your works. Here we observe your strength and beauty, not
in things made by human hands but in the spirit of love that abides in this place.
The earth trembles before you, O God. We are nothing without you, but we are
staggered by the immensity of who you are. Let us here glorify your name, so that
we may sense the reality of your presence wherever we go. Abide with us here and
everywhere, we pray. Amen.

CALL TO CONFESSION

How easily we desert the one in whom we first believed! Our doubts and disobedience take us far from awareness of God. Our restlessness and rebellion cut us off
from our spiritual roots and from close involvement in the family of faith. Let us
return to God, who is waiting to hear from us.

PRAYER OF CONFESSION

Holy God, are you really here? How is it that we miss your appearing? Surely we
have ignored the meaning and power of the gospels in our attempts to win human
approval. We have passed on to others not our faith but our confusion. We have
tried to find truth apart from you, but mere information does not satisfy. We
repent of our arrogance and seek your forgiveness. Come to us now with cleansing power, we pray. Amen.

Assurance of Forgiveness

By the revelation of Jesus Christ, we are a forgiven people, washed clean and empowered to begin anew. Whether newcomers or lifelong communicants, God welcomes our earnest prayer and empowers us to live beyond our highest aspirations. Let us accept God's gift of spiritual health, that all our brokenness may be overcome.

Collect

God of all nations and all peoples, break into our narrow understandings of who you are and whom you welcome as disciples. As we listen for your Word, may we hear your welcoming "Come," but also your command to "Go; do this." By your grace and peace, empower our witness, that the world may embrace good health and abundant life. Amen.

Offertory Invitation

We are all debtors. All we have and all we are belong to God. We owe to others the heritage of faith that surrounds us. The gift of life lays on us an obligation. Yet we give not to pay off our debts but because we have learned to be thankful. Our offerings are tokens of an inexpressible gratitude.

Offertory Prayer

How great you are, O God, and how generously you have blessed us! We bring our offerings with joy and thanksgiving. May they extend a welcome to friends and neighbors, strangers and foreigners. Let the message we send to the world be an authentic witness to the gospel. Bless the work we do and the ministry of others on our behalf, we pray in Jesus' name.

Commission and Blessing

Go into the world to share faith and good news.
Jesus Christ sends you to witness to the gospel.
> *We are not worthy to carry such a message.*
> *Who will believe what we have to say?*
Let all your words and deeds praise God.
May your life be a song of joy and thanksgiving.
> *We will pass on what is revealed to us.*
> *Surely God will go with us and help us.*
The Creator of all things keeps covenant with us.
God's steadfast love will sustain and inspire us.
> *Grace and peace are poured out on us in abundance.*
> *We believe God will empower our ministry.*
Amen. **Amen.**

(See hymns 43, 44.)

LAST SUNDAY AFTER EPIPHANY (TRANSFIGURATION)

Exodus 34:29–35   2 Corinthians 3:12–4:2
Psalm 99   Luke 9:28–36, (37–43)

CALL TO WORSHIP

We come together, a community of faith.
We have gathered to talk and listen to our God.
> *May our faces shine in anticipation.*
> *Our God has invited us to this moment of meeting.*

We share in a new covenant of promise and hope.
Our spirits have been set free for worship and praise.
> *We come with boldness to encounter our Creator.*
> *We assemble here, eager to be changed by God.*

Our fears melt into awe and wonder before God.
Our failures become opportunities for learning.
> *Let us praise God's holy name in chorus.*
> *Let us share in the glory of life. What a gift!*

INVOCATION

Holy are you, O God of all time and space. Before the vastness of your creation, the earth is as nothing. Yet you have lavished your energies upon it, shaping interdependent systems within systems. The mysterious gift of life is ours to handle with care. You have revealed yourself to us. You have created us for justice and equity. You have drawn us to the mountaintop to commune with you. O God, we are here, waiting for your further revelation. Come to enlighten and empower. Amen.

CALL TO CONFESSION

When we come before God, we can hold nothing back. God knows us better than we know ourselves. There is no hiding place. All our cunning and deceit are exposed. Our exploitation of others is known. Our misuse of God's gifts is evident. We can only repent and seek forgiveness.

PRAYER OF CONFESSION

We tremble before you, O God, for we have sinned. You already know what we have done and what we have failed to do. Hear us now as we recognize and admit our actions and inaction in violation of the trust you have placed in us. Enter into our excuses and our pretensions, Holy One, that we may be saved for ministry and mission. Amen.

Assurance of Forgiveness

God provides moments of transformation, sacred times when we sense the cleansing power of the Spirit restoring life and energy. We are even now being changed, lifted up from one degree of glory to another. Believe the good news. Live it. Do not lose heart but embrace your ministry, by the grace of God.

Collect

Transforming Spirit, who awakened Jesus' disciples on the mountaintop, awaken us here that we may discern the vision you place before us. We listen for the Word Christ has for us amid the perils of our day. We dare to question our call and examine ourselves, for we want to share your truth, not our own biases and manipulations, with the world.

Offertory Invitation

How much the church could accomplish with greater resources! How our shared ministry could blossom if our thanksgiving to God exceeded our fear, greed, and ambition. We have taken a small step toward faithfulness in coming to the mountaintop. Will we now be open to let God transform our giving?

Offertory Prayer

Thank you, God, for choosing us to speak for you and to act on your behalf. It is an honor to share with others what you have entrusted to us. Our offerings represent our selves and the depth of our commitment. We rededicate to you the talents, abilities, and resources you have placed in our hands. May we be faithful in our mutual ministry. Amen.

Commission and Blessing

We have been talking with God; what a privilege!
We have glimpsed eternity; what a joy!
> *How awesome to worship at the footstool of God!*
> *The veil has been lifted, but the mystery remains.*
Where the Spirit of God meets us, there is freedom.
In the presence of God's glory, we are made new.
> *We go out into the world, singing and rejoicing.*
> *Our faces and our manner declare God's glory.*
We have a ministry, by the grace of God.
We are missionaries to a needy world.
> *We will not fear or lose heart.*
> *We have found within us the dwelling place of God.*
Amen. **Amen.**

(See hymns 45, 46.)

THE LENTEN SEASON

Joel 2:1–2, 12–17 or Isaiah 58:1–12   2 Corinthians 5:20b–6:10
Psalm 51:1–17   Matthew 6:1–6, 16–21

CALL TO WORSHIP

Welcome to a season of self-examination;
this is a time for reconciliation with God and neighbor.
>   *Welcome together, elders and children, to meet God,*
>   *longing for the abundant mercy of our Creator.*

Seek to know God's presence here and everywhere;
let the wisdom of God guide you in truth.
>   *Through hardship, affliction, and calamity,*
>   *we reach for the power of God to steady us.*

Prepare yourselves for a period of testing.
Be open to the grace that enables your growth.
>   *With fasting, with weeping, and with mourning,*
>   *we seek the steadfast love of God.*

INVOCATION

With eagerness, yet trembling, we return to you, O God, not just as individuals, but as a family of faith. In this season of personal piety, we would enter into corporate disciplines of prayer and praise and service. May our prayers be honest and full of care for others. May our praise involve emotions as well as intellect. Guide our service, that we may invest ourselves in ways that are worthy of your investment in us. Amen.

CALL TO CONFESSION

Christians are sometimes labeled hypocrites. Do we appear pious only in church? Do we call attention to our good deeds for recognition and reward? How do our private lives and working relationships fit the picture we want others to see? God invites honest self-reflection and struggle toward authentic living.

PRAYER OF CONFESSION

Help us, awesome God, to be honest with ourselves and with you. We want to change our wasteful, destructive ways. We want to be rid of the evil that weighs us down, the guilt that crushes our spirits. Have mercy on us as we remember and confess our sins in these moments of silent struggle. Purge us of all the garbage from our past. Wash us in the flowing streams of your forgiving love. Create in us clean hearts, O God, and fill our lives with a new and right spirit. Sustain our hearts day by day in renewed focus on your steadfast love. Amen.

ASSURANCE OF FORGIVENESS

Do you sense changes happening deep inside you? Can you feel new life surging among us? God's forgiveness is real. God is gracious and merciful, restoring us to the joy of salvation. The one who created us sees our brokenness and helps us put the pieces back together. God works with us on new designs for living. We are free to become new people. Praise God!

COLLECT

God of secret places, you know the hidden depths of our hearts and are acquainted with all our ways. You know when the face we present to the world is different from the reality inside us. Bring together our private conscience and public image. Open to us the treasures of your Word and make them the central value of our lives, that our ministry may be pleasing in your sight and draw others to your reconciling love. Amen.

OFFERTORY INVITATION

As we have been directed to pray in secret, so, too, we are invited to give without letting the right hand know what the left hand is doing. When we bring an offering, we are responding to God's generosity, not trying to impress our neighbors. Our tithes already belong to God. Our extra gifts are treasures laid up in heaven. Worship God with your offering.

OFFERTORY PRAYER

As you have been bountiful toward us, loving God, we would be generous in supporting the programs and mission of your church. You have made us rich, even in the face of poverty. You have given us all we need, even when it seems we have little. Help us to find the right priorities for all you entrust to us, that our hearts may follow our treasure to their rightful home. Amen.

COMMISSION AND BLESSING

Now is the acceptable time, the day of salvation:
Go out to tell the world of God's grace.
> **God restores to us the joy of salvation**
> **and sustains us with a willing spirit.**
As our worship ends, our service continues;
the Holy Spirit goes with us wherever we go.
> **By the grace of God, we will do what God intends,**
> **with kindness, purity and genuine love.**
May Lent be not an outer show but an inner discipline,
a time for spiritual growth and shared commitment.
> **We will fast and pray and give,**
> **knowing that God who sees in secret will reward us.**
Amen. **Amen.**

(See hymns 48, 49, 50.)

Deuteronomy 26:1–11
Psalm 91:1–2, 9–16

Romans 10:8b–13
Luke 4:1–13

Call to Worship

Gather to remember and share stories of faith;
rejoice in the goodness of the loving God.
>   *Before our stories began, there was God;*
>   *through all our days, God walks with us.*
Worship the one who gives and sustains life;
sing praises to the one who is our refuge.
>   *There is no place we can go where God is not;*
>   *amid life's terrors, God's promises hold true.*
Delight in God, whose protection we enjoy;
dance with the God, who frees us for new possibilities.
>   *We call out to God, expecting to be heard;*
>   *we listen, knowing there is truth to be received.*

Invocation

God of history, whose Word is alive in us, write your truth into our lives this day. Work your signs and wonders in our midst. Show us your salvation. Be present in our troubles and in our triumphs. Lead us away from bondage to things that do not matter. Show us the better land you intend for us, where barriers no longer divide and true community is born. Amen.

Call to Confession

Come, all who have inflicted or accepted oppression; we share in the world's sin. Come, all who make distinctions among people; we participate in the brokenness of God's family. Come, all who respond to the false voices of the world; God is calling us away from our former limitations.

Prayer of Confession

Sovereign God, we confess our desire to reshape your world to our own advantage. We are more concerned with what we eat than with who will get to eat today. Our own security is more important to us than the health and safety of all your children. The first fruits of our labor grace the altars of our own desires instead of honoring you. We prefer that you keep your distance from us unless we need you. We like promises without commands, gifts without responsibilities. O God, we confess that our ways don't work. Turn us around for true worship and service, as forgiven and forgiving people. Amen.

ASSURANCE OF FORGIVENESS

All who call on God will know salvation. Those who cling to God will be delivered. How great is the joy of people who are loved, forgiven, and set free to become a new creation, through Christ Jesus. God's gifts are for you. Receive them in trust, knowing that God's presence and protection are yours to enjoy every day.

COLLECT

Spirit above all spirits, revealed to us in the faithfulness of Jesus and in the testimony of our ancestors in the faith, keep us from temptations that block our worship and silence our witness. Inspire us to share both bread and meaning, to worship with pure motives, to serve without need for recognition or reward, that your name may be glorified and your will be done among us and through us. Amen.

OFFERTORY INVITATION

All we have is from God. Our best is to be returned to God, freely given to minister in Christ's name. Out of gratitude for a land flowing with milk and honey, we bring our first fruits to be blessed in the outreach of the church.

OFFERTORY PRAYER

From the abundance entrusted to us, we offer up the best we can give. Guide our use of this precious trust, that it may be spent in ways you choose, in places where you would send us, for the sake of people among whom you wish to dwell. May we bear witness to your abiding love, not only with money but with dedicated lives. Allow us to be instruments of assurance and compassion in our homes and wherever our journeys lead. Amen.

COMMISSION AND BLESSING

Depart to the places of your inheritance;
God will dwell with you there and bless you.
> **All that we have is a gift from God;**
> **everywhere we go, we are with our Creator.**
Walk in the ways of God, rejoicing in God's goodness;
the Most High will honor your calls and protect you.
> **We call on God's name as we scatter once more;**
> **our prayers will continue in every day and place.**
Know that Christ Jesus was raised from death for you.
Continue in faith, sharing the good news.
> **We rejoice in our salvation and claim our healing.**
> **We offer renewal and hope to the world.**
Amen. **Amen.**

(See hymns 51, 52.)

Genesis 15:1–12, 17–18   Philippians 3:17–4:1
Psalm 27   Luke 13:31–35 or 9:28–36

CALL TO WORSHIP

Put away your hesitation to come before God;
quiet your fears and anxieties, for God welcomes us.
>*God is our light and our salvation;*
>*whom shall we fear?*

Look to the heavens for inspiration and assurance;
look around you, for God's presence is everywhere.
>*God is the stronghold of our lives;*
>*of whom shall we be afraid?*

Let us watch and wait with our Creator;
let us trust in the one who gives life and hope.
>*Teach us your ways, O God,*
>*and lead us on a level path.*

INVOCATION

In this place, our hearts take courage. Your goodness is all around us. The trials
and cares of life are stilled before you. Show us your face, O God; let your love be
known to us. We need this hour to remember who we are, to let you gather us
under your wings. We need this time to feel close to one another, to recognize
ourselves as brothers and sisters. We need reminders of the humanity and glory of
Jesus Christ that empower our discipleship. Hear our cries and help us. Amen.

CALL TO CONFESSION

God has drawn the church into covenant, calling us to be a faithful people who
walk in the ways of Christ. Yet how often do we explore what that means or
examine our behavior against the example of Jesus? A time of confession gives us
the opportunity to reclaim and grow in our relationship with God.

PRAYER OF CONFESSION

God of all people, we confess that we would like to claim your majesty and power
for our exclusive benefit. We relish the good things of life and are reluctant to
share with those who seem less deserving. We resist the prophets who point out
our greed, even when we feel we are being generous. We resent persons in
positions of authority over us who seem not to have our best interests at heart. We
are angry about ones whose evil deeds seem to go unpunished. O God, how can
we receive your mercy when we are so reluctant to pass it on? Help us to center
our lives in your love more than on our own desires. Amen.

ASSURANCE OF FORGIVENESS
God does not cast us off or forsake us but is with us in our suffering and adversity. Even when we live as enemies of the cross, the God of Jesus Christ does not give up on us. Surely there is shelter for us in the midst of our troubles and forgiveness when we have gone our own way. Lift up your eyes to behold God's promises. Praise God with songs and shouts of joy.

COLLECT
Self-revealing God, whom we meet in quiet retreats and on busy streets, take us now to the mountaintop. Be to us an overshadowing presence that gathers us into community so we may hear your voice and receive your Word. So empower us that we may be authentic witnesses for Jesus Christ wherever you send us. Amen.

OFFERTORY INVITATION
All who find a home in the house of God are invited to extend its sheltering and serving ministry to the world. We are challenged to do this in person but also by sharing the wealth God entrusts to us. What sacrifices do we offer in the name of Jesus Christ, who risked everything for us?

OFFERTORY PRAYER
In the confidence that you will multiply our best efforts, we bring our offerings for the work of your church in the world. Holy God, it is a joy to present our sacrifices, for we are as blessed in our giving as we have been in receiving abundant goodness from your hand. Keep us from seeking to build permanent structures that might block spontaneous responses to your love. Amen.

COMMISSION AND BLESSING
Be strong and let your hearts take courage.
The God of our salvation has met us here.
> *Our hearts will not fear, for God is our shelter.*
> *Our spirits are confident, for God is our shield.*
God's blessings for each of us outnumber the stars.
The commonwealth of heaven is our dwelling place.
> *We will lift up our heads with shouts of joy.*
> *May our witness win others to God's realm.*
Go on your way with Christ as your companion.
Seek opportunities for witness and service.
> *We find our example and inspiration in Jesus.*
> *In the valleys of every day, we will show God's care.*
Amen. **Amen.**

(See hymns 53, 54.)

Isaiah 55:1–9   I Corinthians 10:1–13
Psalm 63:1–8   Luke 13:1–9

CALL TO WORSHIP

Ho, everyone who thirsts, come to the waters.
You who have no money, come, buy, and eat!
> *Our souls thirst for God in a dry and weary land.*
> *We seek God's power and glory in the sanctuary.*

Listen carefully to God and eat what is good;
delight yourselves in the rich food God provides.
> *Here our souls are satisfied as with a rich feast.*
> *Together our mouths praise God with joyful lips.*

God offers us steadfast love and a covenant relationship.
We are called to be faithful witnesses and leaders.
> *We have come to meditate on the living God.*
> *We seek inspiration and empowerment to do what God asks.*

INVOCATION

We come before you, gracious God, seeking what money cannot buy. Only you can provide nourishment for our souls. There is no other source of meaning in our mixed-up world. We can find no fountain of strength or sustenance apart from you. Surely you can be found where two or three are gathered together. As a community of faith, we call on you, believing that you are nearer than our next breath, more available to us than we can think, more caring than we ever dare to imagine. Uphold us now that we may worship on wings of joy. Amen.

CALL TO CONFESSION

God's gifts are available to all, yet some do not use them for the common good. God is faithful, extending love to everyone, yet many of us create idols to occupy our time and attention. We are blessed far beyond our deserving, yet we grumble and complain. How desperately we need to turn around and find new direction!

PRAYER OF CONFESSION

We have been tempted, loving God, to go our own way without reference to eternal truths. We seek our own gratification rather than the well-being of all your children. We compare ourselves to others and find their failures but seldom discover our own shortcomings. We seek to build our lives by our own limited design rather than by your larger purposes. We engage in immorality in the name of freedom and become enslaved by our selfish ambitions. The ground on which we stand is crumbling under our feet. O God, forgive us and grant us a firmer foundation. Amen.

Assurance of Forgiveness

God grants us strength to overcome temptation and offers us a second chance to produce the fruits of repentance. Receive these gifts from God who is faithful, in covenant with us and all people. Open yourselves to the continued guidance of the Holy One, for God's steadfast love is better than life. God's mercy is abundant; God's provision for us is extravagant. God's ways are higher than our own. Praise God with joyful lips.

Collect

Eternal God, whose call comes to us through the scriptures, in the remembrance of our baptism and in our shared life in the church, feed us now with your Word, that we may bear fruit. Confront us with your truth and keep us from being tempted beyond our strength, for we seek to be faithful in our covenant with you and responsible in our relationships with one another. May we together witness to your steadfast love in ways that transform evil into good. Amen.

Offertory Invitation

Why do we use our money for things that do not satisfy, or invest our time in activities without meaning or purpose? God offers us a way of life that satisfies. What we cannot buy, God freely gives us. Our offerings are one way of expressing our thanks.

Offertory Prayer

All that we present to you now, O God, we have received from your hand. We give so the hungry may eat and the thirsty may receive pure water. We share to send the good news of your Word to those who have not heard. We invest in just causes, that your mercy may be known among all people. Most of all, we give because passing on your gifts in generous response is necessary to life. Amen.

Commission and Blessing

God sends us out as witnesses to good news.
May our lips praise God as long as we live.
> *God's steadfast love is better than life;*
> *God's mercy and pardon break through life's clouds.*

Call on God in the midst of each day's tasks;
meditate on God's presence through the night.
> *God is our help in all times and places;*
> *we will call on God's name wherever we are.*

God will grant us strength to resist temptation
and vision to labor for what truly satisfies.
> *Praise God, whose waters quench our thirst.*
> *Thank God for the bread of life that feeds our souls.*

Amen. **Amen.**

(See hymns 55, 56.)

Joshua 5:9–12   2 Corinthians 5:16–21
Psalm 32   Luke 15:1–3, 11b–32

CALL TO WORSHIP

A new day has dawned, God's gift to us;
the fruits of the land are ours to enjoy.
> *We are a new creation in Jesus Christ;*
> *the old has passed away, the new has come.*
This is a day for forgiveness and reconciliation;
celebrate God's love for the lost who are found.
> *The glad cries of deliverance surround us;*
> *shouts of joy arise from our hearts.*
Let all who are faithful offer up prayers;
may all who are in Christ give thanks.
> *We will be glad and join the dance of life;*
> *with the upright of heart, we rejoice and sing.*

INVOCATION

Welcoming God, we have gathered together so that you may teach us the way we should go. In our times of distress and need, you have provided. When we have stubbornly followed our own plans, you have curbed our impulses. From our days of confusion and aimless wandering, you have rescued us and restored us to our true identity. Meet us now as we worship together to shape us into a righteous, reconciling people. Amen.

CALL TO CONFESSION

We pause to consider how far we may have wandered from our home with God. Are we sometimes like a horse or mule whose temper must be curbed? Have we turned away from responsibility in order to seek shallow pleasures and selfish gratification? Or do we consider ourselves above reproach, looking down on those mired in the pigpens of life? Wherever we are, whoever we are, there is much to confess.

PRAYER OF CONFESSION

O God, we will not try to hide from you the wrong we have done or the good we have neglected. You know our transgressions. You have observed our pretensions. We have claimed too lightly the label "Christian," for often we cut ourselves off from you and from people we disdain. At times our rebellion leaves us hungry, alone, and friendless. O God, we are not worthy to be called your children. Grant us, we pray, your forgiveness and pardon and a renewed sense of who you intend us to be and to become. Amen.

Assurance of Forgiveness

We are assured that God forgives the guilt of our sin. Happy are those whose transgression is forgiven, whose sin is covered. Happy are those to whom God imputes no iniquity and in whose spirit there is no deceit Rejoice, for God has brought us back to life!

Collect

God, whose love for us never fails, even when we wander far from home, teach us compassion for all who are lost and confused. Keep us from living as competitors for your favors, that we might participate joyfully in your forgiving, reconciling work. Make us ambassadors for Christ, that all your children may come home to your welcoming arms. Amen.

Offertory Invitation

We have been granted more than our share of the world's wealth. Often we have forgotten the source of our bounty. We grasp and spend as if all were ours to indulge our desires. This is the time to reexamine our management of what is really God's property, entrusted to us for a little while.

Offertory Prayer

Thank you, God, for proclaiming our worth when we do not value ourselves. Thank you for welcoming us to a celebration of life with so many precious gifts. Thank you now for the privilege of sharing so others may be led to your joyous embrace. Help us to be generous in gratitude for your lavish provision for all our needs. Amen.

Commission and Blessing

Stay near to God during the week that lies ahead;
be faithful in your times of prayer.
> **God is our hiding place and present help;**
> **we will speak to God and for God this week.**
Live as ambassadors of Jesus Christ every day;
rejoice when a sister or brother returns home to God.
> **We will seek to love as we have been loved;**
> **we will welcome, not judge, our brothers and sisters.**
We have been reconciled to God through Jesus Christ;
God's love and compassion will be with us always.
> **We will be glad and rejoice in God's goodness;**
> **we will share the joy of God's love.**
Amen. **Amen.**

(See hymn 57.)

Isaiah 43:16–21   Philippians 3:4b–14
Psalm 126   John 12:1–8

CALL TO WORSHIP

God's spirit is moving among us; give thanks!
Our God is about to do a new thing in our midst.
How good it is to be chosen by God;
we gather to sing our praises and thanks.
God has done great things for us; we are glad!
Now God is pointing us toward new goals.
We are waiting to hear what God would have us do;
we are ready to risk new behaviors to be faithful.
Into the wilderness of our lives comes living water.
Into the sorrow of our days comes reason for joy.
Forgetting what lies behind, we greet our future;
we press on, responding to the upward call of Christ.

INVOCATION

Powerful God, we give thanks that you have called us to be your people. In our times of gloom, you have sent your light. When we are weary and discouraged, you lift us up. In our thirst for meaning and purpose, you bring us to living water in Jesus Christ. Set before us now the joy of discovery and a vision of future possibilities. Unite us in friendship with one another, with Christ as our center and inspiration. Amen.

CALL TO CONFESSION

How much easier it is to criticize others than to see our own faults. How quickly we bemoan our suffering and struggles instead of rehearsing all our reasons for gratitude and joy. How often we cling to the past rather than heeding God's call to new life. We are invited to confess our destructive attitudes.

PRAYER OF CONFESSION

O God, whose upward call in Christ Jesus we have so often chosen to ignore, we confess that we settle for lesser goals while you summon us to embrace the realm of heaven. We seldom look beyond our own interests to the well-being of our sisters and brothers. We can see the wasteful acts of other people but not our own selfish habits. We exaggerate the contributions we make but ignore the sacrifices of others. We need forgiveness, O God. Do a new thing within and among us. Amen.

ASSURANCE OF FORGIVENESS

God summons us to return and welcomes us with joy. We are restored to full communion with the saints and are united in the heavenly call of Christ. Together, we find our horizons expanded and our priorities refined. God forgives us and sets before us once more the promise of fullness of life. Embrace God's pardon with renewed faith and joy.

COLLECT

God of the poor and oppressed, whose mercy and pardon are for all those who put their trust in you, teach us to be faithful to all we have learned from Jesus Christ. We seek the power of resurrection faith and the strength to achieve the goals you set before us. May we answer your call and bear fruit for your realm, attracting others to your loving embrace. Amen.

OFFERTORY INVITATION

The most lavish gifts we can bring are never enough to thank God for all we have received. Yet the tiniest offerings we present do not escape God's notice when presented with full commitment and devotion. Let us give as we are able.

OFFERTORY PRAYER

Beneficent God, we are glad for all the good things you have done for us. We count everything as loss before the surpassing value of knowing Jesus Christ. Receive our costly offerings and our best efforts, here dedicated for your use. May Christ be proclaimed and the poor be saved from the terrors of suffering and neglect. Fill the hearts of all your children with laughter and joy. To that end, bless our offerings. Amen.

COMMISSION AND BLESSING

The spirit of God sends us forth, a thankful people;
God goes with us, accomplishing new things among us.
> **We are God's chosen people, appointed for service.**
> **May our lives proclaim our thanks and praise.**
The great things God has done for us inspire our work.
We stretch and strive to reach new goals.
> **Day by day, we will listen for a new word from God;**
> **hour by hour, we will dare to be faithful to God's call.**
God will feed our hunger and quench our thirst
and will comfort us in our need and uplift us.
> **God's praise will continually be on our lips.**
> **We will embrace God's future as we seek to follow Christ.**
Amen. **Amen.**

(See hymns 61, 62.)

SIXTH SUNDAY IN LENT (PASSION SUNDAY)

Isaiah 50:4–9a
Psalm 31:9–16

Philippians 2:5–11
Luke 22:14–23:56

CALL TO WORSHIP

God awakens us and calls us to this time of worship.
Our ears are opened to hear God's Word of truth.
> **Speak to us, gracious God, and arouse our attention;**
> **teach us your way and excite our response.**

God has given us the tongues of teachers,
that our words may sustain and comfort the weary.
> **Open our lips, O God, to praise you;**
> **loosen our tongues to speak your Word of love.**

God has come to us in Jesus Christ to open our minds;
let us empty ourselves of pretense that we may learn.
> **Expand our minds and hearts, Sovereign God.**
> **Instruct us through the power of the cross.**

INVOCATION

In this season of distress and sorrow, we bow before you, all-knowing God. As we remember Jesus' walk toward Calvary, we are tormented by the inhumanity so easily evoked among us. As we recall our own times of suffering and grief, we identify with Christ. We bring to you this day our questions and rebellion as well as our faith and quiet longing. Deliver us, O God, from all that detracts from our full humanity. Help us grow toward the design for which you created us. Amen.

CALL TO CONFESSION

We invite God to examine our hearts, knowing we will not be put to shame. We are ready to discover and admit our sinfulness, for we realize the one who vindicates us is near. Come, then, in response to steadfast love, trusting that there is a way to move beyond guilt to forgiveness and acceptance.

PRAYER OF CONFESSION

God, whose fullness is far beyond our tiny glimmers of understanding, we bring to you our pretensions, our doubts, our fears. We have lived as if we were the center of all things. We have doubted any reality beyond what we can see. We have cringed in fear before the forces that deny you. We find it easier to betray Christ than to witness to the power of love. We are quick to take up the sword rather than risk a reconciling word. Our actions condemn us. We can only look to you to save us from ourselves. Amen.

ASSURANCE OF FORGIVENESS

When we know not what we do, God in Christ forgives us. When we know all too well what we have done, there is pardon if we face our guilt. The realm of God is ours to receive—not just as a future hope but as an emerging reality right here, right now. Accept the gift of new life and praise God!

COLLECT

God of light, whose majesty transcends all earthly powers and brings to naught the pretensions of all who rule in shadows, walk with us through the cruelty of temptation and denial and betrayal and bitter weeping, that we may not falter or lose hope but rather witness to the world that Jesus Christ is the Savior. Draw us into humble obedience and steadfast devotion, that your ways may be honored among us and be shared with all your children. Amen.

OFFERTORY INVITATION

What can we give to our Creator, who owns all things? How shall we honor the Christ who moves among us as one who serves? Will our offerings give wings to the spirit when we retain so much for our own benefit? Let us give that this church may be empowered to do the will of God.

OFFERTORY PRAYER

Loving God, we recognize that we lack nothing we really need. When we ask that your will be done, our vision is stretched beyond our immediate situation. We are thankful that we can give in Jesus' name. We are grateful that our wealth can ease the hunger of our sisters and brothers. We celebrate the promise that lies beyond the cross. Bless the offerings we bring Amen.

COMMISSION AND BLESSING

Go boldly into a world that does not understand you;
go in the name of love that is for all persons.
> *We reclaim the covenant of Christ's table.*
> *We will ignore mocking whispers to follow Christ.*
Be willing to stir up the people to claim their gifts;
live among them as one who is sent to serve.
> *We will speak words of salvation and faith;*
> *we will live, trusting the love we have received.*
The forgiveness and blessing of Christ go with us.
The power of prayer is ours to seek and use.
> *We will not be confounded, for God helps us.*
> *We will trust the steadfast love of God.*
Amen. **Amen.**

(See hymns 61, 62.)

Isaiah 50:4–9a   Philippians 2:5–11
Psalm 118:1–2, 19–29   Luke 19:28–40

CALL TO WORSHIP

Morning after morning, God grants us a new day;
wake up to the joys and challenges life presents.
> **This is the day that God has made;**
> **let us rejoice and be glad in it.**

God equips us to face whatever the day may hold;
watch and listen as God offers to teach us.
> **We gather, seeking a blessing in the name of God.**
> **We come, thanking God for the gift of salvation.**

See the gates of righteousness thrown open for us;
enter to praise God's marvelous works.
> **God's steadfast love endures forever!**
> **Blessed is the one who comes in God's name.**

INVOCATION

We stand together, mighty God, for you have sustained us through weary days and anguished nights. We join the shouts of welcome, "Blessed is the one who comes in God's name. Peace in heaven and glory in the highest." This is a day of celebration. There is joy in the air. We have witnessed the transforming power of Jesus' compassion. But there are ominous overtones. There are voices that say peace is a mirage and love will not endure. We cling to our faith that your steadfast love embraces life and death, that we are surrounded and upheld by your goodness. Meet us here, we pray. Amen.

CALL TO CONFESSION

Come, all who are waving branches to welcome the Savior. When the light shines on us, we see the shadows we create. We sense our need for a faith more deeply grounded and a love more fully committed.

PRAYER OF CONFESSION

We confess, O God, that we identify with times of optimism and applause. We like a religion that makes us feel good. We prefer safety and security and certainty. Then Jesus comes, riding on a donkey, reaching out to outsiders, proclaiming humble obedience as a virtue, challenging powerful people to change their ways. We sense danger. When Christ upsets our craving for stability, we turn away from the risks. We do not want to be rejected or face a cross. We are not sure we really want to be Christians. O God, help us! Amen.

ASSURANCE OF FORGIVENESS
God contends with us in our fears, identifies our rebellion, and transforms our contrition into courage. Our Creator does not give up on us when we are discouraged or reject us when our pretensions get out of hand. God, who exalted Jesus, is ready to forgive and lift us up. Christ walks with us on the way of faithfulness, empowering us to become the disciples we are called to be.

COLLECT
God of peace and glory, who sent Jesus to teach and inspire the multitudes and call us all to discipleship, help us to celebrate the triumph of humility and the satisfaction of servanthood. We rejoice that Christ shared our humanity and lifted the self-esteem of the lowly. May all the world receive Christ's spirit and give thanks for your steadfast love. Amen.

OFFERTORY INVITATION
If Jesus Christ is to reign among us, much more will be needed than our praise and rejoicing when we are together. How do we witness and serve when we are apart? How much of ourselves and our substance will we invest?

OFFERTORY PRAYER
Grateful for your grace that is new every morning and thankful that the gates of righteousness are open to us, we bring our gifts to your altar, O God. We dedicate our offerings and ourselves, that the reign of Jesus Christ may be realized and celebrated wherever Christians gather to worship and everywhere we scatter to serve. May every knee bow at the name of Jesus and every tongue confess that Christ is the world's salvation. May the needs of all your children be addressed by those who confess Jesus Christ. Amen.

COMMISSION AND BLESSING
We have testified to God's mighty works in Christ;
we go into the world to carry on what Jesus began.
> *We have learned what Christ has taught;*
> *God's Word is in our hearts and on our tongues.*
Have the mind of Christ who did not grasp for power;
reach for your full humanity, in humility and praise.
> *The one who was rejected is head of the church;*
> *we will follow in faith and trust where Christ leads.*
Be assured of God's continuing help and blessing;
the steadfast love of God endures forever.
> *We celebrate the name of Jesus above all other names.*
> *Blessed is the one who comes in God's name.*
Amen. **Amen.**

(See hymns 61, 63.)

Sixth Sunday in Lent (Palm Sunday)   69

Isaiah 42:1–9   Hebrews 9:11–15
Psalm 36:5–11   John 12:1–11

CALL TO WORSHIP

Come, God is calling us to a new day;
the gifts of breath and spirit are ours to enjoy.
>   *How great is the steadfast love of God;*
>   *whatever we do, God is righteous and faithful.*

The past is behind us, and the future is not yet;
today, God declares to us new possibilities.
>   *Through Christ we share in a new covenant;*
>   *our eternal inheritance is already evident.*

God invites us to join in proclaiming justice;
we are appointed as bearers of light and love.
>   *Our eyes have been opened to see others' needs.*
>   *Our hands and hearts are equipped to help them.*

INVOCATION

God of heaven and earth, we seek your light amid the gathering gloom of this
week. Yet it is much easier to take refuge in the shadow of your wings than to
stand exposed in the light. It seems safer to stay in the prisons we have made or
accepted for ourselves than to risk passage through the open doors of the freedom
you offer. Call us into the warmth of your light where your acceptance and
empowerment may be fully known. Amen.

CALL TO CONFESSION

Jesus challenged those who thought the old ways were the only ways. He exposed
the limited vision of religious leaders and stretched the perceptions of men and
women who became disciples. Christ comes to us now, breaking into our self-
protective routines. Our timidity is conquered and our temptations to arrogance
are confronted. We are invited to face ourselves honestly in dialogue with our
Creator.

PRAYER OF CONFESSION

How can we bear your judgment, O God? You expect so much of us. You
commission us to work for justice for all your children. We are not sure what is
just or who is worthy. We want to pronounce judgment on those whose priorities
are different from our own. We grow weary and discouraged when no one
responds to our efforts. At times, God, we do not like ourselves. Sometimes we
are jealous of others. We are not at all eager to change our ways. Minister to us in
our confusion and fear. We confess our need. Amen.

ASSURANCE OF FORGIVENESS

God delights in us in spite of our mistakes and misjudgments. With steadfast love, God turns us from dead works to a living faith. Through Christ, we are saved and welcomed into a new covenant. Redeemed from our transgressions, we are promised an eternal inheritance. We are commissioned once again to carry light to the nations. Glory to God in the highest!

COLLECT

Giver of life, whose love celebrates our gestures of devotion, take us by the hand to lead us to deeper understanding and greater faithfulness. Help us so to identify with the servant ministry of Jesus that we, too, may give our best to establish justice among our brothers and sisters throughout your world. Amen.

OFFERTORY INVITATION

All of us have received the gift of life through no merit of our own. An eternal inheritance awaits us. As we feast on the abundance God provides, let us give thanks for the opportunity to share in the ministry of healing. Our offerings can make it possible for others to drink from the rivers of God's delights.

OFFERTORY PRAYER

Thanks be to you, O God, that you continue to call people like us to share in your transforming work. Even when our witness is but a dimly burning wick, you commission us as lightbearers to the world. We dedicate our offerings that eyes may be opened, ears unstopped, and prisoners released. We rededicate ourselves to serve wherever you direct. Amen.

COMMISSION AND BLESSING

Go out with confidence into God's new day;
breathe in God's spirit to empower your ministry.
We go out to share God's steadfast love;
in all things, we will seek to be faithful and true.
Remember that you are accepted and loved;
God values what you give for others.
We seek recognition and justice for all people;
the needs of our sisters and brothers are our concern.
We are a part of God's covenant with the world;
an eternal inheritance is God's promise to us.
God continues to grant us the light of Christ;
we will walk by faith as Christ lights our way.
Amen. **Amen.**

(See hymns 64, 65.)

Isaiah 49:1–7   1 Corinthians 1:18–31
Psalm 71:1–14   John 12:20–36

CALL TO WORSHIP

People far and near, listen for God's call;
your Creator knows your name and bids you come.
> *We gather here, for God is our refuge;*
> *we come to worship God, our rock and fortress.*
All who love life are invited to this celebration;
all who believe in light are welcome to enjoy it.
> *God is our light, our strength, and our salvation;*
> *God is the source of our life in Jesus Christ.*
Assemble in this place of worship and learning.
God is eager to teach us to become children of light.
> *We bow before God, the source of all blessings;*
> *we rejoice that God chooses us to be servants.*

INVOCATION

We glorify you, Sovereign God, for you have cared for us from our birth and blessed our lives with good things. Our mouths are filled with praise as we celebrate your wisdom and rejoice in your presence with us. O God, we wish to see Jesus. We want to know the one who took on our humanity for our sake. Our highest desire is to follow where Christ leads and to serve where we are sent. May this time of worship equip us for our ministry. Amen.

CALL TO CONFESSION

How often God has called and we have not answered! How often we have spent our strength in pursuits that dull our hearing and blind our eyes to God's presence and purpose! The wonders of God surround us, but we do not perceive them. God's strength is our support, but we claim to walk alone. Draw near, that the separation we have caused may be overcome.

PRAYER OF CONFESSION

Our souls are troubled. What shall we say? We have ignored you, O God, the source of life. We have boasted of our own accomplishments. We spend our energies for nothing and vanity. We seek to become powerful and important in the eyes of others. The cross seems a foolish mistake and a monument to weakness. O God, do not let the night fall on our infidelity and confusion. Save us, we pray. Amen.

ASSURANCE OF FORGIVENESS

Jesus Christ brings salvation to the ends of the earth and to each one of us. God turns seeming weakness and foolishness into strength and wisdom. Hope is renewed and life is restored when we realize God's faithfulness. Praise be to God, our rock and fortress.

COLLECT

Glory be to you, mighty God, whose ways turn our values upside-down. We wish to see Jesus, that we might learn the course of eternal life and bear fruit for your realm in our daily living. Let your voice be heard in the proclamation and performance of this congregation, to lead many of your children to walk in the light. Amen.

OFFERTORY INVITATION

According to popular wisdom, life is enriched by what we can accumulate. Success is measured in strength, power, and possessions. But God makes foolish the wisdom of the world. It is not what we hoard but what we give away that makes us rich. The church challenges us to care and to share.

OFFERTORY PRAYER

Strange and compelling God, we would not measure our worth in money. Rather, our wealth is a tool that makes possible some of the works of care and love that you expect of us. We want to spread your seeds of truth. May they take root among us and far beyond our small circles. Use our offerings to bring light to our shadowy world. Amen.

COMMISSION AND BLESSING

God has called us together to strengthen us.
Now God commissions us and sends us out to serve.
> *God has been our fortress and our refuge.*
> *We carry to the world good news of saving grace.*

Our human foolishness gives way to the wisdom of God. Our weakness becomes a channel for God's working.
> *Our mouths will be full of praise to God.*
> *Our daily lives will show forth God's glory.*

When we die to self, we give life to those around us.
Surely God will lift us up to walk in the light.
> *May God use us as a light to all nations.*
> *Shine through us, O God, that all may worship you.*

Amen. **Amen.**

(See hymns 66, 67.)

WEDNESDAY OF HOLY WEEK— A, B, C

Isaiah 50:4–9a
Psalm 70

Hebrews 12:1–3
John 13:21–32

CALL TO WORSHIP

Seek God with gladness and rejoicing.
Wake up to God's presence and help.
> *From our weariness, we rise to new life.*
> *God awakens our ears and opens our eyes.*

Listen for the Word that sustains and delivers us.
Recognize the presence who raises and inspires us.
> *From our rebellion, God calls us to come home.*
> *God meets us in our hostility, poverty, and need.*

Lay aside all that weighs you down and troubles you.
Turn away from contention to a community of friends.
> *God ministers to us in our confusion.*
> *The fainthearted find courage and renewed faith.*

INVOCATION

Come among us, Sovereign God, to teach us. Make haste to help us, for we are deeply aware of our need. The race of life appears to us too demanding. Our defeats are difficult to bear. Enemies surround us, and even our friends seem not to understand. Only you can deliver us from depression and despair. May all who seek you rejoice and be glad in you! May all who search for truth know your greatness and embrace your salvation. Amen.

CALL TO CONFESSION

The downfall of Judas stemmed from misunderstanding and impatience. His desire for power and greed for gain closed his ears to Jesus' teaching. His selfish ambition led to betrayal of the one he had loved and served. When we view his sin, do we sense our own?

PRAYER OF CONFESSION

We have wanted to be loyal to you, powerful God, but it is easy to forget that you are in charge. The ways of love and nonviolence do not seem to work. The shame of the cross has no appeal. We want to enjoy our advantages, not risk them for people we do not know. We like some of the things Jesus did and said, but we turn from following when opposition comes and danger looms. O God, save us from the temptation to betray and defect. Grant us courage to live as disciples. Amen.

ASSURANCE OF FORGIVENESS

In Christ, your guilt is taken away. Your shame and confusion are lifted. Your good intentions are affirmed. Lay aside the weight of sin and dare to stand with Jesus Christ. Support one another as pioneers of a new and better way. God will help you and grant you joy.

COLLECT

God of Glory, whose presence sustains us in the face of opposition, betrayal, and suffering, feed us now with your Word of life, that we may not succumb to temptation. Nourish us as disciples of Jesus Christ so we may grow in faithfulness and witness to your saving love for all people. Amen.

OFFERTORY INVITATION

Our offerings bear witness to the sustaining influence of one who was denied and betrayed by his friends. We give—not out of guilt for having likewise, ourselves, denied and betrayed—but out of thanksgiving that these sins have been forgiven and overcome. Out of the rich resources God gives to us, we bring our response. May our offerings express the joy of giving.

OFFERTORY PRAYER

In our poverty, you have come to us, great and mighty God. When our spirits are crushed by the harsh realities of a sinful world, you restore our hope. When we think we have nothing to give, you shower us with riches beyond our imagining. So now, with joy, we reclaim gifts of the Spirit as we dedicate the gifts of our hands. All that we have and all that we are becoming are yours already. We bring these offerings before you because we need to give in order to live fully the life you grant to us. Amen.

COMMISSION AND BLESSING

We have received our Savior's love.
God has given us tongues to share that gift.
> *Thanks be to God for the love we have received.*
> *It is a joy to tell others of that love.*
Go out, then, as people who are not confounded by evil.
Lift up those who are weary and fainthearted.
> *We will run with joy the race of life.*
> *Jesus is our model, our guide, and our strength.*
Speak of God's saving grace to all who will listen.
Live God's saving grace among all you will meet.
> *May Christ be glorified in all we do and say.*
> *God is great; God is our help every day.*
Amen. **Amen.**

(See hymns 61, 62, 68.)

Exodus 12:1–4, (5–10), 11–14   I Corinthians 11:23–26
Psalm 116:1–2, 12–19   John 13:1–17, 31b–35

CALL TO WORSHIP

Come to God, who has loved us through Jesus Christ.
Present yourselves to the Spirit who understands your need.
> **God has heard our voices and heeded our cries.**
> **We will call on God's name as long as we live.**

Come to prepare yourselves for the journey of faith.
God sets before us a memorial feast.
> **We will pay our vows to God at the table of Christ.**
> **We will offer our sacrifices of thanksgiving.**

Come to embrace the new covenant God offers.
Eat and drink in remembrance of Jesus Christ.
> **We come to be washed and cleansed and healed.**
> **God will equip us here to love one another.**

INVOCATION

We have gathered, O God, in answer to your mandate that we love one another as you have loved us in Jesus of Nazareth. We gather as disciples awaiting a word of assurance and promise. We seek protection from all who insist on conformity to their narrow points of view. We seek empowerment at the table of remembrance and celebration. We long to love as we have been loved, to serve as Christ has served among us, to live lives of thanksgiving that fulfill our vows to you and to one another. We pray in Jesus' name. Amen.

CALL TO CONFESSION

God calls into judgment all that distracts us from true worship: our possessions, our favorite activities, our love of comfort and security. Christ's way of humble service challenges our desire for recognition and applause. We are summoned before God to rid ourselves of our pretenses, that we may be empowered for discipleship.

PRAYER OF CONFESSION

God of love, we confess that we have been slow to turn to you with our sacrifices of thanksgiving. When things go well for us, we give credit to our own efforts rather than pay our vows to you. In times of difficulty, we resist your claims on us and deny your covenant. We want our own way, as if our desires should rule your world. We have not learned to love others without conditions or to serve them without pretense. Forgive us, we pray, and free us to know the blessing and joy of following where Jesus leads. Amen.

Assurance of Forgiveness

God has heard our voices and listened to our supplications. We are welcomed by Jesus Christ to the table where all may eat and drink and find a welcome. Our host bows down to wash our feet and invites us to do the same for one another. Embrace this opportunity to love as we have been loved. Lift up the cup of salvation, for we have been freed from our sin to praise God.

Collect

Loving God, who gave all things into the hands of Jesus and inspired him to wash the feet of the disciples, draw us now into the story as participants, not as mere observers. Help us to recognize one another as sisters and brothers united in the body of Christ for service in the world. As you love us into wholeness and joy, enable us to love others in ways that evoke their response to your love. Amen.

Offertory Invitation

As the congregation of Israel brought the best lambs from their flocks as offerings, we are invited to bring our best in thanksgiving to God. This is a time to express our gratitude for all God's bounty that we enjoy. In this act of worship, we share the love of God through the ministries and outreach of the church.

Offertory Prayer

Thank you, God, for sending Jesus Christ to meet with us on this holy night. In communion, we share once more in the new covenant intended for all your children. We are linked with them in a kinship made evident at the table and in acts of caring every day. Inspire your church to use our offerings to spread love in your world. Amen.

Commission and Blessing

We have received the mandate to love one another.
Christ sends us out as disciples of love.
> *We are messengers of the new covenant.*
> *We will share Christ's invitation to the table.*
We have observed Christ's example of servanthood.
Now we are sent to serve in Christ's name.
> *We are eager to live for Christ today.*
> *We commit ourselves to walk in Jesus' way.*
In the shadow of death, God's love is made real.
Before the cross, we are blessed and empowered.
> *The love of God goes with us everywhere we go.*
> *In Jesus Christ, we are strengthened to love.*
Amen. **Amen.**

(See hymn 69.)

Isaiah 52:13–53:12   Hebrews 4:14–16, 5:7–9, or 10:16–25
Psalm 22   John 18:1–19:42

CALL TO WORSHIP

The God our ancestors trusted is with us.
The servant, despised and rejected, calls us together.
> *We cry out to God and find no answers.*
> *Jesus, whom we seek, has been taken from us.*

We are people of the new covenant in Jesus Christ.
Therefore, have confidence to enter the sanctuary.
> *God seems so far away from our groaning.*
> *How can we believe what we have heard?*

God will fulfill all that is promised.
Trust in God, who will rescue and deliver you.
> *How can another die to save us?*
> *We stand at the cross in terror and confusion.*

INVOCATION

In the loneliness of Good Friday, we come to you, God, wondering how to find your will in the midst of tragedy. All the grief and sorrow we have known is rekindled at the cross. The pain is more than we can bear. Where can we find any meaning in all of this? Thorns and nails and bitter tears cannot be your intent for your children. Whatever happened to love? Where is truth to be found in all of this? Silent God, answer our cries. Amen.

CALL TO CONFESSION

Do you, like Peter, hear the cock crowing? How often have your good intentions been denied by your own words and actions? As the prophet said, "All we like sheep have gone astray." God invites us to lay aside the burden of our sin and come home.

PRAYER OF CONFESSION

Distant God, we repent of small misdeeds to satisfy our consciences, for we cannot deal with our denial of you. We seek to find life apart from you, for the cross is too threatening for us. We want comfort, not sacrifice. We embrace privilege, not pain. Yet the love of Christ brings us to our knees in awe and wonder. O God, we want to lay aside our preoccupation with self to become full participants in your realm. Rescue us from ourselves, O God. Deliver us from sin and bring us home. Amen.

ASSURANCE OF FORGIVENESS

In Jesus Christ, we know the forgiveness of God brought near. God dwells within and among us, the power of love, always available. Surely one has borne our griefs, carried our sorrows, and offered us healing. Receive once more the gift of wholeness. Find your strength renewed and your hope rekindled. Be bold to accept your call to discipleship.

COLLECT

Suffering God, whose compassion is with all your children in their times of grievous need and whose purposes will prevail in spite of opposition, injustice, and death, take us once more to Gethsemane and to Calvary to face the cross. Let us share the experience of loneliness, rejection, and pain in such a way that we are strengthened to live as people of the covenant who provoke one another to love and give encouragement to those facing bitter trials. Forsake not your children, we pray, for we trust you and want to respond to your leading. Amen.

OFFERTORY INVITATION

Love knows no limits to its giving. Insistence on the way of love for all people sent Jesus to the cross. There God's Servant poured out life and died that we might learn to live as whole, trusting, faithful people, eager to share what has been given to us. Today we bring ourselves with our offerings in thanksgiving for all we have received.

OFFERTORY PRAYER

With our gifts and our lives, we wish to follow the living way Christ has opened for us. We respond to the call of love that we have heard, reaching out to one another in the programs of this church and extending our helping hands to our community. May our mission be expanded beyond the reaches of our sight to share in causes and outreach that benefit all your children. Give wings to the testimony of our words and deeds, that the world may believe the good news. Amen.

COMMISSION AND BLESSING

Go as disciples into a world that rejects Christ's message.
Go as defenders of the faith that heals and saves.
> *How can we love when love is ridiculed and rejected?*
> *How can we face disappointment and scorn?*
Live as people of hope, serving a faithful God.
Know that you are loved and sent on a mission.
> *We are growing to believe what we have heard.*
> *Jesus has borne our griefs and died to make us whole.*
Make your witness to the truth you have heard.
Your service will prosper and bear good fruit.
> *We will trust in the God who delights in us.*
> *We will follow our Savior in love and service.*
Amen. **Amen.**

(See hymns 70, 71, 72.)

Job 14:1–14 or Lamentations 3:1–9, 19–24   I Peter 4:1–8
Psalm 31:1–4, 15–16   Matthew 27:57–66 or John 19:38–42

CALL TO WORSHIP

In the midst of gloom, seek the light.
From the shadows of death, reach out in hope.
> **God is our refuge, our rock, and our fortress.**
> **We will call to God and cry out for help.**

The steadfast love of God never ceases.
God's mercies never end; they are new every morning.
> **We trust in God to lead us and guide us.**
> **Our times are in God's hands.**

Worship the one who delivers and blesses us.
Come home to God who listens and welcomes us.
> **We want to hear God's will for our troubled times.**
> **We ask to be equipped for whatever life holds.**

INVOCATION

Incline your ear to us, gracious God, and do not be angry with us. Our souls are bowed down by the troubles we have experienced and observed. There is suffering and affliction among your children, and hope lies buried in the shadows of the tomb. When mortals die, where are they? Will they live again? O God, you are our God. You know what we cannot know. Let your face shine on us here, lest we stumble on crooked, rocky paths. Grant us light and renew our hope. Amen.

CALL TO CONFESSION

Amid the confusion and despair of Holy Saturday, our lives are judged. In the uncertainty of in-between times, our complacency is shattered and we must face ourselves as we really are. How is our inaction involved in the death of others? Does the way we live send Christ once more to the cross and the grave?

PRAYER OF CONFESSION

Distant God, we cannot escape the shame of this day. We have neglected the causes for which Christ lived. Our discipleship has been sporadic at best. We have not disciplined ourselves for a life of prayer and service. We seal off our spiritual needs from the rest of life and follow our deceptive human desires. Neither our speech nor our actions would reveal to those we meet that we are Christians. O God, by your steadfast love, save us. Amen.

ASSURANCE OF FORGIVENESS

God is faithful, even to those who are spiritually dead. Even God's anger is for our salvation, not our destruction. In righteousness, God delivers us. God's love is poured out for us day by day. Love covers a multitude of sins. Let love rule in your lives. By the will of God, live in the Spirit, reaching out to minister to the Christ you find in others and for the Christ who dwells in you.

COLLECT

Persistent God, whose call to discipleship finds answer in unexpected places, in lives once focused on other loyalties, bring light to the shadows. Grant us courage to act in response to needs you reveal to us. Awaken faith where before there were only questions. Stir us to constant love for one another, so all may find support in times of suffering and meaning in spite of loss. May hope be the character of our common life. Amen.

OFFERTORY INVITATION

Secret disciples brought costly spices for the burial of Jesus. How much more should we bring gifts to honor the spirit of Christ in our midst. We have known a presence that brings out the best in us. Thank God for Jesus Christ! There are needs in the world that we can help to meet in Christ's name. Let us give as we have been blessed.

OFFERTORY PRAYER

With love in our hearts we bring our offerings. In spite of our worries and fears, we dare to give away a part of what we think we need for ourselves. In the face of death, our priorities are changed. The love of Christ awakens an answering love within and among us. Thanks be to God, who delivers us and guides our steps. We trust you, God, to lead us beyond death to life. May our gifts bring hope to others. Amen.

COMMISSION AND BLESSING

Life, as we know it here and now, does not last.
Yet God's mercies are new every morning.
> **Hope endures through and beyond the shadows.**
> **Great is God's faithfulness and steadfast love.**
The tomb may be sealed and secured,
but death cannot contain the spirit of love.
> **We will discipline ourselves to live in the Spirit.**
> **We will seek God's will for ourselves and all people.**
Live, then, as children of the light.
Trust in God, who is our refuge, our rock, and our guide.
> **We will take the risks of faith and we will witness.**
> **If we must suffer for truth, we will do so.**
Amen. **Amen.**

(See hymns 73, 74.)

THE EASTER SEASON

Acts 10:34–43 or Isaiah 65:17–25   I Corinthians 15:19–26 or Acts 10:34-43
Psalm 118:1–2, 14–24   John 20:1–18 or Luke 24:1–12

CALL TO WORSHIP

Sing the glad songs of victory;
God is creating a day of newness and joy.
> **God is our strength and our song;**
> **this is the day of our salvation.**

Christ has been raised from the dead,
the first fruits of those who have fallen asleep.
> **The one who was rejected assures us:**
> **we are accepted and beloved by God.**

We are chosen by God as witnesses to good news.
We will live and recount the deeds of our God.
> **God reigns; let all nations and peoples rejoice.**
> **In Christ, all shall be made alive.**

INVOCATION

With thanksgiving, praise, and joy, we worship you, marvelous God. How amazing is all your creation! How glorious is this day of new life! Come among us now, we pray, to raise us up from our fears and doubts and perplexity. We want to believe. We want to trust. We want to dare. We want to live. Touch us today with a spirit of hope, that our discipleship may honor Christ, in whose name we pray. Amen.

CALL TO CONFESSION

Doubters, believers, disciples, deceivers: come to the one who makes all things new. The gates of righteousness are open to us, and a welcome awaits all who truly enter the presence of God, seeking forgiveness. The God whom we have rejected offers acceptance and healing.

PRAYER OF CONFESSION

Dazzling God, we are blinded to your majesty. We have taken for granted the amazing wonder of life, without seeing you as the source of all things. We shrink from the chastening judgment we deserve. We resist the changes we know we must make to receive new life. Save us from the calamity of our selfish ways. Rescue us from all hurtful and destructive habits. Forgive our broken promises, heal our broken relationships, lift our broken spirits, so we may share in the resurrection of Christ. Amen.

Assurance of Forgiveness

Everyone who lives by trust in Jesus Christ has already received forgiveness of sins. Accept this gift God offers. You are chosen by God to receive it. Your prayers are answered, and your salvation is assured. Christ reigns over death, filling you with newness of life. Rise up! Rejoice! Witness to the good news!

Collect

God of empty tombs; God of promises fulfilled; strong, impartial, accepting, loving Creator of all things: roll away the stones that lock us in tombs of prejudice, limited vision, and unbelief. Help us to recognize Christ in our midst, that we may feel your touch, hear your Word, and be moved to respond. Amen.

Offertory Invitation

We who enjoy the work of our hands do not labor in vain. We who invest the fruits of our effort in the sharing of good news are doubly blessed. May our gifts represent our commitment, even as they bear witness and offer healing. Let us give thanks through our offerings.

Offertory Prayer

Thank you, God, for resurrection. We rejoice in Christ as the first fruits of all that you make available to us. As you offered Christ to the world, so we would offer ourselves. May we, along with our gifts, testify to good news of your forgiving love and empowering acceptance. Amen.

Commission and Blessing

Spread the message: Christ is alive!
Live the good news: our lives are renewed!
We have seen and heard the good news.
We have been touched by the presence of Christ.
Share the Word: God's peace is offered to all.
Communicate the power of love: be transformed.
We are saved and reconciled and empowered.
God has chosen us to make all things new.
Announce and proclaim: God is our strength.
Rejoice in the promise: we shall triumph over death.
We will tell friends of our discoveries.
We will witness to God's surprising activity.
Amen. **Amen.**

(See hymns 75, 76.)

Isaiah 25:6–9
Psalm 114

1 Corinthians 5:6b–8
Luke 24:13–49

CALL TO WORSHIP

Long we have waited for God in this place.
Week after week we gather, seeking a presence.
> *Sometimes God seems far away.*
> *Sometimes we know that God is very near.*

We have gathered in times of loss and tears.
We have dared to come together in moments of disgrace.
> *We tremble in awe and wonder before our Creator.*
> *We arise in grateful joy when we sense God's welcome.*

Today God's salvation has been announced to us.
This night we rejoice that Christ is alive.
> *We celebrate the festival of life's renewal.*
> *Jesus Christ is glorified in our hearts and lives.*

INVOCATION

Gracious God, you are our beginning and our destination. You are with us during every step of our journey. How often we miss the signs of your presence and turn away from the joyous encounter you offer. Stay with us, for it is evening and the day is far spent. Open us to your truth, that we may participate in the joy you offer. Amen.

CALL TO CONFESSION

When we feel cut off from our best selves, crushed by circumstances, filled with malice and anger, devastated by our losses, there is hope. We are invited to face our brokenness, to turn from evil, to live beyond our losses. Come to receive and extend forgiveness.

PRAYER OF CONFESSION

Amazing God, we confess that we have ignored your presence and have sought to live apart from you. When mountains tremble and our lives are shaken, we give in to despair. When others offend us, we nurse our resentment. When we feel empty and bereft, our vision is narrowed and our hearing impaired. O God, we cannot save ourselves. Grant us your salvation. Amen.

ASSURANCE OF FORGIVENESS

God will wipe away our tears and our disgrace. A rich feast is ours to enjoy. Let us be glad and rejoice in the salvation God offers. Let us open ourselves to a presence that is never far away. Forgiveness is ours to receive and to share. Christ promises that we will be clothed with power from on high.

COLLECT

God of mighty deeds and quiet encounters, who came to us incarnate in Jesus of Nazareth, open our ears and eyes to your presence that we may not be startled and frightened but rather gladdened and empowered to share good news. Make us messengers of forgiveness, the embodiment of truth, representatives of the best you intend for humankind. Amen.

OFFERTORY INVITATION

Christ, our paschal lamb, has been sacrificed. We who seek to follow respond in gratitude. Our offerings are an expression of thanks, an opportunity to invest a portion of all God entrusts to us in celebration of God's saving love. What will we sacrifice that others may live?

OFFERTORY PRAYER

Our hearts burn within us, O God, in thanks for your gift of Jesus Christ. The threat of death has been taken away. How great is our salvation! Lead us in your truth, awesome God, that we may serve and sacrifice in joyous sincerity. We seek the power Christ promised, that we may share the forgiveness and grace we have received. We dedicate ourselves with our offerings. Amen.

COMMISSION AND BLESSING

God has met us here in our celebration of worship.
We have experienced good news: Christ is alive.
> *We have met Christ in worship and in one another.*
> *Our lives are renewed and inspired.*
The Scriptures have been fulfilled among us.
Let all who have seen and heard respond with joy.
> *We believe and celebrate good news.*
> *Our lives are made whole in Christ's presence.*
May the love of God continue to burn within you.
May the presence of Christ sustain you.
> *We have good news to share, in sincerity and truth.*
> *God is empowering our witness and our service.*
Amen. **Amen.**

(See hymns 77, 78.)

SECOND SUNDAY OF EASTER

Acts 5:27–32   Revelation 1:4–8
Psalm 118:14–29 or 150   John 20:19–31

CALL TO WORSHIP
God is our strength and our salvation;
let everything that breathes praise our God!
> **This is the day that God has made;**
> **we will rejoice and be glad in it!**
Praise God for mighty deeds and extravagant love.
Praise God for loving care and answered prayer.
> **We will give thanks this day, for God is good.**
> **The steadfast love of God endures forever.**
Grace to you and peace from the one who is
and who was and who is to come.
> **We are witnesses to the God who acts.**
> **We are here to offer our worship and praise.**

INVOCATION
God of all our beginnings, may this day and every day begin with our praise to you. Let every breath become a witness to your Spirit, dwelling within and among us. Open our hearts to receive your saving gifts. Loosen our tongues to proclaim your unsurpassed greatness. May the noise of our celebration help your people to sense your powerful presence and to claim the joy of serving you, in Christ's name. Amen.

CALL TO CONFESSION
We who have listened to the siren calls of our culture have neglected a faithful witness to Jesus Christ. The frantic pace of our busyness has left little time or energy to ponder the marvelous works of God. We have closed the doors of our hearts to a presence who longs to claim us. Come with me now to the throne of grace as we join in humble confession.

PRAYER OF CONFESSION
God of our ancestors, how easily we have made you a relic of the past. We act as if you were unreal, or at least irrelevant. By our inattention, we have rejected you and the one whom you sent to teach us. We are ruled by fears more than faith, by hostility more than peace, by a sense of failure more than feelings of accomplishment and victory. Forgive our misuse of the precious days you have entrusted to us. Help us to see the signs of your presence and to witness with joy to our Leader and Savior, Jesus Christ. Amen.

ASSURANCE OF FORGIVENESS

We are loved. We are forgiven, freed from our sins by the sacrifice of Christ Jesus. New life is ours. Let us recount the deeds of our God and respond to the Holy Spirit with joy and thanksgiving. The steadfast love of God endures forever. Fill the sanctuary with joyous praise!

COLLECT

God whom we have not seen, whose gifts we take for granted and misuse, speak to us your Word of peace, that our inner turmoil may be stilled, our eyes opened, our ears alerted to make faithful response. May our witness be authentic, that the world may come to know your glory and dominion and respond with joyous obedience to your Word. Amen.

OFFERTORY INVITATION

As the apostles filled Jerusalem with their teaching about Jesus, we are called to bring good news to the world. Our witness is in word and deed, in time and treasure. Give thanks in all things, for God is good. With our gifts we express thanks for God's steadfast love which endures forever.

OFFERTORY PRAYER

For the breath of life, for eyes to see, for insight to believe, for courage to witness, we give thanks, gracious God. The signs of your presence are everywhere. Your glory and dominion are forever and ever. May this offering witness to your grace and peace. Grant your Spirit as a transforming power among us that inspires and enables our service. Amen.

COMMISSION AND BLESSING

Go out in the strength God provides.
Praise God's mighty deeds by the way you live.
> *In loving obedience, we will witness to our faith.*
> *We will give thanks each day for God's goodness.*
The steadfast love of God goes with us everywhere.
The Holy Spirit empowers our worship and service.
> *God is our strength and our might.*
> *God answers our prayers with salvation.*
Grace to you and peace from the one who is
and who was and who is to come.
> *This day is a precious gift from God.*
> *We will rejoice and be glad in it.*
Amen. **Amen.**

(See hymn 79.)

Acts 9:1–6, (7–20)   Revelation 5:11–14
Psalm 30   John 21:1–19

CALL TO WORSHIP

Sing praises to God, O you saints of God.
Give thanks to God's holy name.
> **Praise God for the joyous gift of a new day.**
> **Thank God for healing and ever-present help.**
Extol the one who lifts us up from defeat.
Praise the one who upholds us when we are discouraged.
> **God sees and hears our weeping.**
> **God lifts our souls from the pit of despair.**
Give thanks to God who turns mourning into dancing.
Praise God who hears our cries and answers our prayers.
> **We have cried to you in our need, O God.**
> **We believe you are working to make us whole.**

INVOCATION

Come to us as a light from heaven, Sovereign God. Pierce the shadows of doubt
and despair, anger and scorn, that we allow to rule in our lives. Turn us from ways
that deny your rule among us. Awaken us from dull routines to worship that is
alive with awe and wonder, spontaneity, and joy. Surprise us with a presence we
cannot avoid, a summons we dare not evade, a mission we may not escape. We are
gathered by the love of Christ, that we may feed others as we have been fed.
Amen.

CALL TO CONFESSION

What questions is God asking us as we examine our faith and faithfulness? Have
our attitudes been rigid or flexible? Have we been motivated by self-sacrificing
love or self-serving lies? Do we live by a self-limited agenda or by a God-given
mission? Surely we have much to confess.

PRAYER OF CONFESSION

Loving God, we admit to attitudes that exclude rather than embrace. We prefer to
associate with others who think and act as we do. We turn away from those who
are different from us. We identify some as enemies to be avoided or even de-
stroyed. Forgive us, God, for seeking to limit your family. Awaken us to the limits
of our understanding and the narrowness of our dealings. Show us the better ways
you intend and make us bold to respond, we pray in Jesus' name. Amen.

ASSURANCE OF FORGIVENESS

Let the scales fall from your eyes. God has offered you new sight. Unplug your
ears. God is claiming you as a beloved servant. Warm to the community that

surrounds you. God has given you sisters and brothers to love. Reach out to feed and care and follow where Christ leads. You are forgiven and claimed and sent.

COLLECT

God of love, who raised Christ from the dead to reign in power, we honor and bless you, even as we seek wisdom to follow where Christ leads. May your favor rest upon us, your joy fill our lives, your love motivate all we do. Make us instruments of good news who carry your name to others and share your blessing with delight. Amen.

OFFERTORY INVITATION

Who will carry the name of Christ into the marketplace? Who will try new ways of faithfulness? Our offerings involve all who give. They empower those who serve. They express our praise and thanksgiving while witnessing to the reign of love in our midst.

OFFERTORY PRAYER

We bring our offerings to feed your lambs and tend your sheep, gracious God. May these gifts extend love in the form of food, pure water, shelter, and acceptance. Let them provide outreach to the world and opportunities for growth within this congregation. Help us focus on what is important, that we may work together to make a difference in the world. Amen.

COMMISSION AND BLESSING

Rise and go where God directs.
Your caring may be the answer to someone's prayer.
> *We will extol our God in word and deed.*
> *We will reach out to our neighbors with love.*
Be alert to the needs of people you meet.
You may be God's chosen instrument of healing.
> *We will praise God's faithfulness day by day.*
> *We will listen with compassion to those who suffer.*
Blessed are those who believe without seeing.
Blessed are those who trust without proof.
> *We will follow where Christ leads us.*
> *Blessing, honor, glory, and power be to our God.*
Amen. **Amen.**

(See hymns 81, 82.)

Acts 9:36–43   Revelation 7:9–17
Psalm 23   John 10:22–30

CALL TO WORSHIP

Arise, people of God, to greet the one who calls us;
come alive to the Spirit's energy among us.

> *God awakens us and restores our souls.*
> *Surely God's goodness and mercy are with us here.*

The shepherd is calling us to new ventures.
We are invited to a higher quality of life.

> *We will not fear to walk through shadowed valleys.*
> *God's love in Christ is with us everywhere.*

Come to drink from springs of living water.
Gather to find comfort and blessing here.

> *Surely God will guide our search for truth.*
> *We seek eternal values within our daily walks.*

INVOCATION

Draw us together, Eternal One, from paths of aimless wandering. Lead us today toward the community you intend. Draw the fragments of our lives together into some meaningful whole. Help us deal with present concerns in constructive ways yet point us beyond ourselves to engage with you in larger issues. Help us feel the hunger and thirst of others; then lead your church to make a caring response. May your love fill us and overflow into other lives. Amen.

CALL TO CONFESSION

How often it is winter in our lives. The good we would do seems frozen within us, and our faith is cold and sluggish. A voice calls us to believe and to care, to confess our doubts and awaken the potential within us.

PRAYER OF CONFESSION

O God, we look at events around us and cannot perceive you within them. We shed tears and find no comfort. We listen for your voice and are greeted by silence. The world seems full of enemies waiting to devour us. On every hand, there are problems too complicated for us to solve. We live in fear rather than faith. We cry out to you for answers. O God, do you hear us? Amen.

ASSURANCE OF FORGIVENESS

In the silence, there is presence too deep for words. The works of God surround us even now, bearing witness to an unseen hand. Multitudes of people from every nation and time join in chorus: "Salvation belongs to our God!" The shepherd will guide us to springs of living water, and our tears will be wiped away. We are freed to live boldly and courageously, through Christ!

COLLECT

Great God, unknown to us except in fleeting glimpses, we live for the moments when your voice is heard and your will is clear. We long to walk with you beside still waters and to lie down in green pastures. Nourish us now by your Word and Spirit, that we may join the heavenly chorus singing your praises while being of some earthly good to those who cannot hear the joyful sounds. Amen.

OFFERTORY INVITATION

Surely the goodness of God overflows in our lives. Take time to count your blessings. The works of God are all around us. In these moments, we have the opportunity to offer ourselves and our substance to extend God's work on earth.

OFFERTORY PRAYER

Make these moments a feast of dedication to your purposes among us, loving God. May we serve you night and day, wherever we are, in all we do. Blessing, glory, wisdom, thanksgiving, honor, power, and might be to our God forever and ever! Amen.

COMMISSION AND BLESSING

Go forward from this place as praying, caring people.
Let good works and charity abound.
> *We believe God calls us to make a difference.*
> *God wants us to change the world.*
Your deeds bear witness to God's love.
Others will believe because of your faith.
> *We trust the shepherd to lead and guide us.*
> *We look to God for the strength we need.*
Surely goodness and mercy will follow us.
Our eternal home is part of us right now.
> *God's salvation has come to us. Alleluia!*
> *We will praise and honor our God forever and ever.*
Amen. **Amen.**

(See hymn 83.)

Acts 11:1–18   Psalm 148
Revelation 21:1–6   John 13:31–35

CALL TO WORSHIP

Come to praise God, all you faithful people!
Come, for God welcomes you and offers to draw close.
> **Praise to God, who rules over all the earth.**
> **Praise to God, who is as near as our next breath.**

Sun and moon and stars shine in praise to God.
God created them and established for each a place.
> **God has a place for us in this world;**
> **we have come that God may instruct and equip us.**

Mountains and hills, trees and animals praise God.
Let all the rulers of the earth do so as well.
> **God provides abundantly for our needs.**
> **God makes of one family all who dwell on earth.**

INVOCATION

We praise you, O God, and celebrate your presence with us. Your glory fills all heaven and earth, all time and space. Your gifts surround us and dwell within us. We are your children. Come to wipe away our tears and comfort us in our distress. Come to heal our divisions and overcome our prejudices. Come, that we might be loved into discipleship. Amen.

CALL TO CONFESSION

The God revealed to us in the pages of Scripture is a welcoming and inclusive God who directs us to love one another. So we gather to seek removal of all barriers to that love. Come to confess all that separates you from others and from your own best.

PRAYER OF CONFESSION

We admit, holy God, that we find it hard to hear your promise of new life. Even when we are dissatisfied with our lives, it is easier to cling to what we know than to risk the unknown. You challenge us to accept people who are different from us, but we are not eager to associate with them. You command us to love one another, but some people are not lovable. O God, melt our defenses so we can accept your love and let it flow through us. Grant us courage to embrace newness. Amen.

Assurance of Forgiveness

God promises to dwell with us, to ease our pain and wipe tears from our eyes. Dare to trust, for God accepts us as we are, that we might become all we are meant to be. God grants us the opportunity to repent. It is a gift that leads to new life. Accept God's offer of new life in Christ.

Collect

Loving God, glorified on earth by the witness of Jesus Christ, touch our lives with the love that creates disciples, that we may learn to love one another. Teach us new attitudes so we will welcome the new heaven and new earth you have promised and work together to live as your people. Amen.

Offertory Invitation

God has called us to a ministry of service: water for the thirsty, comfort to those who grieve, healing for ones in pain, acceptance for persons who have not accepted themselves. This is the time to offer our time and strength as well as money, that God's will may be realized among us.

Offertory Prayer

Thank you, gracious God, for making your home with us and claiming us as your own people. We dedicate ourselves and our gifts toward the new world you are creating among us—a world where peace emerges from mutual respect and honest encounters. May your love be reflected in our attitudes and actions when we are together and when we are scattered. Amen.

Commission and Blessing

We go out as disciples of Jesus Christ.
The world will recognize you by your love.
> *Love has created us and makes us whole.*
> *We grow in love when we share love.*
Praise God whose abundant mercies meet our needs.
Commune daily with the one who heads our family.
> *When we know God's presence, we are unafraid.*
> *Newness is welcomed as God's gift to us.*
God is Alpha and Omega, beginning and end.
God refreshes us daily with the gift of living water.
> *We have been baptized with water and the Holy Spirit.*
> *We are ambassadors of love to all we meet.*
Amen. **Amen.**

(See hymn 84.)

Acts 16:9–15   Psalm 67
Revelation 21:10, 22–22:5   John 14:23–29 or John 5:1–9

CALL TO WORSHIP

Come to this place of prayer; God is calling us.
Come, all who are burdened; there is healing here.
>   *We have come to hear the Word of God.*
>   *We have brought with us all that weighs us down.*

Let voices of praise greet the one who calls us.
Be glad together and sing for joy.
>   *Our hearts respond with hope for a new day.*
>   *Our voices join in thankful prayers and praise.*

God reigns among us and fills the world with light.
We are invited to make our home with the living God.
>   *May God's ways be known within and among us.*
>   *May God guide all nations in ways of peace.*

INVOCATION

Maker of all things, Ruler of all peoples of the earth, we bring our prayers of thanksgiving and praise. You have provided the water of life for our baptism. You have fed us with the fruits of the earth and nourished us through your Word. Meet us again in the joyous encounter of worship, lest we forget the source of all we have and all that we are. Let the peoples praise you, O God; let all the peoples praise you! Amen.

CALL TO CONFESSION

All who keep God's Word know God's love and live by it. But obedience is not easy amid all the world's distractions, and the gift of love is not incorporated into our lives without effort. There is gap between intention and reality, a chasm we create between ourselves and God. That is why we observe a time of confession.

PRAYER OF CONFESSION

Almighty God, we have wandered far from your love. We have neglected your Word in the torrent of words that we hear and read every day. Our hearts are troubled amid the conflicts and violence of our world. Sometimes we find it easier to withdraw from everything, to resist change, lest it require more of us. We know you are reaching out to heal us; help us to respond. We know we are surrounded by your love. Let us feel it deep within, that we may reflect that love to all we meet. Amen.

Assurance of Forgiveness

Jesus invites us to stand, to feel our own strength, to understand our own power, to sense the changes that love is accomplishing within us and among us. The Holy Spirit has come to teach us all that we need in order to be faithful. We are loving servants of God, who claims us and sends us on a journey of peace. Praise God, who has blessed and forgiven us.

Collect

God of love and peace, whose healing Word is offered to every person and group and nation, we long to hear and see and feel your presence with us. Send your Holy Spirit to overpower our excuses, lend new perspective to our troubled thoughts, and equip us to walk into the future with courage. Reign among us that we may proclaim good news to all who need it. Amen.

Offertory Invitation

What do we have to give? Only what we have received. The earth has yielded its increase. God has blessed us in more ways than we can count. Let us offer to God more than support of a church. Let us offer ourselves for the healing of the nations.

Offertory Prayer

For the hospitality of your good earth, for the people you have given us to love, for the tasks you have called us to do, we give thanks, gracious God. Our offerings are a measure of our faith and an evidence of our gratitude. We dedicate ourselves with our gifts, that your reign of light may be realized in the places where we live and work and far beyond our personal reach. Amen.

Commission and Blessing

Worshippers of God, we are called into the world.
We cannot stay here; God has work for us to do.
> *God invites us to follow where Jesus leads.*
> *Our presence is needed in unexpected places.*
If we love God, we will live by God's Word.
If we have met God here, our lives are being changed.
> *God's Word of love is finding a home in our hearts.*
> *God's light is leading us on new ventures of service.*
The peace of God goes with you, today and always;
let not your hearts be troubled or afraid.
> *God is blessing us every day; praise God!*
> *We will carry God's saving power to all nations.*
Amen. **Amen.**

(See hymn 86.)

Sixth Sunday of Easter 97

ASCENSION (OR SEVENTH SUNDAY OF EASTER)—A, B, C

Acts 1:1–11   Psalm 47 or 110
Ephesians 1:15–23   Luke 24:44–53

CALL TO WORSHIP

Clap your hands, all you people of God.
Sing praises to our Ruler, sing praises!
> **God reigns among us and far beyond us.**
> **We celebrate the immeasurable greatness of God!**
We are called to be witnessing people.
Testify, then, to God's loving purpose in Jesus Christ.
> **Christ is head over all things for the church.**
> **We celebrate Christ's resurrection and ascension.**
Worship with eager anticipation of empowerment.
Give thanks for the promised coming of the Holy Spirit.
> **This is a day for revelation and renewal.**
> **We await the baptism of the Holy Spirit.**

INVOCATION

Most high God, Ruler of all worlds, Mother and Father of glory, we seek to know you more fully in this time of worship. Reveal yourself to us here. Grant us knowledge beyond words, a presence that transcends description, a hope that empowers faithful service. With your praise on our lips, we reach out with longing hearts to know the power of the Spirit which you have promised to the church of Jesus Christ. Amen.

CALL TO CONFESSION

Our worship celebrates God's rule over all creation. We are a part of that creation. We can choose whether or not to acknowledge God's sovereignty in our individual lives and in the church. Do our deeds reflect the immeasurable greatness of God's power? Do they mark us as disciples of Jesus Christ? Join me in admitting the shallowness of our commitment.

PRAYER OF CONFESSION

O God, you are judge over all things. That strikes terror within us when we realize how poorly our church has lived as the body of Christ in the world. We have been more interested in institutional survival than in proclamation of the gospel, more attentive to numbers than to individuals, more eager to speak than to listen. What is true for all of us together is also true for most of us individually. We do not seek or accept your daily guidance. Our witness to Jesus Christ is a pale reflection of the joy expressed by the early disciples. Forgive our pretenses. Amen.

ASSURANCE OF FORGIVENESS

Repentance opens the way for forgiveness. God is restoring all who are truly penitent. Drink from the streams of living water. Receive the power of the Holy Spirit, that you may forgive as you have been forgiven.

COLLECT

Parenting God, whose promises are trustworthy, we pray for baptism of the Holy Spirit to empower our ministry. Fill us with the joy of serving in Christ's name, that we might become powerful witnesses, offering forgiveness and healing to all your children. Grant us the joy that accompanies faithfulness to your Word and will, through Jesus Christ. Amen.

OFFERTORY INVITATION

There are times when it is appropriate to stand gazing into the heavens. There are seasons for withdrawing to pray. But there are also times to get to work. As we offer ourselves in the service of Jesus Christ, we return our tithes and extra gifts to extend ministry beyond the limits of our own reach.

OFFERTORY PRAYER

For the life you have offered, for the vision you have granted, for the ministry of Jesus Christ that empowers our witness, we give thanks. May these offerings of gratitude extend the positive influence of Christ's church into parts of the world that have not experienced good news. By the act of giving, may our own commitment be deepened. Amen.

COMMISSION AND BLESSING

Christ is alive; share the good news.
Revelation and wisdom are given to us; pass on the gifts.
> **We are witnesses to the difference Christ makes.**
> **Daily life is changed; the earth is a better place.**
Let your joy be spontaneous and genuine.
Clap your hands and shout your praise.
> **We will bless God together in the temple.**
> **We will let our daily lives preach Christ's name.**
You will receive power from the Holy Spirit.
The eyes of your hearts will be enlightened by hope.
> **We will not shrink from God's empowering spirit.**
> **We will carry Christ's inclusiveness to all people.**
Amen. **Amen.**

(See hymn 87.)

Acts 16:16–34   Psalm 97
Revelation 22:12–14, 16–17, 20–21   John 17:20–26

CALL TO WORSHIP

The grace of Jesus Christ be with all the saints!
We have gathered in that grace to worship God.
> *Rejoice in God and give thanks to God's holy name.*
> *Let all heaven and earth behold God's glory.*

God is Alpha and Omega, the beginning and the end.
All creation is subject to God's rule and reign.
> *We bring our prayers and praise to God most high,*
> *We lift our voices in hymns of celebration.*

Come, all who hunger, all who thirst;
Be nourished and renewed in this time of worship.
> *We bring joys and sorrows, fullness and needs.*
> *We come with successes and failures; we come seeking.*

INVOCATION

We come seeking a presence that shakes foundations and helps us build new ones.
We come with all our wounds, asking for healing. We come, remembering our
baptism and wanting to claim the difference that makes in our lives. We come
through the shadowy clouds of our unbelief, seeking the brightness of your glory,
O God, We want a faith to sustain us through times of trial and testing. Be
powerfully present with us, gracious Spirit. Amen.

CALL TO CONFESSION

We who have fashioned idols to occupy our time and energy are invited to
examine our priorities before God, who expects to be first in our lives. We who
have used others for our own pleasure and gain are summoned before our Creator,
who calls us to treat all our brothers and sisters with the love of Jesus Christ.
Friends, we have much to confess.

PRAYER OF CONFESSION

Hear our individual confessions, O God, as we recall the ways we ignore you
every day. Listen to our regrets over the abuse we have heaped on others by our
words, actions, or neglect. We join together in asking forgiveness for the ways our
church inflicts injury on members of the household of faith while excluding many
who differ from us. We live by our own devices rather than taking risks to follow
where Christ might lead us. Deliver us, O God, from empty forms to receive the
fullness of your grace and the power to live as you intend. Amen.

ASSURANCE OF FORGIVENESS
Rejoice, O righteous ones, and give thanks to God's holy name. You are forgiven, saved from the wrath of one before whom mountains melt and the earth trembles. Through Christ, God's forgiving love is poured out on all who earnestly seek to be changed. We are drawn into a unity that transcends our differences and a faithfulness beyond our ability to achieve. Praise God!

COLLECT
As Christ prayed that believers might be one, we ask, O righteous Parent, that our church may know a unity of spirit amid our diversity. Make your ways known to us, fill us with your love, and send us out in your name. We seek to bring others to the tree of life and to salvation, through Jesus Christ. Amen.

OFFERTORY INVITATION
Christians sometimes bring peace in the midst of turmoil. At other times, we disturb the peace with our work for justice and our championing of the oppressed. As we pool the resources God has given us, we become a powerful influence for good. Our offerings proclaim our faith. Let us give faithfully.

OFFERTORY PRAYER
With joy and gladness we dedicate our gifts to the service of Jesus Christ. May the abused find solace and courage; abusers be led to new awareness, sensitivity, and change; prisoners know release from bondage; and all humankind be led to accept the saving grace of Jesus Christ. To this end, we offer ourselves with these gifts. Use us as ambassadors of your love. Amen.

COMMISSION AND BLESSING
Believers, you have been endowed with the gospel.
Go out, with unity of spirit, to share good news.
We are awed and amazed at God's gifts to us.
With fear and trembling, we dare to represent God.
In the name of Jesus Christ, take love to the world.
With the spirit of truth, offer peace to the nations.
We seek to live in peace with our neighbors.
We offer our best selves to proclaim love for all.
Invite the thirsty to receive the water of life.
The grace of Jesus Christ be with all the saints.
We have received abounding grace.
With joy and thanksgiving, we pass it on.
Amen. **Amen.**

(See hymns 88, 89.)

PENTECOST AND THE SEASON
FOLLOWING

Acts 2:1–21 or Genesis 11:1–9
Psalm 104:24–34, 35b

Romans 8:14–17 or Acts 2:1-21
John 14:8–17, 25–27

CALL TO WORSHIP

We gather together because God has called us.
We wait in expectant awe for God's appearing.
> *We are together, old and young, rich and poor.*
> *We have come, believers and skeptics, to this place.*

On the first Christian Pentecost, there were surprises:
the rush of a violent wind and tongues of fire.
> *We tremble before the power of the Holy Spirit.*
> *What will happen if we let the Spirit in?*

On this Pentecost, we can receive the surprises of God.
We can be moved to speak and act in new ways.
> *With hesitant eagerness, we welcome the Spirit.*
> *We will risk stepping into God's vision for us.*

INVOCATION

Amazing God, who created humanity as one people, come among us now to reunify us. Out of our differences, create understanding and eagerness to explore the variety among us. Out of our narrowness, fashion a breadth of involvement to feed our spirits. May we dream dreams and see visions. May we truly hear our sisters and brothers and respond to them with empathy and love, in Jesus' name. Amen.

CALL TO CONFESSION

How often this week have we pondered the manifold works of God? How have we cared for this amazing planet? What have we done to encourage life at its fullest and best? We violate God's purposes by our neglect as well as by overt acts. God invites our confession.

PRAYER OF CONFESSION

O God, we have built cities for ourselves. We have sought fame and fortune. We have rushed through our days with unseeing eyes, stopped-up ears, and dulled emotions. We are more often enslaved by our fears than freed by your grace. We demand proof of your existence but ignore the work of your hands. We reject Jesus Christ as an impractical visionary. Your Holy Spirit is unreal to us because we insist on being in charge. Have mercy on us, holy God, and save us from ourselves. Amen.

Assurance of Forgiveness

God promises to us an outpouring of the Spirit. We will see signs and experience wonders that we have not observed before. When we call out to God, our healing, our salvation, will come. God approaches us with open hands filled with good things. When we are ready to be taught, God grants new insights and a deep, abiding sense of peace. Praise God!

Collect

Holy Spirit, counselor, revealer of eternal truth, show us God and we will be satisfied. Call to our remembrance all that we have seen and heard and felt that gave us glimpses of your work in our world. Bring a new Pentecost among us so we will be empowered to witness to the world. Amen.

Offertory Invitation

God has made us heirs of great abundance in order that we might use the resources entrusted to us to benefit humankind. We are children of God, called to share with the world the manifold works of our Creator. Our offerings are one expression of our commitment.

Offertory Prayer

God of wind and fire, may new life be breathed into the world because of these gifts we return to you. Grant us enhanced capacity to carry your revelation to others in ways they can understand. We seek to be to one another channels of your love and peace, both in person and through the outreach of our offerings. Amen.

Commission and Blessing

All who believe in Jesus Christ are commissioned.
We are sent out to live and work as Jesus did.
> *We are sons and daughters of God.*
> *We are heirs with Christ of all God has made.*
The Holy Spirit has come to inspire and equip us.
We are empowered for greater works in Jesus' name.
> *We will praise our God while we have being.*
> *We will testify to the good news of God's love.*
The power of the first Pentecost is ours to claim.
The Holy Spirit offers us new ability to communicate.
> *We will heed the Spirit's promptings this week.*
> *We will call on God's name day by day.*
Amen. **Amen.**

(See hymns 90, 91.)

Proverbs 8:1–4, 22–31

Romans 5:1–5

Psalm 8

John 16:12–15

CALL TO WORSHIP

God finds delight in humanity, and in each of us.
Let us rejoice before the majesty of our Creator.
> **God of grace and glory, who made all things,**
> **How majestic is your name in all the earth!**

In Christ, we are called to endure and to hope.
Let us give thanks for a faith that brings peace.
> **God of grace and glory, Savior of your people,**
> **How precious to us is your gift of Jesus Christ!**

The Holy Spirit is present to guide and direct us,
Let us listen that we may hear and do what is true.
> **God of grace and glory, ever present with us,**
> **How reassuring is the love with which you surround us!**

INVOCATION

Amazing God, revealed to us in more ways than we can count, yet binding in unity all that was and is and yet shall be, we worship you. Source of mountains and seas, giver of light and darkness, we marvel at the work of your hands. Reconciler and Redeemer, we are awed by the forgiving love that draws us to you and empowers us to care for one another. Spirit of truth, whose guidance is available to us every day, we rejoice in your transforming presence. Triune God, bless, we pray, this gathering of your disciples. Amen.

CALL TO CONFESSION

Who has truly listened for the voice of God? Who among us is attentive to the heights and depths in which we are called to live? Who are we that God cares for us? Let us draw near in humility and faith, confessing the distractions that separate us from the mind of God.

PRAYER OF CONFESSION

God of Wisdom, our choices have denied you. We drink from the shallow waters of instant gratification when you offer springs of living water from the depths of your love. We pursue our own fame and glory, which crumble into dust when we view the sacrifice and service that build true character. O God, we confess that we have not put first things first. We have not lived up to the crown of glory and honor you offer us. Recall us to awe and wonder and guide us in the ways of truth. Amen.

Assurance of Forgiveness

The glory of God is revealed anew to us in the birth of children. We are reborn when we pause to marvel at the gift of life, when we look beyond ourselves to gaze at the stars. Before the vast mystery of time and space, we are amazed that God cares for us, forgives us, and entrusts to us the stewardship of the earth. God's love is poured into our hearts through the Holy Spirit. Praise God!

Collect

Spirit of truth, you open to us the Word of life and help us to see the possibilities of each day. Guide us now that we may hear your truth and embody it. As we face suffering, help us to endure, to hope, and to love. Grant wisdom and strength of character to overcome former limitations, that we might represent you well each moment we live, doing the work you call us to do. Amen.

Offertory Invitation

Our God, who is mindful of us and our needs, sends us into the world to attend to the needs of others. Where there is enmity or suffering or spiritual poverty, we may become channels through which the Holy Spirit acts. When we give our earnings, we extend our influence beyond our own reach. Let us give thankfully and generously.

Offertory Prayer

Giving God, we are grateful for wisdom, for beauty, for the ways in which we see your glory in all creation. Most of all, we thank you for caring for us and for entrusting to us the ministry of caring for the earth and for one another. May these offerings extend the faith and honor you: Creator, Savior, and Sustainer. Amen.

Commission and Blessing

God's love has been poured into our hearts.
When we give it away, we have even more for ourselves.
> **The Holy Spirit has blessed us with love.**
> **The Spirit dwells with us and enables our loving.**

The Spirit of Truth promises to guide us.
When we respond, our lives are deeply enriched.
> **God has crowned us with glory and honor.**
> **We are given responsibility to care for God's creation.**

Wisdom continues as a partner in creation and re-creation.
Let us praise the one who has dominion over all.
> **How majestic is God's name in all the earth!**
> **We accept the grace and peace God offers.**

Amen. **Amen.**

(See hymn 92.)

PROPER 4

I Kings 18:20–39	(or I Kings 8:22–23, 41–43	Galatians 1:1–12
Psalm 96	Psalm 96:1–9)	Luke 7:1–10

CALL TO WORSHIP

Sing a new song to God, all the earth.
Bless God's name from day to day.
> **God is doing marvelous works among us.**
> **Let all nations declare the glory of God.**

Our God is to be praised as Creator of all things.
Let us turn away from our idols to worship God.
> **Honor, majesty, beauty, and strength belong to God.**
> **Let us worship together in God's sanctuary.**

Tremble before God, all people and nations.
God will judge us all with righteousness and truth.
> **Let the heavens be glad; let the earth rejoice.**
> **God is with us and will answer our prayers.**

INVOCATION

Come this day to rule among us, holy God. As you lit the altar fires of the prophets, light a fire in our midst that will turn our hearts to your truth and energize our lives for your service. Awaken us from easy conformity to the norms of our society so we may encounter the gospel with fresh integrity. Grant us faith that expects great things from you and dares great things for you. Amen.

CALL TO CONFESSION

Come closer to God. Sense anew the wonders of creation and the marvels of human life. Have we not taken it all for granted? Have we not misused the gifts of God? Where is the faith that transforms, the trust that changes the way we view everything, the gladness that radiates through all we do. Confession and forgiveness can reattune us to the grace of God.

PRAYER OF CONFESSION

God of all people, forgive us for claiming to be Christians when our faith is so shallow and our good works so limited. We have not dared to trust you fully. We have not expected your promises to be fulfilled among us. We have not accepted the freedom that is ours in Christ Jesus. Instead, we have guarded our own interests, relied on limited understandings and lingering doubts, reined in our emotions, and settled for a lukewarm relationship that we do little to cultivate. O God, forgive us and draw us closer to you. Amen.

*If the Sunday between May 24 and 28 inclusive follows Trinity Sunday, use the service for the Eighth Sunday after Epiphany.

ASSURANCE OF FORGIVENESS

Let the heavens be glad; let the earth rejoice. God answers prayer. What we have truly prayed with conviction has been heard by God. Remember that Jesus Christ gave life itself for our sins, to set us free from the evil of our present times. The good news is ours to receive, to integrate into our lives, and to pass on to others. Accept your forgiveness and sing a new song to God.

COLLECT

Almighty God, whose power and authority are greater than we can discern, we come to your Word with eagerness to hear more than words. Move among us with healing energy. Awaken in us a dynamic trust that allows your Spirit to reign in us and work through us to create an inclusive, ministering community. Speak your transforming Word, we pray. Amen.

OFFERTORY INVITATION

Bring an offering pleasing to God, who has entrusted much to our care. Bring your gifts, expecting great things to happen because of our common sharing. Bring all that you have to glorify God and to extend awareness of God's rule over humankind. Praise God through your giving.

OFFERTORY PRAYER

Thank you, God, for welcoming us into your household. You have given us all the good things we enjoy, and we are grateful. You have sent Jesus to demonstrate your healing love for all people, and we want to respond as disciples. We seek your approval as we present our offerings. May we be as generous in furthering the ministry of your church as you have been with us. Amen.

COMMISSION AND BLESSING

Declare God's glory among the nations.
Celebrate God's marvelous works among all people.
> **Great is our God and greatly to be praised!**
> **We will notice and announce God's activity among us.**
Reenter your everyday world with renewed faith.
Encounter the people in your life with new appreciation.
> **God has turned our hearts toward important things.**
> **We seek to respond to God in all we say and do.**
Grace to you and peace from God who loves us.
The God of our ancestors is responding to us today.
> **There is one gospel, which we seek to know and represent.**
> **There is one God, whom we honor and serve.**
Amen. **Amen.**

(See hymn 93.)

PROPER 5

I Kings 17:8–16, (17–24)   (or I Kings 17:7–24   Galatians 1:11–24
Psalm 146   Psalm 30)   Luke 7:11–17

CALL TO WORSHIP

Sing praises to God, all you faithful ones.
Give thanks to God's holy name.
> *We will praise God as long as we live.*
> *We will pour out our joyous thanksgiving.*

Do not put your trust in rulers of this age.
Do not rely on things that are perishable.
> *God keeps faith with us today and forever.*
> *The oppressed and hungry receive from God what they need.*

We have received grace to minister in Jesus' name.
We are called to proclaim the faith to others.
> *We want to rise to the challenge set before us.*
> *We seek to keep the faith by sharing it.*

INVOCATION

Gracious God, whose plenty meets us in our poverty with all that we need, open
our eyes and lift up all who are bowed down. Watch over us that we may speak
your word of hope and freedom. Come to uphold the grieving and forlorn,
confront the self-satisfied, and challenge us all to authentic, caring, prophetic
ministry. Help us to live as your faithful children. Amen.

CALL TO CONFESSION

When we live by our fears, we are challenged instead to live by faith. When we
put our trust in the rich and famous of our day, we are called instead to worship
God who made all things. When we are intent on our own agenda, God summons
us to wider awareness and larger service. How do we stand with God?

PRAYER OF CONFESSION

Giver of life, we have not thanked you enough for each breath we can take, each
moment we live, each experience we enjoy or endure. We are more likely to
complain than to appreciate, to wallow in cries of agony and loss than to pour out
joy and gratitude. We repeat our mistakes instead of learning from them. We try to
keep you out of our lives instead of turning to you daily and trusting your
providence. Turn us around, God; we want to experience the confident joy of
living for you. Amen.

ASSURANCE OF FORGIVENESS

God set you apart before you were born and calls you by grace to serve where God sends you. When you turn to God, your emptiness can be filled and your life restored. God lifts up those who are bowed down and has compassion on those who weep. Praise God today! Praise God all your life long!

COLLECT

Compassionate God, whose healing Word is meant for all humankind, let your servants be restored to life this day, that we may not rely on our own traditions but hearken to your voice. Gird us with gladness so we may praise you and not be silent when the world needs to hear you through our voices. Make us bearers of your compassion, we pray. Amen.

OFFERTORY INVITATION

The revealed gospel needs human transmitters. The dispossessed of the world need practical compassion. God calls us to use our abilities and our accumulated resources to reveal the good news of Jesus Christ in daily acts of love. Our offerings support many ministries.

OFFERTORY PRAYER

We praise you with joy, holy God, for the gospel that extends our human vision and challenges our cherished traditions. We commit ourselves and our gifts to the sharing of life-giving good news. May we be equipped to preach the faith in word and deed. Amen.

COMMISSION AND BLESSING

Take what has been revealed into your daily life.
Be zealous for the new life of God's faithful ones.
> **No matter what happens, God keeps faith with us.**
> **We will praise God's continuing grace and love.**
Share the compassion of Jesus with those you meet.
Let God visit them through you.
> **As Christ was revealed through ordinary people,**
> **we seek to be channels of revelation in our day.**
The Word of God will strengthen and equip you.
The Spirit will breathe new life into your soul.
> **We go out as people sent on a mission.**
> **We trust God to supply all that we need.**
Amen. **Amen.**

(See hymn 94.)

PROPER 6

I Kings 21:1–10, (11–14),   *(or 2 Samuel 11:26–12:10, 13–15*   Galatians 2:15–21
15–21a   *Psalm 32)*   Luke 7:36–8:3
Psalm 5:1–8

CALL TO WORSHIP

The steadfast love of God surrounds us;
be glad and shout for joy, all you upright in heart.
> *We celebrate the good things of life that God provides.*
> *We give thanks for God's steadfast love.*
Let all who are faithful offer prayers to God.
Come to listen for God's counsel and instruction.
> *We are here to encounter the one who made us.*
> *We are open to the Word God will speak.*
God hears our cries and answers our pleas.
Rejoice, O righteous, in God's justice and grace.
> *Surely God is our strength and our hope.*
> *We will trust in the one who provides all things.*

INVOCATION

Gracious God, who has provided for us a bountiful inheritance, help us in this time of worship to be fully aware of your rule in all of life and to be fully responsive to your Word. Listen to our cries, O God, and hear our voices as we plead our case to you. Be for us a hiding place in our times of distress. Lead us and make your way straight before us. Increase our faith through this time of joyous praise. Amen.

CALL TO CONFESSION

God does not delight in wickedness, whether it be large offenses or small deceits. With God, evil will not sojourn, and lies and boasting have no place. Neither is there room for arrogant comparisons among the followers of Jesus. We who have violated God's law of love come now to seek forgiveness.

PRAYER OF CONFESSION

O God, there is much for which we need to be forgiven. We have coveted what belongs to others while wasting what we have. We are eager for personal gain, even at another's expense. We seek to justify ourselves through good works rather than serving joyously and gratefully to honor you. We speak when we should keep silent and are silent when we should speak. O God, our actions are at war with what we believe. Draw us close to you, that we might avoid the disaster we are inviting. Amen.

ASSURANCE OF FORGIVENESS

Happy are those whose transgressions are forgiven, whose sin is covered. God forgives and makes our way straight before us. In awe and reverence, let us accept God's gift and allow our ways to be changed. May we live by grace, recognizing and embracing the peace God offers.

COLLECT

Lover of humankind, whose care extends to saints and sinners, and whose judgment spares no one because of rank, open our eyes and ears and hearts to receive all people as brothers and sisters, to honor them as your children, and to seek their well-being as diligently as we seek our own, that all of us together may appreciate and share the good news of your realm as we minister in Christ's name. Amen.

OFFERTORY INVITATION

Our possessions are given to us that we might know the joy of sharing. Our faith is tested by the response we offer to God's generosity. Come, share the joy of thankful giving. Join now in the outreach ministry to which God calls us.

OFFERTORY PRAYER

We give thanks, generous God, because we owe you more than we can ever repay. We give because we love you and want to show our devotion. We give because there are needs to be met among us and in other places where we cannot go. We give because we need to be generous in order to be whole. Loving God, bless all givers who provide for others out of their means, and multiply these resources in your service. Amen.

COMMISSION AND BLESSING

How good it is that we have been together in worship!
Go, now, in peace; your faith is saving you.
   We will continue to pray this week.
   Surely God will be with us, saving and healing.
The steadfast love of God surrounds you always.
Be glad, rejoice, and trust in God's mercy.
   Let our shouts of joy be heard among all people.
   We have good news to share about God's realm.
By the grace of God, Christ lives in you.
Deliver the gospel in joyous acts of caring.
   We have received forgiveness, assurance, and peace.
   Now we seek to live out the message and pass on the gift.
Amen. **Amen.**

(See hymn 95.)

PROPER 7
Sunday between June 19 and June 25
(if after Trinity Sunday)

I Kings 19:1–4, (5–7), 8–15a	(or Isaiah 65:1–9	Galatians 3:23–29
Psalm 42–43	Psalm 22:19–28)	Luke 8:26–39

CALL TO WORSHIP

God is ready for us to seek what is eternal.
God wants us to find the truth beyond ourselves.

> *Our spirits long for God, as a deer longs for water.*
> *We cry out for some evidence of God's presence.*

God seldom comes as earthquake, wind, or fire.
Rather, in moments of sheer silence, God is revealed.

> *We come in quiet expectation to this holy place.*
> *We approach the altar of God, hungering to be fed.*

All are welcome here as brothers and sisters in Christ.
Here is a place to find healing and promise.

> *Our hope is in God, who gives us life and identity.*
> *Our help is from God, who is in covenant with us.*

INVOCATION

God, our refuge and our hope, come among us today to give us energy and purpose. Move us beyond the discipline of the law to the discipleship of faith. Free us from the shackles of fear and a sense of failure that keep us from stepping bravely into your future. Grant us the sense that we are not alone but are part of a great company of your faithful people of every nation and tongue. Amen.

CALL TO CONFESSION

When we ask to be delivered from deceitful and unjust people, we need to examine ourselves to see if we are completely honest and just. When we sense demonic forces in our world, we must ask if there is any evil in us. When we are tempted to exclude, we are met by an inclusive God who calls us to repentance.

PRAYER OF CONFESSION

Almighty and Sovereign God, we confess that we have broken covenant with you, despised some of your children, and accused you of forgetting us. Our lives do not praise you, our actions deny you, and our work is carried out without reference to your will. We draw lines of distinction among ourselves rather than celebrating our common humanity. When we are zealous for the faith, we trample on others rather than learning to know and appreciate them. O God, forgive us and change us. Amen.

ASSURANCE OF FORGIVENESS

When we want to be helped, God is ready to pardon us and equip us for new life. Wounded spirits are restored to wholeness. Enemies can become friends. We can grow in faith and love. God puts a song on our lips and confidence in our hearts. Praise God!

COLLECT

Holy God, whose healing presence gathers together our brokenness and restores our integrity, move us once more to proclaim to one another how much you have done for us, that no one will question, "Where is your God?" but will sense your reality among us. May we be attentive listeners and faithful followers. Amen.

OFFERTORY INVITATION

God has richly provided all we need for life's journey. What are we doing with God's bounty? How much of ourselves and the resources we command are we investing in the work God has called the church to do? May our dedicated dollars reflect a consecrated congregation.

OFFERTORY PRAYER

God of all times and places, may our offerings reflect confidence, not cowardice; altruism, not egotism; inclusiveness, not exclusiveness. We devote them to bringing all humanity into harmony with your purposes. May the programs we undertake build up the body of Christ among us and far beyond us. Amen.

COMMISSION AND BLESSING

God has come quickly to aid and instruct us.
Now we depart to help others and to listen to them.
We will share our stories with the congregation.
We will witness in God's name to one another.
God's family includes those outside the church.
With God, there are no outsiders or insiders.
We will carry the grace of God without distinction.
God's abundant steadfast love will sustain us.
Daily God asks, "What are you doing here?"
Moment by moment, God is with us to help us.
We will hope in God and sing God's praises.
We will look up with hope and confidence.
Amen. **Amen.**

(See hymn 96.)

PROPER 8

2 Kings 2:1–2, 6–14   *(or I Kings 19:15–16, 19–21*   Galatians 5:1, 13–25
Psalm 77:1–2, 11–20   *Psalm 16)*   Luke 9:51–62

CALL TO WORSHIP

Call to mind the mighty acts of God.
Remember the wonders God has revealed in your life.
> **All the ways of God are holy.**
> **Nothing in heaven or earth is so great as God.**

With a strong arm, God redeems the people.
Day by day, God leads us with a shepherd's care.
> **Even when the earth trembles, God is with us.**
> **When lightning flashes, we are confident of God's care.**

We have inherited the mission of the prophets.
We need the prophet's mantle from our God.
> **We have come to be equipped for our tasks.**
> **We have gathered for renewal of our lives.**

INVOCATION

We cry aloud to you, O God. Hear our prayers. In times of trouble, we need your comfort. Amid our confusion, we seek your clarity. From temptations of the flesh, we beg for liberation. Lead us away from the false gods we create, that we may meet you here with full expectancy and eager responsiveness. Amen.

CALL TO CONFESSION

When our self-indulgence enslaves, when our arrogant pretensions deceive, when our anxiety enfeebles, God calls us to repent, to lay aside our excuses, to seek pardon and freedom at their only source—the love of God, revealed by Jesus Christ.

PRAYER OF CONFESSION

O God, we are so self-centered that we cannot be centered selves. We are so preoccupied with things of little consequence that we cannot appreciate important matters of the heart. We consume other people instead of loving them. We bite and devour while you call us to build relationships and delight in your love. Set us free, O God, from the sin that binds us. Amen.

Assurance of Forgiveness

For freedom, Christ has set you free, brothers and sisters; only do not use your freedom as an opportunity for self-indulgence, but through love become slaves to one another. Follow in the footsteps of Jesus Christ and live from this day forward in the promised realm of God. Amen.

Collect

Parenting God, whose will for us as faithful followers of Jesus Christ is that we live by the Spirit, grant to us love, joy, and peace. Teach us patience, kindness, and generosity. Shape us to be gentle and self-controlled. Turn us from passions and desires of the flesh that separate us from you and violate love of neighbor. Fit us for labor in your realm and keep our hand to the plow. Amen.

Offertory Invitation

The way to Jerusalem was costly for Jesus. The way of Christian faithfulness is costly today. It requires nothing less than the full commitment of our lives. Our offering is a symbol of our life in the Spirit, our total commitment to the reign of God.

Offertory Prayer

Gracious God, we did not know it would cost so much or feel so good to follow Jesus. We are grateful that we have so much to give and so much yet to learn. We dedicate our offerings so that we and our neighbors may be equipped for life in your realm. Amen.

Commission and Blessing

Walk by the Spirit, showing the fruit of the Spirit,
giving thanks to God in all circumstances.
> *We will call to mind the many deeds of God.*
> *We will meditate on the wonderful works of God.*

As those who belong to Jesus Christ,
inherit the realm of God and share it.
> *God walks with us on our daily journey.*
> *God makes a path for us through deep waters.*

God grants true freedom to those who love,
who walk in faithfulness all their days.
> *We accept the prophet's mantle to empower us.*
> *We receive the Spirit's gifts to guide us.*

Amen. **Amen.**

(See hymns 97, 98.)

PROPER 9

2 Kings 5:1–14   (or Isaiah 66:10–14   Galatians 6:(1–6), 7–16
Psalm 30   Psalm 66:1–9)   Luke 10:1–11, 16–20

CALL TO WORSHIP

The realm of God has come near.
Enter this time of worship with joyous expectation.

We will extol you, O God, for you have drawn us up.
You rescued us from the pit and restored us to life.

Sing praises to God, all faithful ones.
Give thanks to God's holy name.

We have known your favor, O God, in many ways.
You have healed us and turned our mourning to dancing.

Rejoice in the work you are given to do.
Give thanks that your names are known to God.

We will praise you, O God, and not be silent.
We will give thanks to you forever.

INVOCATION

Gracious God, our helper, we greet you this morning with joy and thanksgiving. We feel your welcome and anticipate your teaching. Show us this day what you would have us do. Whether it be great or small, we want to do what you command. Let our ears be attentive to your Word, and our hearts be responsive to the opportunities you grant us to bear one another's burdens in the name of Jesus Christ. Amen.

CALL TO CONFESSION

Who among us has not wanted to shape God to our own specifications? How often we have wanted to define truth for everyone else and to judge others by standards we ourselves cannot keep. Whether our sins reside in what we have done, in what we have failed to do, or in prideful comparisons with other people, let us confess them now.

PRAYER OF CONFESSION

Gentle God, angry God, gracious God, we know we have let you down in many ways. We have not lived up to your high intentions for us. You send us out as ambassadors of peace, and instead we pick fights with our sisters and brothers. You commission us to travel light, and we become bogged down with our possessions. You ask us to help ease the burdens others carry, but we add to them. You call us to joy in your inclusive realm, but instead we create our own ghettos. Patient God, will you forgive us again? Amen.

Assurance of Forgiveness

Demons fall when Christians pray and witness together. Lives are healed when pretensions are cast aside. God extends mercy and peace to all who are sincerely penitent. Turn away from temptation, knowing that God will strengthen you in fulfilling the law of Christ.

Collect

God of peace, whose challenges to us are not too great for us to fulfill with your help, speak your transforming Word to us now, that we may be empowered for the mission on which you send us. May the hospitality and compassion of Jesus be so much a part of our nature that others will be drawn to worship you and to keep your commands. Amen.

Offertory Invitation

Our offerings support the ministry of this church as we reach out together to announce the better way God intends for all of us. In our giving, we extend a welcome, practice hospitality, offer healing, become reapers in God's harvest, and extend the peace of God to the world. May our offerings honor the one who gives us all we have.

Offertory Prayer

With gratitude for your gracious favor, we dedicate these gifts. May they help others as we have been helped. May they reach out in a spirit of gentleness to restore to community those who are alienated. May they announce to the world that the realm of God is among us, waiting to be claimed. By these resources, may your name be praised here and in many other places. Amen.

Commission and Blessing

God sends us out as lambs among wolves.
It is not easy to proclaim the gospel.
>   *We will not fear to let our faith be known.*
>   *We want to carry God's peace into our world.*
Your words and deeds can be simple and direct.
Your witness is to be gentle and kind.
>   *We will listen before we speak.*
>   *We will seek to love without judging.*
The peace of God dwells in you and will help you.
The Spirit will grant you authority and power.
>   *We accept God's gifts and promises.*
>   *We will not grow weary of doing what is right.*
Amen. **Amen.**

(See hymn 99.)

PROPER 10

Amos 7:7–17   (or Deuteronomy 30:9–14   Colossians 1:1–14
Psalm 82   Psalm 25:1–10)   Luke 10:25–37

CALL TO WORSHIP

God calls together a divine council to render judgment.
God holds a plumb line to measure our faithfulness.
> *Who can stand before the judgments of God?*
> *How shall we know what God expects of us?*

Lift up your prayers for God's mercy.
Earnestly seek to know the ways of truth and salvation.
> *Can we distinguish faithfulness from popular success?*
> *What must we do to inherit eternal life?*

God's judgment comes to all nations of the earth.
God's covenant with us involves care for all people.
> *Will God deliver us from the hands of the wicked?*
> *Will God put an end to wanton treachery?*

INVOCATION

Almighty God, we tremble with the knowledge that you know all our thoughts and deeds and judge them by your perfect will. Yet we are bold to protest the evil around us that seems to go unpunished. So many innocent and good people die randomly or suffer cruelly. How long will you judge unjustly and show partiality to the wicked? O God, we know this is really your question for us. Help us to take seriously these moments of encounter with you, knowing we can trust you to be just. Amen.

CALL TO CONFESSION

God rightfully expects more from us who call ourselves the church of Jesus Christ. Are we tempted to conform to ways we observe around us? The plumb line hangs straight across all our excuses. How do we measure up before the law of God?

PRAYER OF CONFESSION

Righteous God, we confess our easy compliance with ways of the world. We are happy to accept advantages for ourselves that are unavailable to many. We do not call oppressors to account or recognize our own oppressive ways. We pass by many who suffer, as if their suffering were no concern of ours. Our practice of the faith gives neither offense nor inspiration. We are troubled when we see ourselves this way. Redeem us, O God! Amen.

ASSURANCE OF FORGIVENESS

We are rescued from the shadows of our sinfulness by the grace of Jesus Christ. There is forgiveness for all who accept the gracious gift of a loving God. We open ourselves now to receive anew the gospel in all its power. We will share in the inheritance of the saints as we become good neighbors to the weak and needy, the lonely and destitute, whom God loves along with us.

COLLECT

Sovereign God, whose judgments stretch our thinking and challenge our doing, you have placed us in the midst of your eternal realm to be neighbors to sisters and brothers we have not yet acknowledged. Draw us into a circle of mutual caring, where the suffering of one is felt by all and injustice is confronted at every level, to communicate your mercy to the world. Commission us through your Word to grow, to bear fruit, and to serve. Amen.

OFFERTORY INVITATION

You shall love God with all your heart, and with all your soul, and with all your strength, and with all your mind; and you shall love your neighbor as yourself. This love motivates our giving. As God has loved us, we return that love in our offering of energy, time, and resources.

OFFERTORY PRAYER

May these gifts and our lives bear fruit in many good works, increasing among all people knowledge of God, patience and endurance, wisdom and understanding, love and joy. We would act with compassion toward one another and toward neighbors near and far. Thankful for the mercy you have shown us, we pledge ourselves and these offerings to extend mercy to all. Amen.

COMMISSION AND BLESSING

Grace to you, and peace, from God our Creator.
Continue this day your love for all the saints.
We will love God with our whole being.
We will care for ourselves and others as God's children.
Be filled with spiritual wisdom and understanding.
Bear fruit and grow in good works by God's power.
We pray for discernment and empowerment.
We seek to live with patience, endurance, and joy.
God's compassion surrounds you today and always.
Live as people delivered from the power of evil.
We acknowledge the dominion of Jesus Christ among us.
We will carry the spirit of Christ within us.
Amen. **Amen.**

(See hymn 100.)

PROPER 11

Amos 8:1–12   (or Genesis 18:1–10a   Colossians 1:15–28

Psalm 52   Psalm 15)   Luke 10:38–42

CALL TO WORSHIP

Come, people of faith, trusting God's steadfast love.
Take refuge in the eternal presence.
> **We want to acknowledge God first in our lives.**
> **We seek to rely on a power beyond ourselves.**

Gather in silent awe before the source of all things.
Climb God's holy hill, giving thanks.
> **It is not easy to have faith in one we do not know.**
> **It is frightening to realize God's sovereign power.**

Know that Christ is the image of the invisible God,
the one in whom the fullness of God was pleased to dwell.
> **We are the church, gathered in Christ's name.**
> **We are the body of Christ, seeking to live faithfully.**

INVOCATION

Awesome God, we thirst for your Word. We long to make sense of so much we do not understand. We want our worship to be more than a quick diversion from tasks that seem more pressing. We want to believe there is more to life than seeking personal gain. We bring to you today our troubles and anxieties, our estrangements and hostilities, our boasting and deceits. Meet us here with truth we cannot avoid. Amen.

CALL TO CONFESSION

God calls for our full-time devotion. In all that we think and do, God's will is to hold first place. Our worship is hollow and empty if it is only a small, separate compartment in our lives. No matter how good we are, all of us need a time of reorientation and reconciliation. That is why, together, we confess our sin.

PRAYER OF CONFESSION

Take away our distractions, O God, so we may be confronted by your expectation of us. We realize that our busy striving after things has dulled our awareness of you. We have sought fulfillment in ways that deny you and hurt other people. Sometimes our success tramples the needy and brings ruin to the poor. Even our benevolence becomes self-serving. O God, we want to find our hope in the gospel. Help us, we pray. Amen.

ASSURANCE OF FORGIVENESS

Do you truly want to be forgiven? If that is your honest choice, experience that forgiveness now in the very core of your being. Know that in the mystery of Jesus Christ we are truly reconciled to God. Continue in faith, not shifting from the hope of the gospel. Dwell consciously in God's presence in the midst of all you do every day.

COLLECT

We are gathered at the feet of Jesus to learn what you expect of us, O God. We are here seeking a word of hope amid all the bad news, the senseless suffering, and the evil deceit that surround our lives. We want to become mature in faith and responsible in action so you can work through us to bring changes that are needed in our world. Amen.

OFFERTORY INVITATION

The psalmist laughs at those who trust in wealth. Perhaps we are ones who are objects of that scorn. Let us use our wealth to proclaim the one in whom we really trust, that creative energy of love who fills the whole universe and has been revealed to us in Jesus Christ.

OFFERTORY PRAYER

Through our offerings, loving God, we proclaim Christ to the world. We dedicate all we are giving to preaching, teaching, and outreach that move people toward Christian maturity. We offer ourselves as advocates for the poor and needy, as seekers for justice, as stewards of hope. We turn from false securities to put our confidence in you, that the mystery of your glorious Word may be opened up among all your people. Amen.

COMMISSION AND BLESSING

Choose this day a life of listening and trusting.
Let God have first place on your daily agenda.
> *We will give ear to promptings of the Spirit.*
> *We seek to hear God's teachings and warnings.*
Let your faith be evidenced in all your dealings.
Share humbly and caringly the hope that is in you.
> *We believe others can hear the Word of God through us.*
> *We will be careful to represent the gospel faithfully.*
You have chosen well; receive God's blessing.
Give thanks each day for God's gracious favor.
> *Thanks be to God for both comfort and judgment.*
> *Praise God for both reassurance and challenge.*
Amen. **Amen.**

(See hymn 101.)

PROPER 12

Hosea 1:1–10   (or Genesis 18:20–32   Colossians 2:6–15, (16–19)
Psalm 85   Psalm 138)   Luke 11:1–13

CALL TO WORSHIP

God is eager to restore us to right relationships.
The Creator is waiting to claim us now as God's own.
> *We have come to meet the God who welcomes us.*
> *We have gathered to experience God's steadfast love.*

Listen, for God will speak to those who want to hear.
Turn your hearts toward the one who saves.
> *We bow down to receive God's mercy.*
> *We open ourselves to the source of peace.*

God will answer us and will give what is good.
God restores us to faithfulness and righteousness.
> *We come asking, searching, and knocking.*
> *We seek the good gifts only God can provide.*

INVOCATION

Living God, we come as your children to be reclaimed and blessed. We need the inner strength that comes to us through worship. All week long we have wrestled with emptiness and deceit on every hand. Take away the noisy clamor that would make us captives of human traditions. Turn us toward the source of our salvation, toward your steadfast love and faithfulness. Amen.

CALL TO CONFESSION

God judges the earth. God knows our disloyalty. Our grave sins against others are not unnoticed. Our haughty pretensions are noted. Surely God has every reason to be indignant with us, to pour out anger on us for the many ways we misuse the gifts we have been given. Yet God is eager to spare us from the horrible consequences of sin. Let us seek forgiveness.

PRAYER OF CONFESSION

O God, bring our evil to awareness so we can address it and be rid of its burden. Forgive our iniquity and pardon our sin. Turn us away from false pride and violence, from lies and hardness of heart. Erase the record that stands against us. Restore us to a right relationship with you and with those from whom we are alienated. Grant us also the capacity to extend forgiveness to all who have wronged us. Have pity on us now, O God.

Assurance of Forgiveness

God forgives our trespasses and restores us to life. Our puffed-up pretenses are set aside so we can claim a far greater identity as children of the living God. Our sense of alienation is overcome as we are embraced by steadfast love. Friends, the doors of God are open wide to receive us. We are heard and known. The peace of God is ours to accept and cherish. Thank God with whole hearts!

Collect

Teacher and Friend, whose doors are ever open to receive your children, we want to learn from you today how to pray. We long to sense your answering voice when we call. We are eager to receive a response to our earnest requests. We want to persist in prayer amid all the competing distractions of life. We seek this, not just for our own satisfaction, but that the world might become a more wholesome place for all your children. Amen.

Offertory Invitation

The faithfulness of God elicits our answering faithfulness. The good gifts of our heavenly Parent call for an outpouring of gratitude. May our offerings give evidence of abounding thankfulness.

Offertory Prayer

Holy God, whose name is before all names, we worship you with our offerings. They represent our labor, our investment of time and energy. We want them to be put to the best possible use. May they save many from the course of evil and turn them toward faithful discipleship. May they provide bread for body and soul, that your people may be preserved and strengthened for ministry. Bless and multiply our efforts, we pray. Amen.

Commission and Blessing

Reenter your world as children of the living God.
Greet your neighbors as God's valued creation.
> *God sends us out as bearers of peace.*
> *We will honor God's Word above everything.*
With steadfast love and faithfulness, God strengthens you.
You will receive what you need for each day.
> *We will not hesitate to search and ask.*
> *We will be persistent in prayer.*
God will answer you and give you what is good.
Doors will be opened and good gifts will be received.
> *We rejoice in the opportunities God gives us.*
> *May the glory of God be recognized among us!*
Amen. **Amen.**

(See hymn 102.)

| Hosea 11:1–11 | (or Ecclesiastes 1:2, 12–14, 2:8–23 | Colossians 3:1–11 |
| Psalm 107:1–9, 43 | Psalm 49:1–12) | Luke 12:13–21 |

CALL TO WORSHIP

Listen, all who are fleeing from the Holy One;
God is calling us; God has called us together.
>   *O give thanks to God, for God is good;*
>   *God's steadfast love endures forever.*

God is eager to put loving arms around us.
God is waiting to satisfy our hunger and thirst.
>   *God fills the hungry with good things.*
>   *Our thirsting souls are filled to overflowing.*

Set your minds on things that are above.
Put to death your earthly disobedience.
>   *God leads us to a new identity, to new life.*
>   *We seek renewal in the image of our Creator.*

INVOCATION

Loving God, in whose arms we have found our identity, come among us to direct our faltering steps in the ways you would have us go. Teach us to walk with Christ through the distractions that beckon us in other directions. Turn our vain striving into meaningful service, our foolish greed to the fulfillment of sharing, our confusion to clarity of vision, that we might worship you truly this hour. Amen.

CALL TO CONFESSION

What does God see within us and among us that we do not see? Do you suppose that God is disappointed? frustrated? angry? What defenses have we created to keep God out of our lives? How have we turned away from the life God intends for us? Now is the moment to come out of hiding, for God already knows where we are.

PRAYER OF CONFESSION

Holy God, our lives are far from holy. The thoughts we have held in secret have erupted into hurtful words and deeds. We have not avoided lies and slander. We have given in to pessimism and suspicion. We resent people whose lives seem easier than our own. We hate the thought of passing on to those less worthy the things we have worked so hard to possess. O God, we need your wisdom in order to live peacefully within ourselves. Amen.

ASSURANCE OF FORGIVENESS

God has invited all of us to strip off our old selves to accept renewal in the image of our Creator. Right here, right now, in the warmth of God's love, our greed is melting away, our anger is finding constructive release, our despair is giving way to hope. God delivers us from the folly of self-preoccupation to joyous involvement in our Creator's "wonderful works to humankind."

COLLECT

Compassionate God, whose riches have been poured out among us in unrecognized abundance, help us today to reexamine our stewardship over the things and the relationships you have entrusted to us. Confront our greed, lest it destroy us and rob our sisters and brothers of the good you intend for them. Amen.

OFFERTORY INVITATION

Life does not consist in the abundance of our possessions. All that we currently possess will someday belong to others. We have the privilege in this life to do good with all that God has entrusted to us. We bring a portion now to be blessed by God in the work of our church, Christ's church, here and in other places.

OFFERTORY PRAYER

Help us, O God, to give enough of ourselves and our substance every day that we will not be tempted to embrace the idolatry of greed. We here dedicate not just our offerings but all we possess to causes far greater than our own security. Before all our attachments require "larger barns," help us to reflect on how they might better be used by others than stored by us. Thank you for the abundant opportunity to share. Amen.

COMMISSION AND BLESSING

God has made us rich in so many ways.
Now let us go out to find new ways to be rich toward God.
Let us show our thanks for God's steadfast love.
Praise God for wonderful works to humankind.
We are being renewed in the image of our Creator.
We differ in many ways, but Christ is all and in all.
We have been raised with Christ above earth's deceits.
We will set our minds on learning God's will for us.
God will take us up in loving arms when needed.
By God's kindness, we will be taught to walk.
We look to God for healing and renewed strength.
We seek to walk in the straight ways where God leads.
Amen. **Amen.**

(See hymn 103.)

PROPER 14

Isaiah 1:1, 10–20   (or Genesis 15:1–6   Hebrews 11:1–3, 8–16
Psalm 50:1–8, 22–23   *Psalm 33:12–22)*   Luke 12:32–40

CALL TO WORSHIP

Gather before God, people of the covenant.
Listen for God's Word, O faithful ones.
> **God has summoned us to this place.**
> **We believe God will speak to us here.**

Come to honor God and give thanks.
Seek to learn and follow in God's way.
> **We come as willing and obedient servants.**
> **Let your steadfast love, O God, be upon us.**

God calls us as workers for justice.
God sends us out as advocates for the dispossessed.
> **We are here to be equipped for ministry.**
> **We expect to be empowered for our service.**

INVOCATION

For the rich heritage we have received from your hand, we are grateful, O God. You have fashioned our hearts and observed our deeds. Now we come together, awaiting further instructions from your Word. Teach us here what we need to know in order to live faithfully in this troubled world. Lead us beyond the routines of worship to a genuine, life-changing encounter with you. Amen.

CALL TO CONFESSION

Is this another solemn assembly of people who are quite content with ourselves and unable to confront our hidden sin? Do we live in self-protective rebellion against God's call to rescue the oppressed and devote ourselves to seeking justice for all? Have we become a burden to God?

PRAYER OF CONFESSION

Almighty God, we confess that we have shaped our own standards and values rather than seeking to know your will. We turn from faith in you and rebel against the agenda of your realm. Our hearts focus on the things we can accumulate more than on your mission in which we can share. Lead us, O God, into acts of compassion, that our attitudes may be reshaped and a right relationship with you restored. Amen.

ASSURANCE OF FORGIVENESS

Wash yourselves until you are clean. Seek justice, rescue the oppressed, turn from evil to do good. As you share in God's agenda, your sins of scarlet become as pure as new-fallen snow. God is pleased to welcome you into that realm where all are blessed and where true treasures can be found.

COLLECT

God of all worlds, whose presence in our world we celebrate in Jesus Christ, lead us to deeper faith, fuller trust, and greater responsiveness. May we hear your knock, answer your call, and serve where we are sent. We are ready to share in your promises, claim the homeland you offer, and extend to all we meet the invitation to believe and obey. May all people discern the treasure you offer. Amen.

OFFERTORY INVITATION

Where your treasure is, there your heart will be also. When you invest generously in the work to which God calls us, your whole life is drawn into fulfilling relationships with God and with the people you are helping. Do not be afraid to share.

OFFERTORY PRAYER

Thank you, God, for welcoming us into your caring realm, where we claim the needs of others as our concern. We are finding a homeland in your service and we are grateful. Above all, may our offerings be an outpouring of thanksgiving for a God who does not forget us. Your promises are sure and your faithfulness is to all generations.

COMMISSION AND BLESSING

Enter your everyday world dressed for action.
Let your lamps of faith light up the world.
> *We are ready to meet God at home and at work.*
> *We are ready to serve wherever we are.*

God, whose Word prepared vast worlds beyond our knowing,
welcomes us as covenant partners in this world.
> *Direct our steps, O God, and we will obey.*
> *We respond to your promises in faith and trust.*

Work for justice and peace where you live.
Let your prayers embrace those in need.
> *God is our assurance and our peace.*
> *God is the light along our way.*

Amen. **Amen.**

(See hymns 104, 105.)

PROPER 15

Isaiah 5:1–7   (or Jeremiah 23:23–29)   Hebrews 11:29–12:2
Psalm 80:1–2, 8–19   Psalm 82)   Luke 12:49–56

CALL TO WORSHIP

Return, beloved of God, to the fold.
God welcomes you to this hour of prayer.
> **God calls us by name and awaits our coming.**
> **God summons us out of hiding.**

God is like a shepherd, caring for her flocks.
God is like a gardener, carefully tending his vines.
> **Surely God has provided richly for us.**
> **Our lives are sustained by God's good gifts.**

Worship the one who longs for our coming.
Sing praise to the one who expects our faithfulness.
> **We call on God, who gives us life.**
> **May God's face shine on us to save us.**

INVOCATION

Surrounded by a rich heritage of faith, we seek to know you, God, in this time of worship. Thankful for our spiritual ancestors, we return to our roots to find our true identity. We lay aside all that weighs us down and fills us with doubts so we can give attention to your call and your message. Meet us here, we pray. Amen.

CALL TO CONFESSION

Sometimes we deceive ourselves with pious pretense, but God is not fooled. Sometimes we are led astray by the lies and empty promises of the marketplace, but God does not change the rules to accommodate our whims. We busy ourselves with our own agendas, but God continues to have a better plan for us. Stop now to evaluate your relationship with God.

PRAYER OF CONFESSION

O God, after all you have done for us, we have failed to bear fruit for you. We have turned away from your Word and have forgotten to call on your name. People who are weak, lonely, and destitute receive little help from our hands because we are preoccupied with our own concerns. Lift us from the shadows of our own deceits and let your face shine on us so we may walk once more in your truth. Amen.

Assurance of Forgiveness

When we are penitent, God restores us to our rightful identity as children of the Most High. God lights a fire within us so we can change our world for the better. In the name of Jesus Christ, who endured the cross for us, we dare to come out of hiding to speak up for justice and peace.

Collect

God of abundant grace, whose judgment is a part of your love for humankind, bring fire among us that we may be united in faithfulness rather than divided by competing interpretations of your Word and our present times. Make us not so much predictors of the future as practicers of faithfulness in this present moment. Amen.

Offertory Invitation

We are surrounded by a great cloud of witnesses, people of generations before us who have given their all in faithfulness to God. Much is required of those who make a faith commitment. Much is required of us. We give, however, not out of fear or a sense of duty but because it is a joyful opportunity to express thanks for all we have received.

Offertory Prayer

Gracious God, whose creative energy has filled all heaven and earth with good things for us to enjoy and share, we would honor you with our offerings. May the programs we initiate and the outreach we support bear fruits of justice and peace. We look to Jesus, the pioneer and perfector of our faith, as our model in facing all circumstances and giving ourselves for others. Amen.

Commission and Blessing

God has planted and nurtured a splendid vineyard.
We are vines, expected to bear good fruit.
> *No longer will we be choked out by thorns and briars.*
> *Deceit and lies will not overcome us.*
God's Word is more powerful than fire or earthquake.
It is given to shake us from our complacency.
> *We are aware of the weak and needy among us.*
> *We are determined to work for justice.*
Let the one who knows God's Word speak faithfully.
May all who have heard the Word make response.
> *God will restore us in time of difficulty.*
> *God will perfect and equip us for our service.*
Amen. **Amen.**

(See hymn 106.)

PROPER 16

Jeremiah 1:4–10   (or Isaiah 58:9b–14   Hebrews 12:18–29
Psalm 71:1–6   Psalm 103:1–8)   Luke 13:10–17

CALL TO WORSHIP

Assemble before God, our rock and refuge.
Come together to listen for the voice of our Creator.
The Word of God shakes the foundation of the earth.
We expect to be changed by God's message to us.
God rescues us from cruelty and injustice.
In steadfast love, God delivers us from our enemies.
We remember the rich heritage we have received.
We give thanks for God's grace and mercy.
This is God's holy day, a time to lay aside narrow interests.
How will we honor God in word and deed?
We will delight in the Word and works of our God.
We will join together in praise and good works.

INVOCATION

We are known by you, gracious God, better than we know ourselves. You have
given us life and you have renewed our spirits. You have carried us to the heights
and you have dwelled with us in life's depths. You are our hope and our trust.
Touch us here, for you are far beyond our reach. Dwell with us here to lift our
aspirations and inspire confidence among us. Amen.

CALL TO CONFESSION

How often do our habits and traditions get in the way of God's mercy and
abounding love? Are we more eager to enforce the law than to help people? Are
we full of excuses when we are called to serve? God is waiting for our answers.

PRAYER OF CONFESSION

We bow in awe before you, powerful God. We have forgotten that you are in
charge of the earth. We have neglected the brothers and sisters you have called us
to love. We want them to conform to our way of doing things rather than
reaching out to them where they are. We would rather ignore them than feel
obligated to help. Sometimes we would rather continue our own crippled existence than call on you for help. O God, we need your mercy. Amen.

ASSURANCE OF FORGIVENESS

God forgives, heals, and redeems. Stand straight and tall in your own mind, for God reclaims you and grants you freedom to become all you are meant to be. God crowns you with steadfast love and mercy. God appoints you to speak and act as representatives of the heavenly realm, as prophets of the new covenant.

COLLECT

Ruling God, whose will is broader than our best traditions and whose mercy runs deeper than our finest sympathies, speak your Word to set us free from attitudes that cripple, habits that are hurtful, and dispositions that divide. Enlist us as willing disciples so others may meet Jesus Christ through us. Amen.

OFFERTORY INVITATION

Our gifts speak where we cannot go. They witness to people we will never meet. They praise God who has provided for us every day of our lives. Let us give thanks through our offerings.

OFFERTORY PRAYER

O God, we cannot forget all your benefits. Accept our offerings as expressions of praise and acts of true worship. We pour out our thanks for all you have given us and for all you do for us. We are grateful for the opportunities you grant us to help others. May healing come to all who suffer and freedom be granted to those weighed down and bent over with heavy burdens. Use us and our gifts to bring the changes for good that you intend for our world. Amen.

COMMISSION AND BLESSING

God promises to reign among us and guide us.
God's rule in our midst will not be shaken.
> *We will approach God with reverence and awe.*
> *We will worship God in our daily pursuits.*
God's freeing, uplifting presence is ever with us.
God's transforming power is working among us.
> *We rejoice at the wonderful things God is doing.*
> *We are eager to join in good works for God.*
The Word of God empowers us to speak and act.
God is sending us to people who need our help.
> *We will not be afraid to speak of God's love.*
> *We will dare to act as God directs.*
Amen. **Amen.**

(See hymn 107.)

PROPER 17

Sunday between August 28 and September 3

Jeremiah 2:4–13 (or Proverbs 25:1–7 Hebrews 13:1–8, 15–16
Psalm 81:1, 10–16 Psalm 112) Luke 14:1, 7–14

CALL TO WORSHIP

Sing to God, our strength; cry out to God, our helper.
Rejoice, and do not fear to appear before our God.
> **It is God who led our ancestors through hard times.**
> **It is God who leads us through difficult days.**
God will not leave us or forsake us.
God welcomes us to the banquet of life.
> **God fills our mouths with good things.**
> **God offers us fountains of living water.**
Listen now to the voice of God and submit to God's will.
Hear the Word of God and turn away from worthless things.
> **We will delight in the commandments of our God.**
> **We will share eagerly in the work God gives us to do.**

INVOCATION

Gracious God, our helper, we seek the assurance of your presence in this time of worship. We have come to listen and to receive your counsel. Melt our stubborn hearts to remove the barriers that keep us from seeing your glory and doing your will. Challenge all that is worthless and unprofitable in our lives, that we may become worthy imitators of Jesus Christ, in whose name we pray. Amen.

CALL TO CONFESSION

When we are not in daily communion with God, false gods rush in to claim our loyalty. We chase after things that do not profit. We become cracked cisterns that can hold no water. Only God can fill our emptiness.

PRAYER OF CONFESSION

O God, we are desolate and frightened, for there are evil tidings all around us and we do not know you well enough to count on your help. We cannot hear your voice or sense your presence. There is a void within us that things cannot satisfy. We have reached for honors and recognition, but they provide no lasting fulfillment. Forgive our mistaken priorities and draw us to you, the source of living water. Amen.

ASSURANCE OF FORGIVENESS

Happy are those who fear God, who delight in God's commandments. It is well with those who deal generously with others, conduct their affairs with justice, and care for the poor. When we listen to God, the enemies within and around us are subdued and we can walk with confidence into each new day.

COLLECT

Holy God, at whose banquet table we feast every day of our lives, we have been richly fed with good food and homes, education and work, and so many things we take for granted. Feed us now with your glorious presence and with your Word that humbles us, even as we are lifted up to heights we could not have imagined. Amen.

OFFERTORY INVITATION

Through our offering, we extend to the world God's banquet invitation. As we reach out to people who have not known our advantages, we are blessed. Let us not neglect to do good and to share generously what we have, for such sacrifices are pleasing to God.

OFFERTORY PRAYER

In joyous thanksgiving for the banquet of life, we invite those who live in poverty to share our wealth. We give up some of our luxuries for the sake of brothers and sisters who lack food, shelter, or medical care. We reach out to help, expecting no reward but the satisfaction of sharing what you have so richly entrusted to us. We dedicate our time and abilities along with these fruits of our labor. Amen.

COMMISSION AND BLESSING

Go forth as humble servants of Almighty God.
Those who humble themselves will be exalted.
> **We have no right to boast before God or others.**
> **We are simply privileged to share God's bounty.**

When you give a banquet, invite those who cannot repay.
Give honor to persons not usually recognized.
> **God has created us as sisters and brothers to all.**
> **Everyone is a child of God, deserving of our attention.**

God, who blesses your worship, will bless your service.
God will feed you with spiritual food that satisfies.
> **How good it is to walk in the ways God leads us!**
> **How satisfying to drink from the fountain of living water!**

Amen. **Amen.**

(See hymn 108.)

| Jeremiah 18:1–11 | (or Deuteronomy 30:15–20 | Philemon 1–21 |
| Psalm 139:1–6, 13–18 | Psalm 1) | Luke 14:25–33 |

CALL TO WORSHIP

Hear the choices God sets before us:
life and prosperity or death and adversity.
O God, you have searched us and known us.
You know our thoughts and every move we make.
Listen to the ordinances of our God;
love God and walk in the way God commands.
O God, we will listen for your words.
We will seek to walk on the paths you intend.
Happy are those who delight in God's law;
blessed are all who meditate on God's Word.
Wonderful are all your works, O God.
We are your creation; we are in your hands.

INVOCATION

Like a skilled potter, O God, you have shaped each one of us as a unique design.
You know us better than we know ourselves. You value us more highly than we
can imagine. You weep when we are marred or broken through our own misdeeds
or the world's cruelty. We gather now to assemble our prayers for one another and
all the world's people in a chorus of devotion. Hear us, gracious God. Amen.

CALL TO CONFESSION

Come, all who have plugged your ears or averted your eyes when God's commands intrude on your idolatry. God calls individuals and nations to account. God
expects our complete devotion and faithful obedience. How will we respond?

PRAYER OF CONFESSION

Awesome God, we confess that we have become slaves to our own narrow self-
interest. We pay more attention to our possessions than to you. We try to hide
from your all-seeing eye, for we are guilty of devotion to false gods. We are
attracted to wicked advice and sinful pursuits that direct our steps away from you.
We act without thinking or planning or consulting with you. O God, show us the
way to a better life. Amen.

ASSURANCE OF FORGIVENESS

Grace to you and peace from God our Parent. Refresh your hearts in Jesus Christ our Savior, who is the same yesterday, today, and forever. Receive the living water God offers to all who come in true repentance and searching faith. The Holy Spirit will never leave us or forsake us. Our helper is ever available and eager to respond to our prayers. Come, there is a place at God's banquet table for you.

COLLECT

Creator of all, you have demanded our complete devotion and obedience. You call for risk-taking loyalty and commitment that puts you before family and friends in our attention. We want to build the quality of life you intend for us and for all people. Show us how to become fully engaged as disciples of Jesus Christ. Help us to straighten out our priorities so we can witness faithfully to your will. Amen.

OFFERTORY INVITATION

When we perceive all the good we may do for Jesus Christ, we are eager to share. Jesus welcomes into discipleship those willing to give up all their possessions. What we give today is a symbol of our fuller devotion of all we have and all we are toward the realization of God's reign among us.

OFFERTORY PRAYER

Loving God, there is no way we can settle accounts with you. We have no way to repay you for all we have received from your hands. Yet we want to give our best to the work you call us to do through this community of seekers. We enter, with renewed commitment and confidence, the costly venture of spreading love through your world. Amen.

COMMISSION AND BLESSING

God welcomes your partnership in the gospel;
accept the cross of Christ and carry it.
We have considered the cost of discipleship.
We are willing and eager to pay the price.
God expects to hold first place in our lives.
We put everything we own on the line of faithfulness.
We want to be obedient to the law of love.
We want to show God's love in all we do.
We are held in the thoughts of God.
We are shaped and reshaped by the potter's hands.
We are finding new patterns of faithfulness.
We are discovering new reasons for joy.
Amen. **Amen.**

(See hymn 109.)

PROPER 19

| Jeremiah 4:11–12, 22–28 | (or Exodus 32:7–14 | I Timothy 1:12–17 |
| Psalm 14 | Psalm 51:1–10) | Luke 15:1–10 |

CALL TO WORSHIP

God looks on humankind to see if any are wise.
Who is seeking after God above all else?
> *We look to Jesus Christ for wisdom and truth;*
> *we reach out to be strengthened for service.*

The winds of God blow among us to winnow and cleanse.
They sweep through our midst in judgment.
> *Have mercy on us, O God, and wash away our sin.*
> *Do not let your wrath burn against us.*

Remember your promises to us, O God.
Create in us clean hearts and renewed spirits.
> *We seek to know you and to grow in understanding.*
> *Confront us here and light our way out of the void.*

INVOCATION

Hear our cries, O God, for we recognize our need for your mercy. We are fearful to encounter you, yet we cannot live without you. We are like lost sheep who have wandered away from the best we know and cannot find our way back. We want you to find us, but we fear your punishment. Come, Good Shepherd, to rescue us from ourselves. Amen.

CALL TO CONFESSION

We are to God like precious coins, worth seeking when we are lost. We are like sheep who have gone astray and yet are valued so much that God persists in searching for us. God has come among us here and knows where we are. We can keep no secrets; we can only hurt ourselves by hiding rather than confessing.

PRAYER OF CONFESSION

We have been fools. We have said in our hearts, "There is no God." Our deeds deny you. Our plans do not include you. We grumble and complain, criticizing those who embody your love for all people. We have turned aside from the way you commanded. Our greed is robbing this fruitful land and creating a desert. The world is full of suffering people whom we ignore. O God, is there any hope for us? Amen.

ASSURANCE OF FORGIVENESS

Forgiveness is not offered lightly or superficially. Yet it is always available to those who recognize their spiritual poverty and seek new life in Christ. God is a refuge for those who are truly repentant. God delivers us and restores us with mercy and grace. There is great rejoicing when sinners seek forgiveness and turn to serve God in love.

COLLECT

God of all people, who sent Jesus Christ to be a friend to tax collectors and sinners, fill us with love for all your children, that we may be saved from violence to share in patiently searching for the lost. We would join you in rejoicing when anyone responds to your love and enters into your service. Amen.

OFFERTORY INVITATION

We have the opportunity to join with God in providing for the poor and oppressed. Our gifts carry God's mercy to people who have not known God's love or discovered the joy of living in harmony with God's good earth and with their sisters and brothers.

OFFERTORY PRAYER

Because we have been blessed by you, O God, we are delighted to share. Because there are many who do not enjoy your bounty, we search for ways to help them. Thank you for showing us the way of mercy and patient example, the way of generosity and self-forgetful service, the way of faithfulness and joyous celebration. Bless us and our offerings, we pray. Amen.

COMMISSION AND BLESSING

Rejoice that lost ones have been found.
Give thanks daily that God has found you.
> *How wonderful that the lost have been found!*
> *How exciting that God reaches out to claim us!*
Join in welcoming all people whom God loves.
Go after those who are in need of God's mercy.
> *God will restore their fortunes.*
> *They will receive all they need from God's hand.*
You will share in the joy of salvation.
You will hear the sounds of gladness.
> *Praise God for deliverance from judgment.*
> *Give thanks for the experience of grace.*
Amen. **Amen.**

(See hymn 110.)

PROPER 20

Jeremiah 8:18–9:1   (or Amos 8:4–7   I Timothy 2:1–7

Psalm 79:1–9   Psalm 113)   Luke 16:1–13

CALL TO WORSHIP

God welcomes those whose hearts are sick.

God's invitation comes to people whose joy is gone.

Why is the health of God's people not restored?

Why must we weep day and night for those we have lost?

There is a balm in Gilead. There is a physician who heals.

Jesus Christ is our mediator, healer, and savior.

We bring all our pain and unresolved anger.

We come in all our confusion to seek answers.

Bring all your urgent prayers and honest laments.

God is eager to offer salvation and open us to truth.

We cry out to God for deliverance from our sin.

We cry out for relief from our suffering.

INVOCATION

Into this holy temple, we have come, gracious God. This is not our church but yours. We cannot claim our world; it is a trust from your hand. Our lives, our health, our length of days call forth our stewardship. We are managers, not owners, so we come to you now to give account and seek your further commands. Help us, O God of our salvation. Amen.

CALL TO CONFESSION

"The harvest is past, the summer is ended, and all are not saved." We resist the great physician, for healing requires change and we have not been ready to give up our favorite vices. We have not been eager to do things God's way. Join me as we seek forgiveness.

PRAYER OF CONFESSION

O God, we have not managed well the wealth of the earth, which is our trust from you. We have modified your commands to suit our own egos and desires. We have wasted resources while hoarding for our own use what is meant for all to enjoy. Our concerns are narrow and our compassion is weak. We are restless and unfulfilled for we have not tried your ways. Forgive us, we pray, and lead us into your new day.

Assurance of Forgiveness

Let the confusion and despair of your former ways melt into trust in a God who cares. Let go of dishonesty and false riches to accept the wealth of knowing God and responding in faithfulness. God's gift to us is a quiet and peaceable life, full of dignity and godliness. Such acceptance and inner peace enliven our active care for others and our sharing in the joy of service.

Collect

Faithful God, whose mercy is offered to the just and the unjust, help us to reorder our priorities so the wealth we possess becomes a tool, not an idol. We would use our wealth to address problems you call us to solve, to win others to your way of love, and to heal the brokenness of your world. Bless our learning and our doing, we pray. Amen.

Offertory Invitation

As managers for God of the world's resources, we share the hurt of those who are poor, sick, and in mourning. Our wealth is meant to bring good news to them in Jesus' name. We invest in the church's outreach, that our money may serve God, not trap us in idolatry.

Offertory Prayer

We give, loving God, because of your generosity to us. We share because this is your will for us. In faithfulness to your call, we seek to manage the resources you provide for the greatest benefit to humankind. May they bring a bit closer an awareness of your intentions for us and your rule among us. We worship and serve you with all we have. Amen.

Commission and Blessing

God has delivered and blessed us here.
God will assist us every day as we are open to God's help.
> *We will look to God for guidance and direction.*
> *We will seek God's truth for every situation.*
We are invited to pray for others each day.
When we intercede for them, we draw closer to God.
> *We will be sensitive to others' pain and joys.*
> *We will respond in the spirit of Jesus Christ.*
Seek to be faithful in all things, great and small.
Acknowledge God's ownership of all you possess.
> *We seek to be honest managers and generous stewards.*
> *We are grateful servants of a loving God.*
Amen. **Amen.**

(See hymn 111.)

PROPER 21

Jeremiah 32:1–3a, 6–15　　　(or Amos 6:1a, 4–7　　　1 Timothy 6:6–19
Psalm 91:1–6, 14–16　　　　　Psalm 146)　　　　　　Luke 16:19–31

CALL TO WORSHIP

Come, all who live in the shelter of the Most High.
Gather together, all who trust in God Almighty.
> **God reigns through all generations.**
> **We will praise God as long as we live.**

We trust in God, our refuge and our fortress.
We can count on God's faithfulness at all times.
> **God lifts us up when we are threatened or afraid.**
> **We call to God for protection and rescue.**

Worship God, who richly provides us with all things.
Give thanks to the one who dwells in unapproachable light.
> **God, who made heaven and earth, keeps faith forever.**
> **We will pour out our thankfulness in words and deeds.**

INVOCATION

Ever-present God, let your Spirit fill this place, for we need to know that you are in charge. Through the terrors of night, amid the arrows that fly by day, we need to sense your power, your protection, your higher purpose. Show us here your saving, healing strength. Grant to us such confidence and contentment that we may look beyond ourselves to become a blessing to others. Amen.

CALL TO CONFESSION

How easily we find our security in things! We are tempted and trapped by senseless and harmful desires. We become indifferent to the plight of brothers and sisters. We lose touch with God. We are in need of God's mercy, forgiveness, and help.

PRAYER OF CONFESSION

All-powerful God, we have become so comfortable with our advantages that we forget who makes them possible. We are so eager for riches that we wander away from faith. We consider ourselves more worthy than others to enjoy your bounty. We look down on people less industrious or differently gifted than we. We turn away from the plight of neighbors who need our helping hand. O God, forgive our misplaced priorities. Have mercy on us and melt our hardened hearts so we may participate in the joy of your realm here and now. Amen.

ASSURANCE OF FORGIVENESS

You were called to eternal life when you made your first confession of faith. Set your hopes on God, who richly provides all things for our enjoyment. Do good; be rich in good works, generous, and ready to share. In so doing, you will take hold of life as it is meant to be and you will realize the ever-present realm of God.

COLLECT

Eternal God, whose will for humankind is that we live within your rule of love, call us out of our preoccupation with riches to sense our common plight with all who suffer. Help us to identify with rich and poor alike as your children, that through mutual care and compassion we might grow toward your eternal realm. May we hear and heed your life-changing warnings and promises. Amen.

OFFERTORY INVITATION

Because love of money is the root of all evil, we seek to make wealth a tool for accomplishing good more than for accumulating things. Because we have been blessed in order that we might share, we bring our offerings with gratitude and rejoicing. Let us give thanks with glad and generous hearts.

OFFERTORY PRAYER

What a joy to have something to give! Thank you, God, for granting us choices in the use of all you have placed on earth for our use. We have chosen this portion to dedicate for the ministry of the church in our community and in outreach throughout the world. Make us aware of the needy at our doors as well as lost ones everywhere who long for the bread of life. Amen.

COMMISSION AND BLESSING

Pursue righteousness and godliness, today and always.
Face life with gentleness and endurance.
> **The love of God sends us out to share love.**
> **The riches of God inspire our generosity.**

Fight the good fight of faith.
Take hold of eternal life in the midst of every day.
> **We are called to life with eternity in it.**
> **We are blessed with God's presence always.**

Good works and caring contain their own blessing.
Our lives dance with meaning when we share.
> **We rejoice in God's healing touch.**
> **We give thanks for salvation so richly given.**

Amen. **Amen.**

(See hymn 112.)

PROPER 22

Lamentations 1:1–6   (or Habakkuk 1:1–4, 2:1–4   2 Timothy 1:1–14
Psalm 137   Psalm 37:1–9)   Luke 17:5–10

CALL TO WORSHIP

God's mercies never end; they are new every morning.
We gather in gratitude, that our faith may increase.
> *We will sing our songs of praise.*
> *We will proclaim the good news of the gospel.*
Take delight in God, who is with us wherever we go.
Trust God, even when we do not feel like singing.
> *We will commit all our ways to God.*
> *We will wait patiently for answers to our prayers.*
By God's grace, we are gathered for worship.
In God's love, we are no longer exiles and strangers.
> *We have been called together by the Holy Spirit.*
> *We will treasure this special time in sacred space.*

INVOCATION

Make your presence known among us, O God, for the foundations of our lives are
shaking. We grieve in loneliness amid the crowds. We huddle in fear because of
the violence that surrounds us. Cities are ravaged, and rural areas are not safe. We
are exiled from the homeland of our dreams. Draw us to yourself, gracious God,
that we may experience your reign among us. Amen.

CALL TO CONFESSION

The evil abroad in our land is not far from any of us. We who claim to have found
a better way of life in Jesus Christ are called to extend life-saving faith to others.
Yet it is so easy to interact with anger, resentment, and self-interest instead. Let us
examine ourselves before God.

PRAYER OF CONFESSION

O God, we face our world with cowardice. We would rather avoid danger than
take a stand against injustice. We want to enjoy privileges not available to others.
We wish to keep away from all the cries for help that bombard us. The problems
around us are overwhelming. The distress within us is staggering. Too often we
lash out at others rather than turning to you for guidance and strength. Now, in
these moments together, we cry out for help. We want to be your people. We
want to live with a clear conscience and right spirit. Remake us, loving God.
Amen.

ASSURANCE OF FORGIVENESS

Commit your ways to God. Be still and trust, for God will act to transform us when we pray. Refrain from anger and forsake wrath, for they have no place in God's realm. Open yourselves instead to the grace, mercy, and peace God offers. Great is the faithfulness of our God.

COLLECT

Astonishing God, whose purposes are often accomplished in unexpected ways, release in us the gifts you have entrusted to us, that we may realize the power, love, and self-discipline that make for meaningful service in Christ's name. Help us to use whatever faith we have to accomplish great things for you and to reduce the hatred and violence of our world. Amen.

OFFERTORY INVITATION

Our wealth allows us the joyous opportunity to invest in ways that will make a difference in the lives of others. If we see the treasures we have received as private property, to be used only for our own benefit, they will entrap us. In the church, we are committed to sharing our faith and the blessings of the Holy Spirit.

OFFERTORY PRAYER

We are grateful to you, O God, for the faith we have inherited. We give thanks for the courage and faithfulness of ancestors who suffered for the gospel that we might know your love. We join with them in putting our trust in you. May we match their generosity and self-discipline, seeking above all else to know your will and do it. To that end, we dedicate our offerings. Amen.

COMMISSION AND BLESSING

We have a holy calling from God, to be lived each day.
Let us serve faithfully, trusting in God's grace.
> **We have received the promise of life in Christ Jesus.**
> **We want to live with joy and a clear conscience.**

God's hands of blessing rest upon each one of us.
The gifts of God are rekindled within and among us.
> **We are not ashamed of the gospel of Jesus Christ.**
> **We will share the good news, relying on God's power.**

Your faith, however small, holds powerful potential.
Your trust in God will grow as you employ it.
> **We will sing the praises of our God.**
> **We will seek to know and follow God's commands.**

Amen. **Amen.**

(See hymn 113.)

PROPER 23

Jeremiah 29:1, 4–7   (or 2 Kings 5:1–3, 7–15c   2 Timothy 2:8–15
Psalm 66:1–12   Psalm 11)   Luke 17:11–19

CALL TO WORSHIP

Make a joyful noise to God, all the earth;
sing your praise to the glory of God's name.
> **Great and awesome are the works of God.**
> **The whole universe sings of God's power.**

Gather to remember all that God has revealed.
Come to discover what God is doing among us.
> **God is faithful and just in all things.**
> **The promises of God are trustworthy and true.**

Present your best selves for God's approval.
Work and witness without shame or pretense.
> **Bless God, all people, and let our praise be heard.**
> **The fear of God is the beginning of wisdom.**

INVOCATION

Awesome God, who has given us life and kept our feet from slipping, we thank you now for bringing us to this place of worship and learning. Inspire us to speak truthfully and listen attentively. Keep us from wrangling over words in ways that divide. May we prove to be faithful workers, devoted to healing and reconciliation in Jesus' name. Amen.

CALL TO CONFESSION

Our God, who called us into covenant, invites us to examine our faithfulness. We who have known God's healing touch are recalled to a life of gratitude. Challenged to be builders and planters, we are faced with our destructive, unproductive habits. Together, we seek a better way.

PRAYER OF CONFESSION

Forgiving God, once more we seek your pardon and protection. We find ourselves in exile from the best we know. We have focused so much of our attention on our own concerns that we have neglected the welfare of our community. We see our own hardships more readily than we feel the vast suffering around us. We forget the mercy we have received. We are angry when we should be grateful. Restore us to covenant faithfulness, we pray. Amen.

ASSURANCE OF FORGIVENESS

We are healed and forgiven by a trustworthy God whose righteousness endures forever. Make a joyful noise to God, all the earth. Remember the resurrection of Jesus and accept the opportunity to be raised to new life in Christ. Our faith makes us well and prepares us for eternal glory.

COLLECT

Merciful God, from whom we have rebelliously kept our distance, we seek you now, for we are needy and afraid. We want to be healed, that we may praise you before the world and be channels of healing among the alienated and forgotten. Implant your Word among us and free us to live by it. Amen.

OFFERTORY INVITATION

Bring gifts of gratitude to honor God. Give thanks for God's awesome deeds. Praise God for salvation in Jesus Christ. May our offerings express the full measure of our thankfulness.

OFFERTORY PRAYER

We bring the first fruits of our labors, the best of all we have, a portion of the bounty you entrust to us. Accept our gifts, gracious God, as a symbol of our renewed commitment. We give thanks for the wholeness you offer us amid a fragmented world. We are grateful for meaningful tasks in the midst of chaos and meaningless suffering. We dedicate ourselves and our offering to your faithful service. Amen.

COMMISSION AND BLESSING

Go your way; your faith will keep you well.
Give praise and give yourselves in thankful living.
> **We will bless God as long as we live.**
> **We will reach out to help others every day.**
Share the gospel of salvation in Jesus Christ.
In humility, seek to embody the Word of truth.
> **We will work for the welfare of God's earth.**
> **We will pray for the well-being of the earth's people.**
Surely God is faithful and will help us.
Live confidently, assured of God's forgiving love.
> **Great are the works of God, which endure forever.**
> **We rejoice that we may abide in covenant with God.**
Amen. **Amen.**

(See hymn 114.)

PROPER 24

Jeremiah 31:27–34   (or Genesis 32:22–31   2 Timothy 3:14–4:5
Psalm 119:97–104   Psalm 121)   Luke 18:1–8

CALL TO WORSHIP

We gather to honor our covenant with God.
We gather to worship the God who has covenanted with us.
> **Our help comes from God who made heaven and earth.**
> **Our wisdom comes from the one who meets us here.**

Open your eyes to meet God face to face.
Open your ears to hear God's instruction.
> **God takes us by the hand to lead us.**
> **The Word of God is written on our hearts.**

Come to taste God's Word, which is sweeter than honey.
Come to touch the reality of God's presence.
> **Surely God will welcome us and protect us.**
> **We will walk with new understanding of truth.**

INVOCATION

Sow your seed in our midst, O God, for we are prepared to receive what you offer. We want to know you and to bear fruit for your reign among us. We want to meditate on your law and keep your commandments. Draw us into the new covenant you have fashioned for us in Jesus Christ so that we may fulfill our ministry. Amen.

CALL TO CONFESSION

God does not tire of our prayers. Rather, God feels neglected when we fail to pray. God does not write us off when we are careless. Instead, God's care of us summons us into new caring relationships. Bring to God in prayer all that causes you shame.

PRAYER OF CONFESSION

We confess, O God, that we are not eager to wrestle with you or to take responsibility for sin in our lives. We see ourselves as basically decent, respectable people. Yet we have bent your commandments to our own conveniences. We listen only to the word we want to hear. We participate in the greed that is destroying your good earth, and we allow evil to triumph through our neglect. Shake us into awareness that brings change, and support us, we pray, on the difficult path toward greater faithfulness. Amen.

ASSURANCE OF FORGIVENESS

Our self-disclosing God proclaims: "I will forgive your iniquity and remember your sin no more. I will be your God and you will be my people. I will put my law within you; I will write it on your hearts." Give thanks for the new life God offers, attuned to eternal values.

COLLECT

Just and listening God, ever more ready to hear us than we are to pray, meet us where we are, lest we decide that you are beyond our reach. We bring our disappointments and complaints, our cries for justice, our concern for the needy, asking for strength and courage to join in a more effective ministry among your people. Amen.

OFFERTORY INVITATION

We do not lose heart amid all the problems that compete for our attention. We have the resources to make a difference in our work of evangelism, teaching, and outreach. What we dedicate here is a symbol of our larger commitment of time and talents to the work of ministry.

OFFERTORY PRAYER

With thanksgiving for your presence in all our coming and going, through all our work and leisure, in our times of faithfulness and when we break covenant, we bring our offerings. May these resources help your people to know you more fully and serve you more effectively. Equip us for every good work, that your church may witness boldly and influence profoundly. Amen.

COMMISSION AND BLESSING

Continue in what you have learned.
Grow in all you have firmly believed.
God's Word provides our daily instruction.
Jesus Christ is our salvation day by day.
Proclaim the message that we are God's people.
Convince, rebuke, and encourage with patience.
We will persist in our teaching and serving.
We seek to be faithful in all circumstances.
Lift up your eyes to know God as your helper.
God has made us partners in a covenant of salvation.
God is granting us life in all its fullness.
We are growing in understanding and faith.
Amen. **Amen.**

(See hymn 115.)

PROPER 25

Joel 2:23–32	(or Jeremiah 14:7–10, 19–22	2 Timothy 4:6–8, 16–18
Psalm 65	Psalm 84:1–7)	Luke 18:9–14

CALL TO WORSHIP

This is God's house, a holy temple.
We are in the midst of God's dwelling place.
> *My soul longs, yea, faints for the courts of God.*
> *My heart and flesh sing for joy to the living God.*

Happy are those whom God has chosen to be here.
Blessed are all whom God has forgiven and named.
> *Our voices rise in praise of God's awesome deeds.*
> *Mountains and seas bow down before the Creator.*

God crowns the year with a bountiful harvest.
Flocks and grain fill the meadows.
> *God's presence is felt to the ends of the earth.*
> *All creation is God's dwelling place, God's home.*

INVOCATION

To you, O God, shall our vows be performed. To you we sing our praises and utter our prayers. Come among us to renew your covenant and offer your signs. Pour out your Spirit on your people gathered here, that we may dream and prophesy and follow the vision you set before us. Amen.

CALL TO CONFESSION

No good thing will God withhold from those who walk uprightly. Let us, therefore, acknowledge our wickedness and leave it behind us that we may set our hope in God and walk with confidence into God's new day.

PRAYER OF CONFESSION

How easily we have forgotten you, O God of our salvation. We imagine that our prosperity is of our own design. We wander into paths of self-righteousness and self-congratulation. We compare ourselves with those whose sins are public knowledge and consider ourselves better than they. O God, rescue us from the evil inside us that alienates us from others and from you. We humble ourselves before you, seeking forgiveness. Amen.

ASSURANCE OF FORGIVENESS

God justifies those who confess their guilt and forgives their transgressions. The God of our salvation delivers us in awesome ways. Those who put their trust in God and center their hope in Jesus Christ are blessed by an outpouring of the Spirit. God equips us to fight the good fight, to finish the race, to keep the faith. Be glad and rejoice in God.

COLLECT

Merciful God, who understands our motives and knows our every thought, we seek in these moments to be attuned to your Word and will, that we may be humbly receptive to the proclamation you would have us share with the world. Grant us strength to persevere in our witness, so others may catch a vision of the joy you offer to all who serve you. Amen.

OFFERTORY INVITATION

The threshing floors are full of grain, the vats overflow with wine and oil, the technology of our day puts the world at our remote control. The choices are so abundant and the possibilities for good and evil so extensive. Will we use the vast resources God puts at our disposal for selfish pleasure or for greater good? The church seeks to exercise wise stewardship to proclaim the reign of God.

OFFERTORY PRAYER

You have dealt wondrously with us, gracious God. We have gathered in your temple to praise you and to join in efforts to share faith with one another and with the world. Through our offerings, we wish to extend the witness made here into our neighborhoods, and, in ever-widening circles, to the ends of the earth. Bless and multiply our efforts, we pray. Amen.

COMMISSION AND BLESSING

Be glad and rejoice in God's wondrous works!
Praise God whose spirit blesses and empowers us!
> *God forgives our transgressions and answers our prayers.*
> *God delivers us from pretense and false pride.*
God stands by us to grant support and strength.
God is the ever-present source of hope and healing.
> *God rescues us from evil attack, from the lion's mouth.*
> *God is with us in times of suffering and loss.*
Return to your homes justified, praising God.
Return to your world, proclaiming good news for all to hear.
> *All who trust in God are strengthened and blessed;*
> *to God be the glory forever and ever.*
Amen. **Amen.**

(See hymn 116.)

Habakkuk 1:1–4, 2:1–4   *(or Isaiah 1:10–18*   *2 Thessalonians 1:1–4, 11–12*
Psalm 119:137–144   *Psalm 32:1–7)*   *Luke 19:1–10*

CALL TO WORSHIP

We cry out to God for the help we need.
How will we know we have been heard?
> **God stands with us through life's trials and temptations.**
> **God sends visions of new possibilities.**

Here we stand watch for God's appearing.
Together we seek a presence and aspire after truth.
> **Surely God is in this place and will give us understanding.**
> **God is recalling us to the values we have neglected.**

God's righteousness is everlasting, and God's law is truth.
Listen to all God would teach us; hear the Word of God.
> **We seek to grow in faith and in love for one another.**
> **We would learn to do good and to work for justice.**

INVOCATION

All around us, we see trouble and wrongdoing. Our world is consumed by violence and destruction. Even in your church, O God, are strife and contention. The iniquity of this generation hangs heavy upon us. We cannot worship you apart from the turmoil that lies so close at hand. Listen to us, God of all people. Hear our longing for a new day in which your reign of love is established among us. Amen.

CALL TO CONFESSION

Our festivals and solemn assemblies are offensive to God when we come with hardened hearts and with blood on our hands. God will not listen to the words of our prayers when our hearts are not attuned to the Spirit. God's welcome is for those who are penitent.

PRAYER OF CONFESSION

All-knowing God, we confess our participation in the hatred and evil that is consuming this planet. We gladly accept for ourselves the power and advantages that come our way. We seldom consider the cost to others of our prosperity. We tolerate poverty, hunger, and homelessness for people we do not know. We think our small efforts too insignificant to make a difference. Wash away, O God, the evil that paralyzes us, that we may become rescuers of the oppressed and seekers after justice. Create in us a right spirit that prompts us to live by faith and to dare great things for you. Amen.

ASSURANCE OF FORGIVENESS

Grace to you and peace from the God who loves us and equips us to become all we were meant to be. God is even now working in us to make us worthy of our high calling in Jesus Christ. Today salvation has come to this house, and we are all being changed.

COLLECT

Transforming God, Parent of our Savior Jesus Christ and Parent to each of us, we find ourselves up a tree, seeking to observe you from a distance, while you compel us to come close enough to welcome you into our homes, our work, and our play. Come into our hearts to reorder our priorities and save us from ourselves so we may be a blessing to those who need the love you will offer through us. Amen.

OFFERTORY INVITATION

Jesus Christ came into the world to seek out and to save the lost. Sometimes those who have much are lost in their possessions. The offering becomes the high point of worship when we are centered on the steadfast love of God. Then our possessions become instruments of grace, for us and for others, and the lost are found.

OFFERTORY PRAYER

Seeking God, all that we have is yours. All your children are our brothers and sisters. We are all inheritors of your grace. You have blessed us abundantly. Now bless what we have been moved to share, that our love for one another may increase. Amen.

COMMISSION AND BLESSING

Hurry home, for a guest awaits you there.
Jesus Christ wants to stay at your house today.
We give thanks to God for this gift of grace.
May our homes be places of self-sacrificing love.
Greet the challenges of this week as opportunities.
Let your faith grow as your love for others increases.
We will pray for one another as we serve.
We will look to God for the strength we need.
God will fulfill your good resolves and works of faith.
The name of Jesus Christ will be glorified in you.
Today salvation has come to this house.
Today our homes are being blessed by Christ's presence.
Amen. **Amen.**

(See hymns 117, 118.)

Daniel 7:1–3, 15–18   Ephesians 1:11–23

Psalm 149   Luke 6:20–31

CALL TO WORSHIP

>Praise God, all people who are called to be saints.
>Sing a new song in the assembly of the faithful.
>>**We will be glad in God our Maker.**
>>**We will rejoice with music and dancing.**
>God takes pleasure in us and receives our worship.
>God lifts up the humble and invites us to share God's glory.
>>**We will not cease to give thanks in all things.**
>>**We look to God for revelation and wisdom.**
>Listen here for God's Word of truth.
>Share with one another the gospel of salvation.
>>**We are here to seek a better way of life.**
>>**We have come to learn and to do what God intends.**

INVOCATION

Grant us today a vision of your reign and an awareness of your presence, mighty God. Draw us away from the distortions of the world to a clearer understanding of your Word of truth. Send your Holy Spirit among us, as you have promised. Knit us together in love so Christ may live in all we do and say. Empower our ministries with deep faith and abiding hope. Amen.

CALL TO CONFESSION

In Christ, the selfish distortions of our times are challenged. The self-centered appetites of rampant individualism are called into question. Christ calls us away from our preoccupation with riches, public approval, self-congratulation, and defensiveness. The world's values are reversed as we turn the other cheek and give more than is asked.

PRAYER OF CONFESSION

Most High God, we confess that we have not aspired to the best that we know. We have neither set our hope on Christ nor treated others with the love and respect we crave for ourselves. We seek to avoid entering into the depths of another's pain or risking our wealth out of compassion for all your saints. We do not want to embrace those we perceive as enemies or do good to those who hate us. We are afraid to trust the working of Christ's power among us. O God, help us to accept the demands of faith that we may experience its joy. Amen.

ASSURANCE OF FORGIVENESS

God executes judgment among us. Forgiveness is not cheap grace, for God continues to expect faithfulness in all things. Yet when we come in humble penitence and sincere desire to change our ways, God gives us the victory. We are inheritors of salvation. We are accepted in the family of God. Our way is enlightened, and we are filled with hope. Our values are put right. Praise God!

COLLECT

God of all who are poor, hungry, and sad, whose compassion extends to those we perceive as enemies, set our minds and hearts on higher values than our own comfort and security, that we may be led to love and serve you with joy. May the way we live attract others to the richness and empowerment known most fully in the community of faith when we truly become the body of Christ. Amen.

OFFERTORY INVITATION

Our inheritance in Jesus Christ prompts us to share the riches of good news with the world. Our pledges and extra gifts witness to the Word of truth, to the gospel of salvation. Because we have received so much, we seek to use our resources among those who hunger for physical or spiritual food. Let us give generously.

OFFERTORY PRAYER

God of glory, in thanksgiving for your abundant goodness, we seek to reach out to others as you have reached out to us. We want to treat our brothers and sisters as we wish to be treated, with dignity, understanding, and grace. May these offerings prove to be a blessing to those who give and those who receive. Amen.

COMMISSION AND BLESSING

Rejoice each day and praise God's name;
leap with joy and dance your faith.
> *We have set our hope on Jesus Christ;*
> *we live each day with the promised Holy Spirit.*
The eyes of your hearts will be enlightened;
God offers you a spirit of wisdom and revelation.
> *We sense the immeasurable greatness of God's power.*
> *We feel that power at work in Christ's body, the church.*
You are blessed in every time of want and need.
You are chastened whenever you put your trust in things.
> *We look to God for consolation, acceptance, and hope.*
> *We seek to know God's reign in our midst.*
Amen. **Amen.**

(See hymn 119.)

PROPER 27

Haggai 2:1–9   (or Job 19:23–27a   2 Thessalonians 2:1–5, 13–17
Psalm 145:1–5, 17–21   Psalm 17:1–9)   Luke 20:27–38

CALL TO WORSHIP

We call on God, who is as near as our next breath.
We gather to meet God, who has promised to bless us.
> **God is great and greatly to be praised.**
> **Through many generations, God has acted among us.**

Meditate on the wondrous works of our Creator.
Marvel at the glorious splendor of God's majesty.
> **God is the Savior of all who seek refuge.**
> **God hears our cries and fulfills our deepest desires.**

Remember God's steadfast love and faithfulness.
Make a joyful noise and break forth in song.
> **Our mouths will speak the praise of God.**
> **Let all flesh bless God's holy name.**

INVOCATION

Give ear to our prayers, gracious God, and attend to our cries. We call on you, knowing that you will answer and make your way known to us. We seek to follow the path you show us. We take courage, knowing that you are kind and just in all you do. When we need assurance, you gather us in the shadow of your wing. As we mature in faith, you give us wings to fly on our own. Meet each one of us in our particular need this hour. Amen.

CALL TO CONFESSION

God invites sinners to reclaim their former glory. All who have stumbled and fallen are welcomed and lifted up. Those who exalt themselves as if they were gods are brought to their knees. God will listen when we repent and will answer when we sincerely desire to change.

PRAYER OF CONFESSION

All-knowing God, we are reluctant to identify weakness or wickedness in ourselves. We do not recognize violent behavior or lawless rebellion as a personal problem. We would not think of elevating ourselves to take your place. Yet we find ourselves viewing the world from the narrow perspective of our own self-interest. Our anger at others spills over into our words and deeds. We ignore you in our decision making and fail to give thanks to you in our daily living. Without your forgiveness and transforming love, there is little hope for us. Hear us and save us, we pray. Amen.

Assurance of Forgiveness

God judges with righteousness and equity. God will strengthen us in every good work and word. By the kindness of our Creator, we are saved from self-centered rebellion and equipped for abundant living. We are called to join the chorus that praises God, proclaims good news, and invites others to share God's grace.

Collect

God of the living and of the dead, whose love embraces countless generations who have looked to you in praise and supplication, lead us beyond divisive debate to eager exploration of your truth. May our lives bear witness to your love, that all flesh may come to bless your holy name forever and ever. Amen.

Offertory Invitation

Great treasures have come to us from God's hand. The air we breathe, the lives we treasure, the love we have known are all gifts from our Creator. We are privileged to say thank you as we dedicate a portion of our resources for the ministry and mission of the church.

Offertory Prayer

For the future glory of your church, we dedicate our gifts. Toward the reign of love in our midst, we consecrate ourselves. O God of all the ages, show yourself to us in our time. Work within us individually and among us as a community of faith, that we may experience resurrection and carry your good news into our world. Amen.

Commission and Blessing

A kind and just God sends us out into the world.
We are bearers of truth beyond our understanding.
We have been comforted and strengthened this day.
We have good news to share with the world.
God watches over those who respond in love.
God fills us with hope and multiplies our good works.
We will praise God as long as we live.
We will witness to the resurrection day by day.
Take courage and sing a new song.
Work in new ways, for the Spirit abides in you.
We will break down barriers with joyous daring.
We will live with a spirit of adventure.
Amen. **Amen.**

(See hymns 120, 121.)

PROPER 28

| Isaiah 65:17–25 | (or Malachi 4:1–2a | 2 Thessalonians 3:6–13 |
| Isaiah 12 | Psalm 98) | Luke 21:5–19 |

CALL TO WORSHIP

God is ready to answer us, even before we call.

God is eager to listen, though we are not ready to speak.

> **The hills sing together before God's presence.**
> **All of nature proclaims God's glory.**

If the seas join in praise, how much more should we.

If hills are alive with song, let us, too, awake to sing.

> **Make a joyful noise to God, all people of the earth!**
> **Break forth into joyous song!**

Be glad! Rejoice in all that God is creating.

Welcome the new heaven and earth God has planned.

> **We worship God with great joy and delight.**
> **We welcome God's healing touch in our midst.**

INVOCATION

God of hosts, our strength and our salvation, there are no words large enough to praise you. No response by us can match the love you have shown us. Gather us now in your warm embrace, that our faith may be renewed and our work empowered to the honor and glory of your holy name. Amen.

CALL TO CONFESSION

We come to renew our relationship with God, knowing we are often led astray by our busyness, our greed, and our hope for gain without effort. Sometimes arrogant, often putting our trust in things, we neglect the spiritual dimension of our lives. Let us confess the emptiness we often feel.

PRAYER OF CONFESSION

O God, our salvation, we confess that we have tried to live apart from you. Our daily habits deny your reality. We toil without seeking your will. We work without giving our best. We compete with brothers and sisters without valuing them as your children or relating to them as our kin. We follow fads and false leaders while neglecting our faith. Forgive our misplaced trust, our hesitation to take the risks of caring witness, and our failure to empathize with others. Restore our connections with all from whom we are alienated. Amen.

ASSURANCE OF FORGIVENESS

Those who revere God's name will find healing when they come to God in heartfelt prayer. Those who model themselves after the saints will grow in love and trust. Be glad and rejoice in what God is creating among us. God grants forgiveness along with wisdom and strength to face life's challenges.

COLLECT

Reigning God, whose presence reassures us in times of uncertainty and terror, we pray for wisdom and courage to discern your purposes in every time and place. Help us to stand for the best we know, even if that evokes derision or betrayal. Keep us from being led astray by competing voices that compromise your intentions for us and all people. May we who seek to be the church of Jesus Christ never become weary of doing what is right. Amen.

OFFERTORY INVITATION

We have the opportunity to give thanks through our offering of ourselves and our possessions to the work God calls us to do. We cannot repay God for our lives, our minds, the beauty of earth and sky, the abundance of resources that we enjoy. But we can respond with acts of gratitude and kindness, with generosity and thanksgiving.

OFFERTORY PRAYER

We rejoice, O God, in the new world you are creating around us and within us. We give thanks for the joy we find in the church as we draw water from the wells of salvation. It is our intention to share the joy, to proclaim your Word among all nations, to work quietly and enthusiastically for a world where your love reigns. To these ends, we dedicate our offerings. Amen

COMMISSION AND BLESSING

Take with you the assurance of healing and wholeness.
God's steadfast love and faithfulness accompany you.
> *We will sing of the victories God makes possible in us.*
> *We will praise God for comfort and guidance.*
Life in God's realm is a gift freely given to us.
It is also a way of relating that we are to share.
> *We want others to come to know God through us.*
> *We want to live in ways that make God's love known.*
God will give you the words and wisdom you need.
By your endurance, you will gain your souls.
> *Praise God with trumpet, lyre, and horn.*
> *Make a joyful noise to God, all the earth.*
Amen. **Amen.**

(See hymns 122, 123.)

PROPER 29 (CHRIST THE RULER)

Sunday between November 20 and November 26

Jeremiah 23:1–6   Colossians 1:11–20
Luke 1:68–79 or Psalm 46   Luke 23:33–43

CALL TO WORSHIP

Bless God, all people of faith and hope.
God has looked on us with great favor.
> **God is our refuge and strength in times of trouble.**
> **God is our guide and inspiration when things go well.**
God gives light to those who live in the shadows.
God offers stillness amid the turbulence of our times.
> **We live in covenant with God, who gives us the best.**
> **We are eager to give our best to God in return.**
By the tender mercy of our God, we meet for worship.
God has brought the dawn of a new day for our use.
> **Praise God for signs and wonders all around us.**
> **Praise God for peace and reconciliation.**

INVOCATION

We worship you with gladness, O God our shepherd, for you have gathered us as
your beloved flock. You have sent a mighty Savior, who has demonstrated among
us the power of love. Send your Spirit now to remind us of your gifts and to
strengthen us for our tasks. May we show our loyalty to Christ by the way we live
every day. Amen.

CALL TO CONFESSION

Come, all who dwell in the shadow of death, whose ways are not God's ways,
whose works scatter and destroy rather than gather and build up. God summons us
to a time of repentance and reconciliation. Let us admit our unfaithfulness that we
might be restored to the flock.

PRAYER OF CONFESSION

Many times you have rescued us, O God. Yet we continue to wander away from
your vision for us. We claim to be followers of Jesus, but we do not speak up when
he is mocked. We do not respond when he summons us from the perilous byways
we have chosen. Our words and deeds deny the faith we proclaim. God of all
nations, deliver us from misplaced loyalties and unacknowledged sin. Forgive our
foolish ways. Amen.

ASSURANCE OF FORGIVENESS

Jesus Christ has claimed for us God's forgiveness and restoration to full partnership. Christ's promises are for today as well as for unknown tomorrows. We have been rescued from enemy hands, that we might serve God without fear. We are citizens of God's realm, where Jesus reigns in the triumphant power of love. Give joyful thanks to God, who has enabled you to share in the inheritance of the saints.

COLLECT

All-knowing God, who sent Jesus to this earth to demonstrate your rule of love, let your chosen one inspire us now to make faithful response to your call for justice and peace. We recognize your beloved child as head of the church and ruler in our individual lives. May we live even now as residents of your realm. Amen.

OFFERTORY INVITATION

The knowledge of salvation is meant to be shared, and we are a people called to extend this good news in every way we can. When we give our money, we give a part of ourselves, for we have traded our labor, our time, and our talent for what we now give away. All we possess belongs to God, to whose purposes we now dedicate our gifts and ourselves.

OFFERTORY PRAYER

For the saving faithfulness of Jesus Christ, we give thanks. For the church that seeks to extend Christ's ministry, we are humbly grateful. All things we have are gifts from you, O God, so we dedicate more than our money. We reinvest ourselves in patient, joyful response to your promises. Hear our prayers and empower our ministry. Amen.

COMMISSION AND BLESSING

Step out into the light that God will provide.
Receive the strength of Christ's glorious power.
> **God is our refuge and strength, our help in trouble.**
> **Christ is our Savior, who welcomes us to God's realm.**
Rejoice in the tender mercy of our God.
Give thanks for the one who demonstrated God's love.
> **God has looked favorably on us and redeemed us.**
> **Christ has prepared the way for us to go.**
Be still and know that God is God.
Let the good shepherd lead you day by day.
> **We will not fear or be dismayed.**
> **We are being recreated in the church of Jesus Christ.**
Amen. **Amen.**

(See hymns 124, 125.)

SPECIAL DAYS

Deuteronomy 26:1–11   Philippians 4:4–7
Psalm 100   John 6:25–35

CALL TO WORSHIP
We dwell in a land God has loaned to us.
Make a joyful noise to God, all the earth.
> *We come with gladness to worship God.*
> *We enter God's presence with joyous song.*

The first fruits of our labor belong to God.
Rejoice in the privilege of sharing God's bounty.
> *God has made us, and we belong to God.*
> *We are the sheep of God's pasture.*

The God of peace greets us in this time of worship.
Enter with thanksgiving and heartfelt praise.
> *We thank God for steadfast love to sustain us.*
> *We praise God for faithfulness to all generations.*

INVOCATION
Our baskets are full, gracious God, with the bounty you have provided. Our hearts are full of thanksgiving and praise. We are eager to meet you here, to learn from you, to be changed by you, to become more fully the people you intend for us to be. Show us how to do the work you have planned for us. Equip us as your faithful stewards. Amen.

CALL TO CONFESSION
Like lost sheep, we stray from the good shepherd. We become aliens to the realm of God. We accumulate advantages over others and resist any lessening of our special privileges. A gentle voice summons us to confession.

PRAYER OF CONFESSION
O God, we like to think we have nothing to confess. If our thoughts are pure, our actions kind, and our thanksgiving genuine, have we not lived up to your standards? Yet you call us to put you first in all things, and we have not done that. You call us to be peacemakers, but we do little more than try to avoid conflict. You call us to a passionate faith and compassionate sacrifice, and both are difficult for us. Feed us, God, with food that endures for eternal life and answer our thirst with life-giving water. Amen.

Assurance of Forgiveness

Do not worry. The God of peace will be with you, guarding your hearts and minds. Let your thoughts center on all that is true, honorable, just, pure, and commendable. Keep on doing the things you have learned. God's transforming spirit dwells with those who seek to be faithful.

Collect

God of signs and wonders, God of everyday surprises, we are eager to hear your Word, thankful that you choose to dwell among us and lead us to your new day. We want to celebrate your bounty, share it with those who have less, and together learn to live as responsible, compassionate people. Amen.

Offertory Invitation

The Bible speaks of first fruits offered before the altar of God. How would our lives change if our first thoughts on receiving a paycheck were of how we could honor and thank God? What if we always linked our material concerns with the spiritual? Does our gratitude begin to match God's generosity?

Offertory Prayer

We rejoice in this opportunity to thank you, gracious God, with a portion of the bounty you provide for our use. We reach out for meaning and purpose in our unsatisfying lives. As we share materially in the work of your church, we are on a spiritual quest to discern your will for us and our world. Thank you for pointing us beyond food that perishes to feed on the bread of life. Amen.

Commission and Blessing

The bread of heaven gives life to the believer.
Receive the bread, eat, and live.
> *We will turn to God daily for nourishment.*
> *We will give thanks with grateful hearts.*
The bread of heaven gives life to the church.
Share the bread; share your stories.
> *We will gather in the community of faith.*
> *We will share the bread and share our lives.*
The bread of heaven gives life to the world.
Pass on the gift with joy to neighbors near and far.
> *We will bless the world with acts of love.*
> *This is our highest thanksgiving to God.*
Amen. **Amen.**

(See hymns 126, 127.)

Related Hymns

THE ADVENT SEASON

1

The Days Are Coming

First Sunday in Advent—C
Lavon Bayler

7.6.7.6.D
(Lancashire)

The days are surely coming
When promises, once made,
Will be fulfilled among us
Where justice is displayed.
A righteous branch from David
Provides the saving grace
To shelter us in safety,
Our deepest fears erase.

We trust that God will teach us
The ways that we should go,
That truth will lead us forward,
God's steadfast love to know.
Then, mindful of the mercy
That overcomes our sin,
We wait, in humble patience,
Our Parent's discipline.

We lift our souls to praise you,
Great God, upright and good;
We witness to your purpose,
For we have understood:
Your covenant invites us,
In faithfulness, to share
Your message of salvation
With people ev'rywhere.
Amen.

(Psalm 25:1–10, Jeremiah 33:14–16)

2

The Realm of God Is Near

First Sunday in Advent—C
Lavon Bayler

6.6.8.6. S.M.
(St. Thomas)

The realm of God is near;
The signs are all around.
Look up to see the Human One,
With love and glory crowned.

Fear not the pow'rs of earth;
Fear not the roaring sea,
But raise your heads and set your hearts
On what is soon to be.

God's Word, in human form,
Will live among us here,
That faith and holiness may grow,
And falsehood disappear.

Then render thanks to God,
For all the joy you feel.
Pray earnestly, both night and day,
And live for Christ, with zeal.
Amen.

(Luke 21:25–36, I Thessalonians 3:9–13)

See "Make Known Your Ways," *Refreshing Rains of the Living Word,* p. 160.

3

Come to the Temple

Second Sunday in Advent—C   6.4.6.4.6.6.6.4.
          Lavon Bayler   (St. Edmund)

Come to the temple, come;
God will appear.
Come to prepare the way,
For Christ is near.
Let the refiner's fire
All our best gifts inspire,
That we may toil and plant,
In covenant.

We our thanksgiving bring,
Glad we can bear
Seed time to harvest tasks,
Joy to declare.
When others wail and weep,
We will our vigil keep,
'Til they are comforted,
Cared for and fed.

Working in partnership,
Seeking God's face,
We for each other pray,
Sharing God's grace,
That hills and valleys may
Seem level plains today,
Where we can find your ways
And sing your praise.
Amen.

(Psalm 126, Malachi 3:1–4, Luke 3:1–6, Philippians 1:3–11)

The same texts inspired "Hear the Voice," *Refreshing Rains of the Living Word,* pp. 160–61.

4

Sing Aloud!

Third Sunday in Advent—C
Lavon Bayler

8.7.8.7.8.7.
(Regent Square)

Sing aloud among the nations.
Come, rejoice with all your heart.
Shout so all the world may hear you,
All God's blessings to impart.
Come rejoicing, come rejoicing,
Let the joyous chorus ring.

Surely God is our salvation.
We will trust and have no fear.
All who once were judged are rescued.
Time for our release is near.
Come rejoicing, . . .

God will bring us home together,
Casting out our enemies,
Evil has no place within us;
Wrong before God's judgment flees.
Come rejoicing, . . .

Greet with joy God's holy presence.
God is still our strength and song.
Let your praise and deep thanksgiving
Echo through the ages long.
Come rejoicing, . . . Amen.

(Isaiah 12:2–6, Zephaniah 3:14–20)

See "Give Thanks to God," *Refreshing Rains of the Living Word*, p. 161.

5

God of Peace

Third Sunday in Advent—C   7.7.7.7.D
Lavon Bayler   (Spanish Hymn)

God of peace, be with us here;
Calm the turmoil of our soul.
Let true loveliness appear,
Lifting up and making whole.
Take away anxiety;
Let us live more thankfully,
Joining all our prayers and praise,
In contentment with your ways.

Keep our hearts and minds in Christ,
Filled with honor, truth, and grace.
All that Jesus sacrificed,
We are eager to embrace.
Keep us pure and just each day;
Let your excellence hold sway,
As we join in prayers and praise,
With commitment to your ways.

Grant us strength in Christ to live,
Whether we are strong or weak.
May we our best efforts give,
As we your intentions seek.
In our hunger, you will feed,
Care for us, and meet our need.
We will raise our prayers and praise,
Thanking you through all our days.
Amen.

(Philippians 4:4–13)

6

When John the Baptist

Second and Third Sundays in Advent—C   9.8.9.8.9.9.
Lavon Bayler   (St. Petersburg)

When John the Baptist heard God's summons
In desert wilderness to preach,
His word was warning to all persons:
Let all your actions match your speech.
God's wrath will fall on all your pretense.
Bear fruits each day that show repentance.

Prepare the way for God to visit;
Make paths of welcome smooth and straight.
All hills and valleys shall exhibit
How God's salvation recreates.
All flesh shall see the wondrous vision,
Calling for generous decision.

God loves all people, claims all nations,
Welcomes the baptized to invest
Their efforts and their expectations
In serving others with their best.
A Savior comes who heals and names us,
Sending the Spirit's fire to claim us.
Amen.

(Luke 3:1–18)

"Bear Fruits of Penitence," *Refreshing Rains of the Living Word*, p. 162, is based on the same text.

7

O God of Hosts

Fourth Sunday in Advent—C
Lavon Bayler

7.6.7.6.6.7.6.
(Es Ist Ein Reis)

O God of hosts, we greet you,
Our shepherd, bright and strong.
We thank you for your promise
To rescue us from wrong.
A ruler shall appear
From lowly place and people,
To save us from our fear.

How long will you be angry
At prayers that we have said?
For we have failed to thank you,
And worshipped wealth instead.
O fill our emptiness,
That we may cry no longer
From insult and distress.

Restore us as your children,
And feed your flock, we pray.
May we delight to welcome
Our neighbors to your way.
Expand our will to care,
That ev'ry race and nation
May in your fam'ly share.
Amen.

(Psalm 80:1–7, Micah 5:2–4)

8

Let Us Rejoice

Fourth Sunday in Advent—C
Lavon Bayler

10.10.10.10.10.10.
(Yorkshire)

Let us rejoice; good news is on its way.
Leap up to welcome Jesus Christ today.
One God has promised soon will reappear,
Challenging all whose faith is insincere,
Lifting the humble in a warm embrace,
While mighty rulers reap a lesser place.

Blest are the people carrying God's gifts,
Who share the joy that raises and uplifts,
Who give themselves as offerings complete,
Pausing to sit, at times, at Jesus' feet.
May we, like them, find moments to be still,
For we are here, O God, to do your will.

Then let us magnify our Savior's name,
In Jesus Christ our destiny to claim.
May we, like Mary, sense fulfillment near,
Daring to serve 'though outcomes be unclear.
Help us believe and trust you day by day,
Rememb'ring you in all we do and say.
Amen.

(Luke 1:39–55, Hebrews 10:5–10)

"Come to Bethlem," *Refreshing Rains of the Living Word,* pp. 162–63, uses themes from all four scripture selections for the fourth Sunday of Advent.

THE CHRISTMAS SEASON

9

Rejoice, People of Light

Christmas Eve/Day—A, B, C
Lavon Bayler

8.6.8.6.7.6.8.6.
(St. Louis)

Rejoice, O people of the light;
Our gloom is washed away.
The shadows of our greed and spite
Have fled as yesterday.
You multiplied the nation,
O God, and granted joy
To young and old, to rich and poor,
Who live in your employ.

The yoke and burden we have worn
Against oppressor's might
Are lifted, for a child is born
To set the world aright.
The bearer of good tidings
Of peace that has no end,
This child will reign on David's throne
And to our cares attend.

O mighty God, our parent, friend,
And helper ev'ry day,
Let justice reign as you intend,
And all our fears allay.
With righteousness abounding,
Your church, we know, will stand
With Jesus Christ as counselor,
And zeal on ev'ry hand.
Amen.

(Isaiah 9:2–7)

10

Let Heavens Be Glad

Christmas Eve/Day—A, B, C
Lavon Bayler

8.6.8.6. C.M.
(St. Anne)

Let heavens be glad and earth rejoice;
Declare God's glory here.
May all creation, with one voice,
Affirm salvation near.

O sing to God a song made new
By God's creative power,
That lifts us to a higher view,
To worship in this hour.

In fear and praise, we bow before
God's majesty and reign,
Confessing idols we adore,
And evils we maintain.

God judges us with equity,
The world with righteousness.
The sovereign one brings unity,
Sends truth to heal and bless.

Profess to all the world today
God's coming once again,
As fields exalt and heavens say
That love and joy will reign.
Amen.

(Psalm 96)

11

Glory to God

Christmas Eve/Day—A, B, C   11.10.11.10.10.
Lavon Bayler   (Peck)

Glory to God, sang angels in the highest,
Peace on the earth to people of good will.
Great is the joy that God in Christ discloses.
Hear once again the song that echoes still.
Hear once again the song that echoes still.

Surely God's grace is meant for our salvation.
Fear is erased, and wonder fills our hearts.
Claim the good news and witness to the story,
Finding delight in truth God's love imparts.
Finding delight in truth God's love imparts.

Keep in your hearts the wonder of this moment,
Sensing in Christ your own integrity.
Follow the shepherd, glorifying, praising.
God's work in time, for all eternity.
God's work in time, for all eternity.

Come, chosen people, who have glimpsed the manger,
Laying aside all lesser loyalties.
Give of your best in zealous deeds of kindness,
Sharing a blessed hope that heals and frees.
Sharing a blessed hope that heals and frees.
Amen.

(Luke 2:1–20, Titus 2:11–14)

See "O Blessed Hope," *Refreshing Rains of the Living Word,* p. 164.

12

Heavens Proclaim

Christmas Day (Proper 2)—A, B, C   8.6.8.6.6.10.
Lavon Bayler   (Antioch)

Heavens proclaim the grace of God.
Be glad, rejoice and sing.
Give thanks to God, as heirs of hope,
Your joyous praises bring,
Your joyous praises bring.
Rejoicing, join the song, your praises bring.

Goodness abounds, light dawns once more;
Let righteousness prevail.
Our God preserves the lives of saints,
Delivered from travail,
Delivered from travail,
Delivers and saves us from all travail.

Washed and renewed, prepare the way
For others to enjoy
God's mercy shown in Bethlehem,
Our talents to employ,
Our talents to employ,
Our talents and joyous service to employ.
Amen.

(Psalm 97, Isaiah 62:6–12, Titus 3:4–7)

"Prepare the Way," *Refreshing Rains of the Living Word,* p. 163, is based on all texts for this occasion.

13

Now, by God's Mercy

Christmas Day (Proper 2)—A, B, C   6.5.6.5.
                 Lavon Bayler   (Merrial)

Now, by God's great mercy,
Earth and heaven meet.
Angels join the chorus,
God's own child to greet.

Shepherds on the hillside,
Watching flocks by night,
In their quiet vigil,
Witness to the sight.

Light consumes the dimness,
Joy replaces fear,
When a tiny baby
Brings God's glory near.

Who will tell the story,
Meant for all to hear?
Gaze in awe and wonder;
God is present here.

Come again, dear Savior;
Make your home in us.
May your church's mission
Gain new impetus.
Amen.

(Luke 2:8–20)

14

Listen for Good News

Christmas Day (Proper 3)—A, B, C
Lavon Bayler

7.7.7.7.7.7.
(Dix)

Listen for good news of joy!
Horn and trumpet now employ!
Lift your voice in songs of praise,
Thanking God for peaceful days.
Hail our God's nativity,
Love's triumphant victory.

Shout it from the mountaintop,
News no earthly power can stop:
God's salvation comes for all
Who will hear and heed God's call.
We are comforted and blessed
By a child, our heavenly guest.

From the founding of the earth,
From the love that gave us birth,
We have gratefully believed
Joyous words that we received,
For the words were matched with deeds
That discerned and met our needs.

Comfort then your people here
Who have felt your presence near.
God, whose righteousness abounds
And all lawlessness confounds,
Change us for the better now
As before the Christ we bow.
Amen.

(Psalm 98, Isaiah 52:7–10, Hebrews 1:1–12)

"Come, O Word," *Refreshing Rains of the Living Word*, p. 166, is based on all the texts of Proper 3.

15

O Word of Light

Christmas Day (Proper 3)—A, B, C   6.6.6.6.8.8.
       Lavon Bayler   (Arthur's Seat)

O Word of light and life,
You shine in deepest night,
Creating children who
Will champion what's right.
As John bore witness to the light,
We, too, your greatness will recite.

May we receive your Word
With joyous gratitude,
Intent to follow Christ,
However we are viewed.
We long to live courageously
Your will, O God, that sets us free.

The grace and truth of Christ
Bring glory to our lives.
The word that makes us whole
Our best intent revives.
Come once again, show us the way
To faithful living every day.
Amen.

(John 1:1–14)

16

Let All the Earth

First Sunday after Christmas—C
Lavon Bayler

7.6.7.6.D
(Aurelia)

Let all the earth together
Sing praises to your name,
Great God of all creation,
Forevermore the same.
With thankful hearts, we bless you,
With psalms and hymns, we teach
Your word of wisdom offered
To all within our reach.

The moon and stars, the heavens
Created by your hand,
The mountains, hills, and valleys
Of this and every land,
Are witness to your power
As, joining in your praise,
They lift your name in chorus
And celebrate your ways.

Our words and deeds give witness
To your forgiving grace
That calls forth our compassion
Toward all the human race.
With lowliness and kindness,
With patience, born in peace,
We now forgive our neighbors
And pray that hatreds cease.

Forbearing one another,
We seek that harmony,
Displayed in your creation,
For all of us to see.
The word made flesh in Jesus
Calls us, your church, to be
One body, bound together,
In loving unity.
Amen.

(Psalm 148, Colossians 3:12–17)

17

Thank God

First Sunday after Christmas—C
Lavon Bayler

Irregular
(Adestes Fideles)

Thank God for our parents,
Leading us as children
To worship and learn and pray while serving our God.
Listening, caring, sacrificing, risking,
Their love equips our journey,
Their trust evokes our trusting,
Their hope will lead us forward in paths yet unknown.

Thank God for our teachers,
Tending to our growing
While patiently guiding us to question and probe.
Praising, correcting, coaching, understanding,
Their love equips our journey,
Their trust evokes our trusting,
Their hope will lead us forward in paths yet unknown.

Thank God for our pastors,
Shepherding, proclaiming,
Conveying a way of life that brings out our best.
Challenging, training, comforting, forgiving,
Their love equips our journey,
Their trust evokes our trusting,
Their hope will lead us forward in paths yet unknown.

We come now to praise you,
God of all our mentors,
Rejoicing that we can grow in wisdom and love.
Children and aged, all of us together,
Commit ourselves to serve you,
Within your house to worship,
Within your world to follow where Jesus will lead.
Amen.

(1 Samuel 2:18–20, 26, Luke 2:41–52)

See "We Come to Praise," *Refreshing Rains of the Living Word*, p. 167.

18

'Tis the Season

New Year's Day (January 1)—A, B, C
Lavon Bayler

8.7.8.7.D
(Austrian Hymn)

'Tis the season to be joyful;
Eat and drink and laugh and dance,
Doing our allotted business,
God's full purpose to advance.
We will plant and build and gather,
When the time is right for each.
We will seek and love and listen,
Knowing God will speak and teach.

We rejoice in birth and dying,
Seeing both as in God's hands.
We will weep and mourn together,
Trusting one who understands.
War, destruction, tearing, hating.
How can these express God's will?
We will trust through times of silence;
God is caring, loving still.

All the matters under heaven,
Have their time and place to be.
Stones, once thrown, can form an altar,
Reaching toward eternity.
God embraces all our triumphs,
Turns our failures toward some good.
We will serve with speech and actions
That reflect God's neighborhood.
Amen.

(Ecclesiastes 3:1–13)

19

God, Our Beginning

New Year's Day (January 1)—A, B, C   11.11.11.6.
Lavon Bayler   (Integer Vitae [Fleming])

God, our beginning, may the year now dawning,
Lead us to sense your Spirit with us dwelling.
Help us discern new earth and heaven 'round us.
Grant us to know your love.

God of all majesty, we sing your glory,
Seeing the stars and moon you have established.
What then are we—mere mortals—that you love us?
Grant us to know our worth.

God of all ages, young and old adore you,
For you have honored us within creation,
Giving dominion over plants and creatures.
Grant us to know our place.

God of all judgment, we would be responsive
To your intention for this fragile planet.
Aid us as stewards, keeping trust with vision.
Grant us to know your truth.

God, at our ending, may there be no crying,
For we affirm your care within our dying.
When our short span on earth is slowly ending,
Grant us to know your peace.
Amen.

(Psalm 8, Revelation 21:1–6a)

20

Shepherd and Judge

New Year's Day (January 1)—A, B, C
Lavon Bayler

10.10.10.10.
(Toulon)

Shepherd and judge, we gather at your throne.
You are the one by whom we're fully known.
You come to judge 'tween faithfulness and sin.
Enter and try our hearts and live within.

You bid us give the hungry food to eat,
Ask us to quench the thirst of those we meet.
Unless we pause along our busy way,
Touching real needs, it does no good to pray.

Our serving seeks to represent your care,
That, in our love, the poor may see you there.
How unexpected when, instead, we find
You are in them and we have been unkind.

Christ, when you come, we want to welcome you,
Giving you honor by the things we do.
May we be humble servants, reaching out,
Daring to follow, even when we doubt.

Now, through our sisters, lonely and afraid,
And through the brothers we are quick to aid,
We hear your voice, Come, blesséd ones, to me,
My realm is yours; your life is truly free.
Amen.

Matthew 25:31–46

21

On This Day

Celebration of Jesus and Mary
(January 1)—A, B, C
Lavon Bayler

8.7.8.7.
(Stuttgart)

On this day of God's own coming,
We are claimed, redeemed, set free.
Bowing at the feet of Jesus,
We become God's family.

Welcomed here as sons and daughters,
We are awed by what we see.
Wondering at the love that saves us,
Wakens true humility.

Drawn beyond our fear and trembling,
We are sent to tell good news.
God is working now among us,
Granting us the power to choose.

Let us, then, decide for service,
Seeking guidance day by day,
Praising, glorifying, doing,
That God's will we may obey.

God will bless and keep us always,
Granting peace along our way.
Grace and love will shine upon us,
Guiding all we do and say.
Amen.

(Numbers 6:22–27, Luke 2:15–21, Galatians 4:4–7, Philippians 2:5–11)

See "May God Bless" and "When God's Time," *Refreshing Rains of the Living Word*, pp. 168–70.

22

We Sing with Gladness

Second Sunday after Christmas—A, B, C   7.6.7.6.D
Lavon Bayler   (Webb)

We sing aloud with gladness,
For God has saved and healed.
God gathered humble people,
And boundless grace revealed.
In Jesus Christ, God offered
True light to all the earth
Empowering us, God's children,
To realize our worth.

Our God has blessed and chosen
The weak, the blind, the lame,
As bearers of the promise,
As workers in Christ's name.
Each one of us has value,
What e'er our age or skills.
God fills our lives with purpose,
And meaning that fulfills.

God's word in Christ confronts us
With truth that we must share.
Our witness to Christ's glory,
Will demonstrate God's care.
The blessings of the Spirit
Are meant for one and all.
Be radiant, be joyful,
In answer to God's call.
Amen.

(Psalm 147:12–20, Jeremiah 31:7–14, John 1:1–18, Ephesians 1:3–14)

"O Sing Aloud," *Refreshing Rains of the Living Word*, p. 170, is based on Jeremiah 31:7–14.

Epiphany and the Season Following

23

Come to God's Glory

Epiphany—A, B, C
Lavon Bayler

5.6.8.5.5.8.
(Schonster Herr Jesu)

Come to God's glory,
Risen now upon us.
Nations shall come to see the light.
Gather together,
Eyes lifted upward,
In Jesus Christ to find delight.

See what the magi saw,
See and be radiant.
Let heart and soul within rejoice.
Poor are delivered,
Needy find helpers,
And those oppressed find strength and voice.

Join in the worship,
Opening your treasures,
Lifting your praise for all to hear.
Proclaim with boldness
Faith that will always
Grant confidence to conquer fear.

All generations,
Parents and their children,
Work for the day when peace shall reign.
When earthly powers
Humbly acknowledge
God's love in Christ life's only gain.
Amen.

(Psalm 72:1–7, 10–14, Isaiah 60:1–6, Matthew 2:1–12)

"Now Arise and Shine," *Refreshing Rains of the Living Word,* p. 171, is based on the Old Testament texts and "When Christ Was Born," pp. 172–73, centers on the Matthew passage.

24

Behold the Mystery

Epiphany—A, B, C
Lavon Bayler

6.6.8.6. (S.M.)
(Festal Song)

Behold the mystery
Of grace in Christ revealed.
God's promises are meant for all;
Our gifts with love are sealed.

To each of us is given
Responsibility.
One body, we, the church, are called
To build community.

To preach to all the world
The wisdom God imparts,
Apostles, prophets, ministers,
Have boldness in your hearts.

As least of all the saints,
With confidence, yet awe,
We seek to share God's purposes
As Christ fulfilled the law.

As stewards of the word,
As heirs with Christ, we pray
That all the human race may find
Your Word in what we say.
Amen.

(Ephesians 3:1–12)

"Proclaim the Mystery," *Refreshing Rains of the Living Word*, pp. 171–72, puts these verses of scriptures together in a different way.

25

God Who Made Us

First Sunday after Epiphany
(Baptism of Jesus)—C
Lavon Bayler

7.7.7.7.
(Vienna)

God who made us, calls our name,
Claims us, saying, "You are mine."
Let God's glory be our aim
As we meet, by God's design.

Formed for true community,
We are precious in God's sight.
Honored and redeemed, we see
Loving us is God's delight.

Therefore, we will never fear,
Though we pass through waters deep.
When we call, our God will hear,
Gently lead and safely keep.

Glory be to God, our peace,
Whose assistance we implore.
May our confidence increase
As we worship and adore.

Strengthen us for every test:
Flood and earthquake, wind and fire.
In your majesty we rest;
To your glory we aspire.
Amen.

(Psalm 29, Isaiah 43:1–7)

26

Live with Expectation

First Sunday after Epiphany
(Baptism of Jesus)—C
Lavon Bayler

10.8.10.8.8.8.
(Margaret)

Live with expectation, O saints below,
That expands life's depth and length.
We are baptized people who seek to grow,
Knowing God is our source of strength.
O send now your Holy Spirit,
Gracious God, to empower our faith.

Jesus met with John to identify
With the sins of humanity.
Said the Baptist, "One more mighty than I
Will bring fire that will cleanse and free."
O send now your Holy Spirit,
Gracious God, to empower our faith.

As the grain is winnowed, so lives are cleansed
When the Christ comes to judge and bless,
And the chaff is burned while our God commands
Our turning from sins we confess.
O send now your Holy Spirit,
Gracious God, to empower our faith.

Let the heavens open to us, we pray,
That your voice we may hear and heed,
While disciples' hands send us on our way,
Spirit-filled, to meet others' need.
O God, blend your Holy Spirit
With the witness we make today.
Amen.

(Luke 3:15–17, 21–22, Acts 8:14–17)

27

Fountain of Life

Second Sunday after Epiphany—C
Lavon Bayler

L.M. 8.8.8.8.
(Duke Street)

Fountain of Life, we see your light,
Torch of salvation, burning bright.
Let every nation understand:
You rule, O God, on every hand.

You are the judge of all we do;
Our vindication comes from you.
Rulers of earth your glory see;
Let all declare your sovereignty.

With steadfast love and faithfulness,
All living things you save and bless,
Crowning with beauty all our days,
As we delight to know your ways.

No more forsaken, desolate,
No longer filled with deep regret,
Blessed by forgiveness you proclaim,
We hear you call us each by name.

So, in the newness you bestow,
Upright of heart, we seek to grow,
Feasting on all that you supply,
Drinking from fountains never dry.

Within the shelter of your wings,
We will rejoice as heaven rings
With your delight in children who
Trust and obey and worship you.
Amen.

(Psalm 36:5–10, Isaiah 62:1–5)

See "How Precious Your Love," *Refreshing Rains of the Living Word,* p. 174.

28

O Holy Spirit, Send

Second Sunday after Epiphany
Lavon Bayler

C.D. 8.6.8.6.D
(Materna)

O Holy Spirit, send once more,
Your gifts that shape and bless.
Our former idols we abhor,
And lingering sins confess.
Forgiven and inspired by you,
We seek to do our best.
Pour out in rich variety,
More talents to invest.

The many ways that we can serve,
The differing works we do,
Are drawn into one common good,
Enriched, empowered by you.
Direction comes from Jesus Christ,
Our Savior, guide, and friend,
Who blends our individual gifts,
To serve a common end.

All wisdom, knowledge, faith, and speech,
And each discernment skill,
All miracles and prophecy,
Are subject to your will.
From you alone come healing gifts
And tongues we understand.
Unite us now to carry out
The mission you have planned.
Amen.

(I Corinthians 12:1–11)

The gospel reading, John 2:1–11, is the subject of "At a Marriage Feast," *Refreshing Rains of the Living Word,* p. 175.

Hymns for Epiphany and the Season Following

29

God, the Heavens Proclaim

Third Sunday after Epiphany—C
Lavon Bayler

7.7.7.7.D
(Martyn)

God, the heavens and earth proclaim
Glory to your holy name.
Knowledge, far beyond our reach
Echoes forth in beauty's speech.
Human words cannot contain
Wisdom that we seek to gain.
Open now each heart and mind
That life's purpose each may find.

God, whose precepts we have heard,
Hearts rejoice to learn your word.
As your love revives our souls,
Your commands transform our goals.
Guide us by your truth, we pray.
Make us clean in every way.
Keep us steadfast, lest we fail.
Let your perfect will prevail.

God, before your majesty
Eyes are opened now to see
Truth we have not sensed before,
Faith to worship and adore.
Filled with awe, our heads are bowed,
Recommitting all we've vowed.
We would all your gifts employ,
Lifting hands and hearts with joy.
Amen.

(Nehemiah 8:1–3, 5–6, 8–10; Psalm 19)

See "We Stand in Awe," *Refreshing Rains of the Living Word*, p. 175.

30

O Christ, We Seek to Be

Third Sunday after Epiphany—C
Lavon Bayler

8.8.8.8.8.8.
(Melita)

O Christ, whose church we seek to be,
Unite us in our ministry.
That ear and eye and nose and hand
May work as one, as God has planned.
Baptized into one body, we
Will seek for all true liberty.

We cannot say we have no need
For ways that others work or lead.
Their acts of simple modesty
Can help deaf hear and blind to see,
While gifts that we acquire and use
May celebrate and preach good news.

Apostles, prophets you appoint,
And teachers, healers you anoint,
Administrators, helpers find
Gifts greater than the human mind,
When we accept your Spirit's power
And let you use us every hour.

O Spirit of the Living God,
Direct our steps where Jesus trod.
That all may use their gifts each day,
Providing joy along life's way.
By word and deed to help and heal,
Fulfilling all that you reveal.
Amen.

(Luke 4:14–21, 1 Corinthians 12:12–31a)

See "As Jesus Worshipped," *Refreshing Rains of the Living Word,* pp. 176–77.

31

God Our Refuge

Fourth Sunday after Epiphany—C
Lavon Bayler

8.7.8.7.8.7.
(Regent Square)

God, in you we take our refuge;
Let us not be put to shame.
In your righteousness, deliver;
Rescue us from harm and blame.
Be for us a rock of refuge,
As we praise your holy name.

Hear us, God, when times are cruel,
When injustice seems to win.
Be our hope, our trust, our fortress;
Save us from the grasp of sin.
From our birth, we've leaned upon you;
Come again to reign within.

Lead us, God, to know your purpose;
Speak your Word that we may hear.
Send us out to do your bidding,
Knowing you are ever near.
Help us plant and build and nourish,
By designs that you make clear.
Amen.

(Psalm 71:1–6, Jeremiah 1:4–10)

These passages are also used for "We Trust and Praise," *Refreshing Rains of the Living Word,* pp. 77–78.

32

If We Speak

Fourth Sunday after Epiphany—C
Lavon Bayler

8.7.8.7.D
(Beecher)

If we speak in tongues of angels,
Eloquent in all we say,
We are only clanging symbols
When your love is not our way.
If we have prophetic vision,
Understand all mysteries,
Have the faith to move a mountain,
Without love we cannot please.

Love is patient, kind, and caring,
Never arrogant or rude,
Not dogmatic, jealous, boastful,
But with faith and hope imbued.
Love does not rejoice in evil,
But rejoices in the right.
Loves endures through many trials,
Bears all things 'til faith brings sight.

All in life that is imperfect,
Soon will cease and pass away.
Tongues and prophecy and knowledge
End, but love is here to stay.
Seeing in a mirror, dimly,
Knowing only partially,
God, we turn to you to lead us
To our full maturity.
Amen.

(1 Corinthians 13)

Another rendering of this scripture can be found in "Faith, Hope, and Love," *Refreshing Rains of the Living Word,* pp. 178–79.

33

Reveal to Us, Jesus

Fourth Sunday after Epiphany—C
Lavon Bayler

12.11.12.11.
(Kremser)

Reveal to us, Jesus, God's presence among us.
Interpret the Scriptures to all who will hear.
Disclose God's intentions, fulfilling within us,
The words that we read and the will you make clear.

Your life and your words fill our worship with wonder.
We ask for your healing among us today.
Let all that divides and would rip us asunder,
Be altered by love and submit to your way.

Help us to accept all the truth you are teaching,
To faithfully trust and refuse to despair.
Stay with us as we, your assistance beseeching,
Find life in its fullness, inspired by your care.
Amen.

(Luke 4:21–30)

34

In Your Holy Temple

Fifth Sunday after Epiphany—C
Lavon Bayler

8.7.8.7.7.7.
(Unser Herrscher)

In your holy temple gathered,
God of hosts, we sing your praise.
Filled with awe, we sense your glory,
Setting human hearts ablaze.
Thresholds shake before your voice;
Rulers of the earth rejoice.

Holy God, you know our weakness,
As we bow before you now.
We confess our sinful actions;
Unclean lips we disavow.
When you speak to reprimand,
Help us hear and understand.

Surely you forgive and heal us,
Taking all our guilt away.
Purifying fires attend us,
As we seek your will today.
Open now our minds and hearts
To the word your love imparts.

Faithful God, amid our troubles,
You deliver us from grief.
When we call, you hear and answer,
Overturning unbelief.
With the faith that you endow,
Here we are, O send us now.
Amen.

(Psalm 138, Isaiah 6:1–13)

See "I Thank My God" and "Holy Are You," *Refreshing Rains of the Living Word,* pp. 179–80.

35

Appear to Us, O Christ

Fifth Sunday after Epiphany—C
Lavon Bayler

8.6.8.6. (C.M.)
(Coronation)

Appear to us, O risen Christ,
That we may hear good news.
Enable us, by saving grace,
Your way of truth to choose.
Enable us, by saving grace,
Your way of truth to choose.

Teach us again, as by the lake,
You taught the crowds before.
Now we, discouraged in our trials,
Your helping hand implore.
Now we, discouraged in our trials,
Your helping hand implore.

We know that you for us have died;
We know that we have sinned.
You bid us put our fears aside,
Before God's mighty wind.
You bid us put our fears aside,
Before God's mighty wind.

Your Spirit comes to us today,
Empowering us to stand.
We seek to leave our past behind,
To follow your command.
We seek to leave our past behind,
To follow your command.
Amen.

(Luke 5:1–11, I Corinthians 15:1–11)

The same passages inspired "By Grace You Called," *Refreshing Rains of the Living Word*, pp. 180–81.

36

Blessed Are the Righteous

Sixth Sunday after Epiphany—C
Lavon Bayler

6.4.6.4.D
(Bread of Life)

Blessed are the righteous ones;
God knows their hearts.
Trust and delight are theirs,
As God imparts
Hope and a faith made strong,
By waters pure.
Led by the risen Christ,
They shall endure.

Cursed are the wicked ones
Whose futile ways,
Like chaff, are blown away,
In dire malaise.
They cannot see beyond
Suffering and death,
One who can raise them up
With reborn breath.

From desert places, God,
Hear now our cries.
Search out our minds and hearts;
Let faith arise.
Water our shriveled lives,
By living streams.
May we bear fruit for you,
And live your dreams.
Amen.

(Psalm 1, Jeremiah 17:5–10, 1 Corinthians 15:12–20)

See "Come, O God, to Bless," *Refreshing Rains of the Living Word*, pp. 181–82.

37

Come to This Level Place

Sixth Sunday after Epiphany—C
Lavon Bayler

6.6.8.6.D. S.M.D.
(Diademata)

Come to this level place
Where all are blessed and healed.
Come, find within this time and space,
The love of Christ revealed.
God welcomes one and all,
Those troubled and distressed.
Disciples answering the call
Are welcomed, touched, and blessed.

Blessed are the humble poor;
The realm of God is theirs.
And hungry ones can now endure,
Filled by the one who cares.
The weeping ones will laugh
And find new joy within.
Protected by God's rod and staff,
Those once despised can win.

Yet, all will not receive
These blessings offered free.
Those laughing now will learn to grieve,
Those rich and full will see
Prosperity at end,
Their prideful ways brought low.
Those falsely praised, from heights descend,
To face our common woe.

When we together stand
As one humanity,
Rejoicing, dancing, hand in hand,
God's sure reward we'll see.
All hatreds will be past,
No evil overwhelm.
Come, leap for joy, now free at last,
In God's inclusive realm.
Amen.

(Luke 6:17–26)

38

God Provides for Us

Seventh Sunday after Epiphany—C
Lavon Bayler

8.7.8.7.D.
(Vesper Hymn)

God provides for us and blesses,
Saves a faithful remnant band,
Guards and guides amid distresses,
Helps us for the truth to stand.
Lift our spirits from the deluge
Of life's problems that devour.
Raise us up, O God, our refuge.
Change our weakness by your power.

Flesh and blood cannot inherit
All that God intends for us.
No accomplishment can merit
Life's transforming exodus.
By your grace, we write our story,
Wondering at our distant fate.
Raise us up from sin to glory,
God in whom we trust and wait.

Saved from evil wrath and anger,
Dwelling in security.
We are not bowed down by slander,
As you grant prosperity.
With new courage none can damage,
We can die with confidence.
Raise us up to share your image,
In that realm where life makes sense.
Amen.

(Genesis 45:3–11, 15, Psalm 37:1–11, 39–40,
I Corinthians 15:35–38, 42–50)

"Gracious God, We Trust," *Refreshing Rains of the Living Word,* p. 182, is based on Psalm 37:1–11.

39

Christians Turn the World

Seventh Sunday after Epiphany—C
Lavon Bayler

7.7.7.7.7.7.
(Ratisbon)

Christians turn the world around,
Doing good to those who hate,
Loving enemies as friends,
God's own will to demonstrate.
They who turn the other cheek
Reconciliation seek.

Christians give to those who ask,
And forgive the ones who take
Coat or shirt or other goods,
Leaving mayhem in their wake.
They who act as God desires
Show the love that Christ inspires.

Christians, by God's mercy, live
With unselfish attitude,
Giving, lending, doing good,
Out of joyous gratitude.
They who meet another's need
Are rewarded, blessed, and freed.

Christians judge not nor condemn,
Daring ever to forgive,
Praying for community,
In which all may grow and live.
They who live by Christ's design
Hear God's promise, "You are mine."
Amen.

(Luke 6:27–38)

The same passage inspired "Your Ways Are Not Our Own," *Refreshing Rains of the Living Word*, p. 183.

40

Thanks Be to You

Eighth Sunday after Epiphany—C
Lavon Bayler

6.5.6.5.6.6.6.5.
(St. Dunstan's)

Thanks be to you, O God;
We sing your praises.
Here we acknowledge your
Love that amazes.
Moved by your faithfulness,
We seek your work to do.
We give ourselves with joy;
Let peace continue.

Seeds you have given and
Bread for our eating.
Let us be sowers, your
Mission completing.
So shall your Word go forth,
Your purpose to fulfill.
We pledge ourselves, O God,
To live by your will.

May all bear fruit, O God,
Both youth and aged.
Trees clap their hands at the
Growth you have aided.
Remove the thorns and the
Briars that get in our way,
For we would faithful be
To all that you say.
Amen.

(Psalm 92:1–4, 12–15, Isaiah 55:10–13)

See "Reveal the Mystery," *Refreshing Rains of the Living Word,* pp. 183–84.

41

Lo, a Mystery

Eighth Sunday after Epiphany—C   8.7.8.7.
       Lavon Bayler   (Galilee)

Lo, a mystery I will tell you.
In a moment, we will change
When the trumpet sounds in glory
We'll be raised from mortal range.

Death is swallowed up in victory.
Sin and grave will lose their sting.
Law no longer holds us captive,
When Christ's song of love we sing.

Therefore, friends, be steadfast always,
That you labor not in vain.
Do the work to which God calls you,
Seeking first Christ's coming reign.
Amen.

(1 Corinthians 15:51–58)

42

Disciples We Are Called

Eighth Sunday after Epiphany—C
Lavon Bayler

8.8.8.8. LM
(Canonbury)

Disciples we are called to be,
Whose eyes are opened wide to see
The ministry that Jesus taught,
As one we share in deed and thought.

The speck we find in neighbor's eyes
May hide the log that in us lies.
We cannot help another know
If we ourselves refuse to grow.

To bear good fruit, we must rely
On God, who will identify
Within our hearts, the good that's there,
And give to us abundant care.

Whoever hears and does not do,
Is blocking God from breaking through
Into our lives, as day by day,
We seek to build by Jesus' way.
Amen.

(Luke 6:39–49)

"Please Teach Us," *Refreshing Rains of the Living Word,* pp. 184–85, is based on the same text.

43

Here We Come

Ninth Sunday after Epiphany—C
Lavon Bayler

7.7.7.7.6.7.6.7.
(Rock of Ages)

Here we come, most holy God,
Singing praises to your name.
All the earth resounds with song,
Telling of salvation's reign.
Glory, glory, glory!
Honor, majesty and power!
Sing we all, joyously,
As we worship you this hour.

Great you are, most gracious God,
Heaven and earth cannot contain,
All you are and all you give,
Our allegiance to retain.
Glory, glory glory!
Beauty, strength, and saving grace!
Sing we all, joyously,
As, with awe, we seek your face.

In your name, we stretch our hands,
Welcoming with glad refrain,
All who keep your covenant,
Seeking peace and ways humane.
Glory, glory, glory!
We would share with all the earth.
Sing we all, joyously,
As your love proclaims our worth.
Amen.

(I Kings 8:22–23, 41–43, Psalm 96:1–9)

44

We Seek Your Word

Ninth Sunday after Epiphany—C
Lavon Bayler

10.10.10.10.
(Morecambe)

We, in our anguish, seek your healing Word.
Turn us away from falsehoods we have heard.
Come now to touch us with your healing hand,
That we your grace and peace may understand.

We are not worthy of your presence here,
Quickly deserting paths that interfere
With our ambitions, for Christ's yoke we dread.
Our age has chosen evil ways instead.

Yet, you have raised your Servant to the skies.
Is there within your realm some great surprise,
Shared only when we humbly work and pray?
Does Jesus truly take our sins away?

Do we have value in this world of strife?
Is there some reason you have granted life,
To us who struggle for some purpose clear?
Where is the gospel we are meant to hear?

Glory to God who justifies and frees.
Yours is the gospel meant for our dis-ease.
Melting confusion, granting faith that heals,
Your will and purpose are what Christ reveals.
Amen.

(Luke 7:1–10, Galatians 1:1–12)

45

Covenant Word

Last Sunday after Epiphany
(Transfiguration)—C
Lavon Bayler

9.8.9.8.
(Eucharistic Hymn)

Covenant word, revealed through Moses,
Shaping our lives by rule of law:
We can but tremble as it shows us,
One whom we hold in holy awe.

God rules the world with truth and justice.
Fear not to talk with God in prayer.
Praise and implore the source of promise,
One who forgives and offers care.

When you have heard the God who answers,
Veil not your face, but let it shine.
Praise and exalt, as joyous dancers,
One of whom Christ is glorious sign.

Covenant word, revealed through Jesus,
Shaping our lives by gift of grace,
Offering pardon's hope that frees us,
Grant us, at last, to see God's face.
Amen.

(Exodus 34:29–35, Psalm, 99, 2 Corinthians 3:12–18)

46

Wake from Sleep

Last Sunday after Epiphany
(Transfiguration)—C
Lavon Bayler

7.7.7.7.
(Mercy)

Wake from sleep to hear the voice,
Claiming Jesus as the Christ.
Listen, let our hearts rejoice,
Never more by sin enticed.

With fresh boldness, hope and act;
God has set our spirits free.
Shameful ways will not distract
Those who know God's sovereignty.

We have seen God's glory near,
With transforming mystery.
May God's image grow more clear
In our lives and ministry.

We will not lose heart or fear
As God's mercy gives us strength.
In the silence, God is here,
Filling all life's breadth and length.
Amen.

(Luke 9:28–36, 2 Corinthians 3:12–4:2)

47

The People Tremble

Last Sunday after Epiphany
(Transfiguration)—C
Lavon Bayler

8.6.8.6. C.M.
(Winchester Old)

The people tremble, nations quake,
O God, before your reign.
Your holy name evokes our awe
As justice you ordain.

The wrongs that you avenge are ours,
The sins that you forgive.
Oh speak once more from clouds of light
And teach us how to live.

As Moses heard your mighty word,
In faith upon the mount,
You guide us on our way today
And call us to account.

In Christ, your chosen messenger,
Your mercy is revealed,
And in the dazzling light of truth,
Our fears and hurts are healed.

Disgraceful, underhanded ways
We now renounce with glee.
Your covenant and your commands
Empower our ministry.
Amen.

(Exodus 34:29–35, Psalm 99, Luke 9:28–36, 2 Corinthians 3:12–4:2)

"Show Us Your Glory" *Refreshing Rains of the Living Word*, p. 185, is based on these same texts.

THE LENTEN SEASON

48

Lift Up Your Voice

Ash Wednesday—A, B, C
Lavon Bayler

6.6.8.6. S.M.
(Trentham)

Lift up your trumpet voice;
Another Lent begins.
Point out the empty righteousness,
That marks our hidden sins.

Why do we fast today?
Why show a humble front,
While we enjoy advantages,
And others live in want?

People are called to share
Clothing and bread and home,
Living in close community,
No more from God to roam.

Where'er injustice reigns,
God bids us break the yoke.
May the oppressed find quick relief,
As we God's will invoke.

Then shall our light break forth,
And God will be our guide.
Healing shall come and make us strong,
As we in God abide.
Amen.

(Isaiah 58:1–12)

49

With All Your Heart

Ash Wednesday—A, B, C
Lavon Bayler

6.6.8.4.D.
(Leoni)

Return with all your heart,
God's Spirit to embrace.
Repent and weep and fast and mourn,
Your sins to face.
For God desires truth
Within each human breast.
May we be washed and cleaned within
From wrong confessed.

Restore to us the joy
That your salvation grants.
May we declare your praise to all
Your supplicants.
The only sacrifice
That God expects of us
Is willing service, caring and
Adventurous.

Be reconciled to God,
Whose grace is not in vain,
Through hardships and calamities
That bring us pain.
While facing life's unknowns
To find our destined niche,
We sense the power of love to make
Us truly rich.
Amen.

(Psalm 51:1–7, Joel 2:1–2, 12–17, 2 Corinthians 5:20b–6:10)

These texts, along with the gospel reading, are addressed in "Receive Our Valued Treasures," set to the tune Aurelia, *Refreshing Rains of the Living Word*, p. 186.

50

Receive Our Treasures

Ash Wednesday—A, B, C
Lavon Bayler

8.8.8.8. LM
(Federal Street)

Receive our treasures with our hearts,
For you, O God, know who we are.
Cleanse us from pretense, pride, and sin,
That we may praise you, near and far.

Lead us to pray with pure intent,
Not to be seen, like hypocrites.
We would, with you, O God, commune,
Learning truth's lasting benefits.

God, you discern our secret thoughts.
You know when self is first concern.
Widen the circle of our care,
That we may others' needs discern.

Jesus, forever with us stay,
Guarding our lives from self-deceit.
May we join hands, your work to do,
Finding a joy, full and complete.
Amen.

(Matthew 6:1–6, 16–21)

51

Bring Your Promise

First Sunday in Lent—C
Lavon Bayler

8.7.8.7.8.7.7.
(CWM Rhondda)

Bring us to your place of promise,
God of our inheritance.
You have led the lifetime journey
Of your loyal supplicants.
We rejoice in all your goodness,
Giving you our first and best,
Giving you our first and best.

From the depths of grave oppression,
From their bondage and distress,
You have freed our righteous forbears,
With intent to save and bless.
We rejoice . . .

Help us share the ancient story,
Lived among us even now.
As our parents loved and trusted,
We before your glory bow.
We rejoice . . .

Ev'ry day we seek to serve you,
Passing on what we receive,
That the world may know your mercy,
Hear your promise and believe.
We rejoice . . .
Amen.

(Deuteronomy 26:1–11)

52

Whoever Clings to God

First Sunday in Lent
Lavon Bayler

8.6.8.6. C.M.
(St. Agnes)

Whoever clings to God in love,
God will protect and guard.
Seek, then, a refuge from above,
When life is fierce and hard.

Angels will have us in their charge,
Bearing us lest we fall.
God will our sense of life enlarge,
Answering when we call.

In every trouble, God is near,
Granting us strength to cope.
God will deliver us from fear,
Filling our lives with hope.

Let us give thanks for length of days,
Which God, in love, imparts.
We celebrate God's saving ways,
Giving our minds and hearts.
Amen.

(Psalm 91:9–16)

New Testament texts for the day are addressed in "Tempt Us Not," *Refreshing Rains of the Living Word,* p. 187.

53

Our Light and Our Salvation

Second Sunday in Lent—C
Lavon Bayler

7.6.7.6.D.
(Lancashire)

Our Light and our Salvation,
O God, we will not fear;
You are our life's true stronghold,
A presence ever near.
When evil foes assail us
And enemies oppress,
In confidence we face them,
For you are there to bless.

We seek within your temple
To see your beauty clear.
You shelter us from trouble;
You listen, help, and cheer.
To high roads you are pointing;
Our hearts are lifted high
To follow where you lead us,
Your name to magnify.

With joyous shouts, we greet you
And ask for your advice.
We hear your call to service,
To risk and sacrifice.
Reveal your high intentions
For each of us today,
For in your gracious answers
To prayer, we find our way.
Amen.

(Psalm 27)

54

Gather Us, Your Children

Second Sunday in Lent—C
Lavon Bayler

6.5.6.5.D
(Penitence)

Gather us, your children,
Safe beneath your wings;
Rescue us from bondage
To our earthly things.
In your name we worship,
Eager to be fed,
Not with loaves and fishes,
But with living bread.

May we face our trials
With a confidence,
Centered in our Savior's
Sure obedience.
Stones and threats and danger
Could not stop the care
Jesus gave to all who
Suffered anywhere.

Blessed is one whose coming
We now celebrate,
And through tears and doubting,
Yet would imitate.
May our hearts be joyful,
Standing firm with Christ,
Who, for our salvation,
Loved and sacrificed.
Amen.

(Luke 13:31–35, Philippians 3:17–4:1)

55

Hear Your Thirsty People

Third Sunday in Lent—C
Lavon Bayler

11.10.11.10.
(Ancient of Days)

God, hear your thirsty people when we call you,
Fainting and weary, seeking strength to live.
You are the source of bread and food and rescue.
We look to you with thanks for all you give.

Grant to your people fuller satisfaction;
For we have labored long without delight.
Filled with ourselves and many a distraction,
We have ignored the joys that you invite.

Help us forsake the wicked ways we cling to.
Turn us away from thoughts that scorn your will.
May we repent and evermore continue,
Living by covenants that we fulfill.

We celebrate your power and your glory,
Singing your praises every night and day,
Telling to all salvation's wondrous story.
Your steadfast love upholds us on our way.
Amen.

(Psalm 63:1–8, Isaiah 55:1–9)

56

Faithful and Loving God

Third Sunday in Lent—C
Lavon Bayler

6.4.6.4.6.6.6.4.
(Something for Jesus)

Faithful and loving God,
We trust your care.
God of our ancestors,
We now declare
Our need for food you give,
Refreshing drink to live,
Knowledge that you forgive,
Help us, dear God.

Testing your purposes,
We now confess
Evil, idolatry,
And faithlessness.
We have forgotten you,
Grumbling, complaining through
Years when your love stayed true.
Forgive us, God.

When we are tempted, God,
Grant strength to stand.
Keep us from falling and
Lead by your hand.
Given a second chance,
May we your cause advance.
In every circumstance,
Help us endure.
Amen.

(Luke 13:1–9, 1 Corinthians 10:1–13)

57

Be Glad, O Righteous

Fourth Sunday in Lent—C
Lavon Bayler

6.6.8.6. (SMD)
(Terra Beata)

Be glad, all righteous ones;
To God, sing joyous praise.
Surrounded by God's steadfast love,
Give thanks through all your days.
Be glad and shout for joy
To God who answers prayer.
Where'er we go, whate'er we do,
Our God is present there.

We cannot hide from God
Or long our silence keep.
Our unconfessed iniquity
Will painful burdens reap.
Oppressed through night and day,
By sins we will not face,
Our strength dries up, and hope is lost
When we disdain God's grace.

Yet God will listen still
And render judgments just
When we acknowledge our mistakes
And turn to God in trust.
God will instruct and teach
The way that we should go.
Be glad, forgiven ones, and praise
The God whose love we know.
Amen.

(Psalm 32)

58

Far from Home

Fourth Sunday in Lent—C
Lavon Bayler

8.7.8.7.8.7.
(Rhuddlan)

Far from home and out of money,
Facing famine, want, and fear,
Once a younger son, despairing,
Thought of those at home and dear.
"Feeding pigs is desperation,
This should not be my career."

Out of wasteful, sinful living,
To a life of frantic want,
Lonely, hungry, in the pigpen,
He could not be nonchalant.
"I will beg my parent's pardon;
Wrong I've done, I will confront."

Going home, disgraced, and humbled,
Feeling his unworthiness,
He would ask to be a servant,
Working with no bitterness.
But his parent saw him coming,
Opening arms to greet and bless.

Robe and ring and shoes were waiting;
Friends were called to celebrate.
But the older brother grumbled,
"He does not deserve this fate."
"Claim your brother," said the father;
"Turn away from jealous hate."
Amen.

(Luke 15:11–32)

59

Praise Our God

Fifth Sunday in Lent—C
Lavon Bayler

7.7.7.7.4. with refrain
(Chautauqua)

Praise our God with joyous song;
Lift our voices loud and long.
Tears are dried; let weeping cease.
Freed from bondage, find release
And turn from wrong.

[Refrain]
Praises, praises, ever shout to God.
Let our laughter ring with joy;
Let our lips full praise employ.
God sets us free!

Through deep waters we have come,
And through suffering troublesome.
Yet our God provides a way
Through the wilderness each day,
Through tedium.

[Refrain]

Former things we leave behind,
God's new way of life to find,
Drinking deeply, dreaming of
Ways to share God's gracious love
With humankind.

[Refrain]

Amen.

(Psalm 126, Isaiah 43:16–21)

See "Lead Us by Love," *Refreshing Rains of the Living Word*, pp. 191–92.

60

Press toward the Call

Fifth Sunday in Lent—C
Lavon Bayler

8.8.8.8. (LM)
(Olive's Brow)

Press toward the upward call of Christ,
Forgetting all that lies behind.
Have faith in one who sacrificed
And suffered for all humankind.

All that I have, I count as loss
To know the one who died for me.
God, grant me strength to face the cross,
That I might share Christ's victory.

May I have confidence to serve
With joyous purpose every day,
To give my best without reserve
And honor Christ in every way.

With awe, I bow at Jesus' feet
To worship Christ with all I am.
Possessions, fear, and vain conceit,
I now disclaim before the Lamb.

In perfect love, I find my goal.
May righteousness and zeal abound.
The one who calls and makes me whole
Will by my daily acts be crowned.
Amen.

(John 12:1–8, Philippians 3:4b–14)

61

The Mind of Jesus

Sixth Sunday in Lent
(Palm/Passion Sunday)—A,B,C
Lavon Bayler

8.7.8.7.D.
(St Asaph)

May we share the mind of Jesus,
And his way of life observe.
We would care for one another,
Finding humble ways to serve.
God awakens us each morning,
Bidding us to hear and heed
All that Jesus taught and modeled,
Reaching out to those in need.

Sovereign God, we pray for courage
While you give us mind and breath.
May we be forever faithful
In the face of shame and death.
Just as Christ became obedient,
Risking life that love might reign,
So may we, with daring boldness
Honor you despite our pain.

We would bow before our Savior
To confess our faith and awe,
For we sense our vindication
In the one whose Word is law.
Grateful for the joy of knowing
One who heals and makes us whole,
We would use our tongues to praise you,
God, whose mission is our goal.
Amen.

(Isaiah 50:4–9, Philippians 2:5–11)

62

Morning by Morning

Sixth Sunday in Lent (Passion Sunday)—C   10.10.10.10.
Lavon Bayler   (Langran)

Morning by morning, we to God awake,
Loved and sustained by one we cannot see.
Let us remember Christ, who for our sake,
Suffered and died from sin to set us free.

When we consider Jesus' sore distress,
Praying that death might be avoided still,
Our inattentive waiting we confess
And our unwillingness to seek God's will.

By word and deed, like Peter, we deny
Any relation to the one on trial.
Standing with those who clamor, "crucify!"
Our silent fearfulness appears as guile.

When, from the cross, forgiving words are said,
While scoffers mock and friends bewail their loss,
We stand convicted, with uneasy dread,
Knowing that we instead deserve that cross.

How long, O God, will followers betray,
Sharing at table, yet with hearts unmoved?
From false pretensions, save us now we pray.
Let your transforming work in us be proved.
Amen.

(Psalm 31:9–16, Isaiah 50:4–9a, Luke 22:14–23:56)

63

Join the Celebration

Sixth Sunday in Lent (Palm Sunday)—C   8.7.8.7.D.
Lavon Bayler   (Hymn to Joy)

Join the festal celebration,
Giving thanks to God this day.
Marvel and rejoice together
At the gifts that light our way.
Gates are opened, righteous enter
To salvation's joyous song.
Blest is one whose peaceful coming
Promises an end to wrong.

Peace on earth, in highest heaven,
Peace to all who do God's will.
Steadfast love endures forever
As a force that none can kill.
O, that people would remember
Times of triumph, days of grace.
God is good, who seeks commitment
From our stumbling human race.

Riding on a lowly donkey,
Heralded as branches wave,
Jesus comes among us ever,
Seeking still to love and save.
Let us be no longer silent,
Thinking faith a private thing.
Rather, join in loving service
As our joyous offering.
Amen.

(Psalm 118:19–29, Luke 19:28–40)

64

Behold God's Servant

Monday of Holy Week
Lavon Bayler

11.11.11.5.
(Herzliebster Jesu)

Behold God's servant, chosen for a mission,
To bring all nations to a just condition,
Led by the Spirit, gently leading others.
Sisters and brothers.

Behold the Christ whose blood is our redemption,
Granting to sinners pardon and exemption,
Leading us from our folly and distortion,
Without coercion.

Be not discouraged, for God's light is given
To warm our weary hearts, by conflict driven.
From timid, fearful, self-protective measures,
God frees our treasures.

With steadfast love, God brings us to a new day.
Called to be servants, we discern God's true way.
Let no external force thwart faith's decision
Or blur our vision.

Covenant living gives us high contentment,
Granting fulfillment, easing all resentment.
God is our refuge; we our all surrender
To our defender.
Amen.

(Psalm 36:5–11, Isaiah 42:1–9, Hebrews 9:11–15)

See "Your Steadfast Love," *Refreshing Rains of the Living Word,* p. 194.

65

To Martha's Table

Monday of Holy Week—A, B, C   8.6.8.6. C.M.
       Lavon Bayler   (Dundee)

To Martha's table Jesus came
For rest and sustenance.
A welcome guest, his presence taught
Love's widening expanse.

Our mission is to help the poor
While bringing hope for life
That offers space for beauty and
Gives peace in place of strife.

In Mary's kind extravagance
That would not hoard or shirk
Expressions of devotion, we
Learn love is costly work.

When Jesus Christ reclaimed a man
From death to live once more,
A grateful Lazarus was freed
Life's meaning to explore.

So curious crowds surrounded them,
And some of them believed
That all things Jesus taught were true.
In giving, we receive.
Amen.

(John 12:1–11)

66

To You, O God

Tuesday of Holy Week—A, B, C
Lavon Bayler

6.6.6.6.
(St. Cecelia)

To you, O God, we raise
Our listening ears and eyes,
That joining here in praise,
We may to light arise.

You rescue us and save;
You shelter us and keep
From all that would enslave,
From vengeance we might reap.

In you, we find true strength,
In steadfast love's employ,
To go to any length
To share our hope and joy.

O be not far from us;
Make haste to meet our needs.
Lead us through exodus
From our half-hearted creeds.

May joyous praise abound
In trust that conquers fear.
May people all around
Know you, O God, are near.
Amen.

(Psalm 71:1–14, Isaiah 49:1–7

67

Creator of Wisdom

Tuesday of Holy Week—A, B, C   11.11.11.11.
Lavon Bayler   (St. Denio)

Creator of wisdom and source of our lives,
Your call in Christ Jesus empowers and revives
The best that is in us and helps us to see
The cross not as folly but great victory.

As seeds in the earth spring to life out of death,
So we, in Christ crucified, find our new breath.
No longer a stumbling block, cruel though it be,
The cross is now witness to God's sovereignty.

The power and wisdom of God are revealed
In weakness and foolishness, not sword and shield.
Through humble obedience, we will receive
A sense of life's purpose and strength to believe.

O God, help us follow where Jesus will lead,
To walk in the light and make service our creed.
The cross is less symbol of what we have lost
Than witness to love that is worth any cost.
Amen.

(John 12:20–36, 1 Corinthians 1:18–31)

"Come, O Christ," *Refreshing Rains of the Living Word,* pp. 194–95, is based on the same texts.

68

The Cross

Wednesday of Holy Week—A, B, C   Irregular
Lavon Bayler   (Need)

The cross: Oh, who can face
It's wretched disgrace?
Our troubled spirits faint
In bitter complaint.
Be pleased, O God, to hear us;
Save us now and help us,
For we are poor and needy
And make our plea.

How easily we blame
And sinful ways disclaim,
In anger and in hurt,
Deny and desert.
Forgive us, God, we beg you.
We would not betray you.
Deliver and empower;
Our passions stir.

We turn to glorify
One unafraid to die,
The one who found pure joy
That death could not destroy.
In Jesus Christ we glory,
Welcoming the story
Of Love's transforming power
To change this hour.
Amen.

(Psalm 70, John 13:21–32, Hebrews 12:1–3)

See "O Sovereign God, Sustain Us," *Refreshing Rains of the Living Word*, pp. 195–96.

69

Remembering the Supper

Maundy Thursday—A, B, C
Lavon Bayler

7.6.8.6.8.6.8.6.
(St. Christopher)

Remembering the supper
Christ shared with friends that night,
When common things found holy worth,
And shadows turned to light,
We gather now in Jesus' name
To find a presence here,
That washes, feeds, and sends us forth
As servants cleansed of fear.

We bring our hungry spirits
To find the bread of life.
We seek a cleansing, healing balm
To ease our pain and strife.
Renew our sense of covenant
As bread and wine are shared,
As towel and basin show us how
Your love is best declared.

Prepare us for our journey
Through life as day by day
We learn and grow to understand
And follow Jesus' way.
Receive our thanks and praise, O God,
And by your love equip
Your children here and everywhere
For true discipleship.
Amen.

(Exodus 12:1–4, 11–14, Psalm 116:1–2, 12–19, John 13:1–17, 31b–35,
1 Corinthians 11:23–26)

70

We Who Have Trusted

Good Friday—A, B, C   14.14.4.7.8.
    Lavon Bayler   (Lobe Den Herren)

We who have trusted your mercy, O God, are dejected.
Will you not rescue your servant, despised and rejected?
How can we bear
Burdens of suffering and care,
Heaped on the one we respected?

Why should one carry the burdens and wounds of our sinning?
When we have turned from the pathway that marked our
beginning?
As sheep astray
Mindlessly chase their own way,
So we reject humble winning.

We have not dared to believe God will heed our deep moaning.
Where is salvation and help in our desperate groaning?
How can we trust?
Will God be faithful and just,
As heartfelt prayers we're intoning?

When evil doers encircle, O God, grant us power,
That we may stand unafraid against sins that devour.
Your love revealed
Shows us how we may be healed,
Turning to you in this hour.
Amen.

(Psalm 22, Isaiah 52:13–53:12)

71

We Live in Covenant

Good Friday—A, B, C
Lavon Bayler

8.6.8.6. CM.
(St. Anne)

We live in covenant with God,
Whose law is in our hearts;
And written in our minds is all
The wisdom God imparts.

Yet we are tempted and we sin;
Our deeds defy God's will.
Through all the wrong that we have done,
Our God is faithful still.

When we confess our brokenness
And sinful, lawless ways,
We look to God with confidence
That sets our hearts ablaze.

Cleanse us from evil, and forgive,
We pray, in faith and trust.
God's grace and mercy meet our need.
Christ leads from ways unjust.

Through Jesus Christ, forgiveness comes,
A new and living way
Unfolds within us and expands
Through love that we relay.

Renewed in hope, made strong by faith,
We gather to impart
Encouragement toward loving deeds,
Disciples, true in heart.
Amen.

(Hebrews 4:14–16, 5:7–9, 10:16–25)

See "Draw Near with Confidence," *Refreshing Rains of the Living Word*, p. 197.

72

From Bleak Gethsemane

Good Friday—A, B, C   6.4.6.4.6.6.4.4.
Lavon Bayler   (More Love to Thee)

From bleak Gethsemane,
Where Jesus prayed,
To priestly courts of law,
Bound, unafraid,
Came one for whom God's call
Issued in love for all:
Inclusive love
For great and small.

Those who would crucify,
Fearing love's claim,
Covet authority
No one dare claim.
For, in the cross, is power,
Strongest in death's grim hour:
Inclusive love,
Raised to full flower.

Will our discipleship
Risk or deny?
Will we stand by or act,
Death to defy?
Witness to truth each day,
Follow Christ's loving way;
Inclusive love
Will not betray.
Amen.

(John 18–19)

Jesus, We Follow," *Refreshing Rains of the Living Word,* p. 198, is based on the same chapters.

73

Few Are the Days

Holy Saturday—A, B, C
Lavon Bayler

8.8.8.8. L.M.
(Olive's Brow)

Few are the days we spend on earth.
Short is our time to grow and flower.
Our troubles oft' deny our worth,
Yet through it all we sense God's power.

In steadfast love and faithfulness,
God both supports and disciplines.
We trust in God amid our stress
And find forgiveness from our sins.

New every morning is the light;
Shadows and gloom are swept away.
As day o'ercomes the dimmest night,
Hope conquers death and points the way.

Lead us where you would have us go,
Guide us in paths made straight by love.
Our rod and refuge here below
Prepare for us a home above.
Amen.

(Job 14:1–14, Psalm 31:1–4, 15–16, Lamentations 3:1–9, 19–24)

74

O Suffering God

Holy Saturday
Lavon Bayler

7.6.7.6.D.
(Passion Chorale)

O suffering God, we ponder
This empty, holy day.
In numbing silence shrouded,
We scarce can think to pray.
Our Savior's death has stunned us;
Your judgment now we fear.
Where can we turn for solace
Or know your purpose clear?

Our human wisdom fails us.
Desires have led astray
Your fledgling young disciples,
Who crave an easier way.
For loving one another
Is difficult at best,
And risking all for others
Is not our chosen quest.

Empower us by your Spirit
To seek to do your will.
Grant disciplines of self that
Enlighten and fulfill.
If we are called to suffer,
Sustain us in our plight.
Let not our sins deceive us,
But grant to us your light.
Amen.

(Matthew 27:57–66, I Peter 4:1–8)

THE EASTER SEASON

75

Let Our Joyous Song

Easter Sunday—C
Lavon Bayler

10.8.10.8.8.8.
(Margaret)

Let our joyous song echo 'round the earth,
For salvation has come today,
And the promises that our God has made
Are fulfilled in a glorious way:
Christ Jesus is here among us
As we gather to sing and pray.

O give thanks to God who makes all things new,
Whose creation continues still,
For the risen Christ lifts our spirits high,
Adding purpose to every skill.
Hope now in the one who saves us,
While rejoicing to do God's will.

May our work bear fruit with transforming power
As we honor our Savior's reign.
May we enter the gates of righteousness
With a trust that is not in vain.
Your call brings our joyous answer:
We will work to make life humane.
Amen.

(Psalm 118:1–2, 14–24, Isaiah 65:17–25, I Corinthians 15:19–26)

"On This Day," *Refreshing Rains of the Living Word*, p. 199, was inspired by Isaiah 65:17–25, Luke 24:1–12, and 1 Corinthians 15:29–26.

76

Give Thanks, Our Savior Lives

Easter Sunday—C
Lavon Bayler

6.6.8.6.4.6.
(Marion)

Give thanks, our Savior lives;
This joyous message spread.
Good news of peace send through the land
And turn away from dread.
Give thanks, give thanks;
Our Savior lives today.

The stone is rolled away;
This is no idle tale.
Christ comes to judge our faithfulness
With love that will prevail.
Believe, believe;
Our Savior will forgive.

Weep not, you chosen ones;
The Savior whom you seek
Equips as faithful witnesses
Those healed and freed to speak.
We hear, we hear;
Our Savior calls our name.

Fear not and do what's right,
God brings our work to flower.
Turn from your unbelieving stance
To serve this present hour.
Fear not, fear not;
Our Savior grants us power.
Amen.

(Luke 24:1–12, John 20:1–18, Acts 10:34–43)

See "Teach Us Again," *Refreshing Rains of the Living Word,* p. 200, which is based on Acts 10:34–43.

77

Gladness and Joy

Easter Evening—A, B, C
Lavon Bayler

SM. 6.6.8.6.
(Boylston)

Gladness and joy we bring
To celebrate this night.
Tears and disgrace are wiped away
In Jesus Christ, our light.

Before the startling news
That Jesus lives and saves,
Our hearts rejoice, our spirits soar,
For wrong no more enslaves.

Mountains and hills convulse;
All nature comes to flower.
Rocks turn to water, seas turn back
Before God's present power.

Long we have waited here
To find new ways to think.
Come, join the feast that God provides:
Rich food, and wine to drink.

Old leaven we discard;
No evil malice here,
But with sincerity and truth,
God's saving love revere.
Amen.

(Psalm 114, Isaiah 25:6–9, I Corinthians 5:6b–8)

78

Join Us Daily

Easter Evening—A, B, C
Lavon Bayler

8.7.8.7.8.7.
(Dulce Carmen)

Join us daily on our pathways,
Risen Savior, Jesus Christ.
Fill our talk, inspire our journey,
Lest we fall, by doubts enticed.
Keep before our vision always
Love for which you sacrificed.

Meet us daily at the tables,
Where we come for nourishment.
Open there our eyes and spirits,
In amazed acknowledgment:
You are present with us always,
Filling our environment.

Send us daily to our colleagues,
Friends and foes on every hand.
Clothe us with the power to witness,
That we may your work expand.
Led by truth, in joyous service,
May we live as you have planned.
Amen.

(Luke 24:13–49)

The same text inspired the hymn, "The Sun Was Sinking," *Refreshing Rains of the Living Word,* pp. 201–2.

79

Praises, Praises, Praises

Second Sunday of Easter
Lavon Bayler

11.13.12.10
(Nicaea)

Praises, praises, praises! Glad songs of victory!
Praise to God, our strength and might, whose love has set us free.
Praise with pipes and trumpets, cymbals crashing loudly,
Praise with each breath, with gladness, joy, and glee.

Grace and peace are given, life in its fullness,
As we sing our thankfulness and every sin confess.
Come we now rejoicing on this day of gladness,
With steadfast love, we know our God will bless.

Christ, the faithful witness, scorned and rejected,
Has become the cornerstone, the firstborn of the dead.
Now we seek to follow, summoned and elected,
Blessing the name of Christ, our living head.

Praises, praises, praises! to God who loves us.
We recount your loving deeds from dawn to exodus.
Alpha and Omega, we will join the chorus,
Praising your glory, great and marvelous.
Amen.

(Psalm 118:14–29, Psalm 150, Revelation 1:4–8)

80

The Doors Were Shut

Second Sunday of Easter—C
Lavon Bayler

8.6.8.6.D CMD
(Geneva)

The doors were shut because of fear;
Disciples were afraid.
The rumors they began to hear,
The claims that some had made,
Confused and shook them to the core.
They knew their leader dead,
Yet Christ appeared through bolted door,
Alive, as some had said.

My peace be with you every day,
My Spirit now I give.
I send you out to teach my way,
My people to forgive.
Live not by doubts or seeking proof;
Let trust fill every thought,
For those involved, not those aloof,
Will do as I have taught.

Be bold, as witnesses to truth;
Be daring to proclaim
The message meant for aged and youth:
Full life in Jesus' name.
O God, receive us now, we pray,
Inheritors of grace.
We seek your mandate to obey,
Disciples in this place.
Amen.

(John 20:19–31, Acts 5:27–32)

"My Peace Be with You," *Refreshing Rains of the Living Word,* p. 202, is based on the same texts.

81

Gathered at Your Throne

Third Sunday of Easter—C
Lavon Bayler

7.8.7.8.8.8.
(Liebster Jesu Wir Sind Hier
[Nuremberg])

Gathered at your throne today,
Hearing praise from angel voices,
We join in without delay,
As the heavenly choir rejoices.
Worthy is the Lamb whose glory
Blesses us and claims our story.

Sing God's praises, all you saints;
Thank God's holy name forever.
Worshipping without restraints,
Forge the bonds that none can sever.
Moved by faith, with joy advancing,
Honor Christ and join the dancing.

You, O God, have drawn us up,
Heard our cries and filled our longing.
Christ has offered us the cup,
Symbolizing our belonging.
When we are by foes surrounded,
They are by your strength confounded.

We extol your power and might
And the help you are revealing.
As a faithful source of light,
You respond to us with healing.
Bless our coming and our going;
Favor us beyond our knowing.
Amen.

(Psalm 30, Revelation 5:11–14)

"Sing Praises to God," *Refreshing Rains of the Living Word,* p. 203, is based on Psalm 30:4–12.

82

When Christ Appears

Third Sunday of Easter—C
Lavon Bayler

6.6.6.6.6.6.
(Laudes Domini)

When Jesus Christ appears
Amid our grief and tears,
Life is forever changed.
When we receive our sight,
And in new tasks unite,
Our goals are rearranged.

Disciples, at their nets,
Confounded by regrets,
Caught nothing through the night.
Then Christ to them appeared,
And when their vision cleared,
Their faith gave others light.

When Christ appeared as light
To Paul, who lost his sight,
It brought bewilderment.
No longer troublesome,
Transformed, he would become
God's chosen instrument.

Good news is what we share:
God's love is everywhere;
It cannot be denied.
To follow, feed the sheep
And prayerful vigil keep,
As God is glorified.
Amen.

(John 21:1–19, Acts 9:1–20)

"Discouraged Fishermen," *Refreshing Rains of the Living Word*, pp. 203–4, is based on the same texts.

83

Thanksgiving and Glory

Fourth Sunday of Easter—C
Lavon Bayler

11.11.11.11.
(St. Denio)

Thanksgiving and glory and honor and power,
Be sung to our Savior in worship this hour,
For God leads and guides us in paths richly blessed,
And welcomes each one to the table as guest.

How long can we live, unbelieving and cold,
When God warmly welcomes each one to the fold?
O, hear now the voice that is calling us home
And shepherding through risky byways we roam.

The waters are pure and the pastures are green
Where Christ walks beside us and goodness is seen.
Anoint us with oil; let our cups overflow,
That mercy and kindness within us may grow.

The voice of the shepherd we answer today,
Intending to follow each step of the way.
Where God will commission disciples to go,
Empower us, we pray, that your love we may show.
Amen.

(Psalm 23, John 10:22–30, Acts 9:36–43, Revelation 7:9–17)

84

Heaven and Earth

Fifth Sunday of Easter—C
Lavon Bayler

8.7.8.7.D.
(Bradbury)

Heaven and earth, in glorious newness,
Praise you, God of faithfulness.
As your love is flowing through us,
We our need for you confess.
Holy Spirit, hear our longing
For the new world you create,
Where all people know belonging
And there is no place for hate.

Young and old together singing
Praises to your holy name,
Set the highest heavens ringing
With your jubilant acclaim.
All creation is your dwelling;
Sun and moon and stars rejoice.
Creatures great and small are telling
Of the one who gave them voice.

Grant us vision and compassion
As you wipe away our tears.
Out of grieving you will fashion
Glorious newness through the years.
You send springs of living water;
On your word we can depend.
You are Alpha and Omega,
Our beginning and our end.
Amen.

(Psalm 148, Revelation 21:1–6)

85

Spirit, You Offer

Fifth Sunday of Easter—C
Lavon Bayler

11.10.11.10.10.
(Peck)

Spirit of God, you offer all your children
Life full and free within your love and care.
No one can say another is unworthy,
For you accept all people everywhere.
For you accept all people everywhere.

We hear anew the word that Christ commanded:
Love one another, just as I loved you.
Then all the world will know you are disciples,
People of prayer: accepting, gracious, true.
People of prayer: accepting, gracious, true.

Grant us the vision, God, to be inclusive,
In word and deed, of all whom you have made.
Keep us from judgments that exclude unfairly
Sisters and brothers who may need our aid.
Sisters and brothers who may need our aid.

Help us to learn from those whose gifts may differ;
Add to our faith the insights they may share.
We would be guided by your Holy Spirit,
That all our lives your glory may declare.
That all our lives your glory may declare.
Amen.

(John 13:31–35, Acts 11:1–18)

86

Be Glad and Sing

Sixth Sunday of Easter—C
Lavon Bayler

SMD 6.6.8.6.d.
(Leominster)

Be glad and sing for joy,
All nations of the earth.
Praise God, all people; shout your thanks
For your God-given worth!
Today God summons us
As bearers of good news:
The way of love that Jesus lived
Is free for all to choose.

We hear the cries for help
That echo through the land.
As servants, baptized in the faith,
We rise to Christ's command:
To keep God's Word of truth,
To share the love God gives,
To walk untroubled, unafraid
Through all the days we live.

We praise you, God, for light
That falls across our path.
And fills with glory all the world,
Dissolving human wrath.
Your Holy Spirit lives
Among us day by day.
Your peace is planted in our hearts;
Your love will show the way.
Amen.

(Psalm 67, John 14:23–29, Acts 16:9–15, Revelation 21:10, 22–22:5)

"Be Gracious, God," *Refreshing Rains of the Living Word,* p. 206, is based on Psalm 67.

87

Gathered as Witnesses

Ascension (or Seventh Sunday
of Easter)—A, B, C
Lavon Bayler

7.7.7.7.7.7.
(Redhead [Ajalon])

Gathered here as witnesses,
With uplifted hands and hearts,
On this great Ascension Day,
When the one we've known departs,
We are filled with joyous calm,
For Christ's love is still our balm.

All that Jesus did and taught
Prompts our joyous songs of praise
We have learned from Christ to live
Faithfully through all our days.
Called to hope in God's great power,
We believe and serve this hour.

Clap your hands and shout for joy;
God who judges also spares
Those repenting of their sins,
And full pardon now declares.
As forgiven sinners, we
Raise our voices thankfully.

Waiting for the Spirit now,
We will trust the promises
That the church will be empowered
For our task as witnesses.
Set our hearts and minds aflame,
That we may God's love proclaim.
Amen.

(Psalm 47 and 110, Luke 24, 44–53,
Acts 1:1–11, Ephesians 1:15–23)

See "We Have Faith," *Refreshing Rains of the Living Word,* pp. 207–8.

88

The Grace of God

Seventh Sunday of Easter—C
Lavon Bayler

L.M. 8.8.8.8.
(Brookfield)

The grace of God be with all saints,
Who love and serve without complaints,
Who thirst for water Christ will give,
And seek for faithful ways to live.

The God we serve is first and last,
The source of all things in the past,
The one who holds our future, too,
The Alpha and Omega true.

God is the Ruler of the earth,
The one in whom we find new birth,
Who guards the lives of those who ask
And meets them in each common task.

Our idols we will cast away
To live with thanks in God's new day.
And as the Spirit bids us come,
Enlist in service venturesome.

With joy, we praise God's holy name,
God's righteousness and peace proclaim.
Rejoice that we are given light
To live by what we know is right.
Amen.

(Psalm 97, Revelation 22:12–14, 16–17, 20–21)

89

Thank You for Jesus

Seventh Sunday of Easter—C
Lavon Bayler

10.11.9.11.9.10.
(Wait on God)

Thank you, God, for Jesus, who made you known
To the common people, whom you call your own.
As Jesus prayed, so, too, we would pray:
Make us one with others, your love to display.
Through all our trials, keep us on course;
Be our life's companion, our sure resource.

Heal our broken spirits; help us to trust,
When our world is shaken and life seems unjust.
Keep us from fear when our days are drear
Take away the terror; let your light appear.
Free us from prisons where we are bound.
Grant us strength to praise you with joyous sound.

God, when we are tempted by greed and wrongs,
When neglect or malice someone's pain prolongs,
Help us to hear words that make it clear:
You are with the sufferer, and your judgment near.
May we repent of evil intent,
And receive forgiveness not punishment.

Thank you, God, for Jesus, who taught us how
We can live for others while we disavow
Pleasing the crowd or authorities,
Standing firm for justice, not for selfish ease.
Unite us now with Christ and with you.
In a love that's shared for the world to view.
Amen.

(John 17:20–26, Acts 16:16–34)

"Make Us One," *Refreshing Rains of the Living Word,* p. 208, is based on all texts for the day.

PENTECOST AND THE SEASON

FOLLOWING

90

Come, Spirit of God

Pentecost—C
Lavon Bayler

10.10.11.11.
Lyons

Come Spirit of God, with tempest and fire;
Unite as one voice humanity's choir
Although different tongues mark the way that we speak,
May Pentecost blend them with power for the meek.

Empower your people, both great and small,
With visions and dreams that answer your call.
If love be the language that all can express,
Together, our mission will know true success.

Let no one aspire to selfishly build
A private domain that you have not willed.
May pretense and greed be erased from the earth,
As we heed your word and accept our new birth.

Show wonders in heaven and signs on the earth,
That loudly proclaim forgiveness and worth,
For all of earth's people who call on God's name.
With awe and amazement, our kinship we claim.
Amen.

(Genesis 11:1–9, Acts 2:1–21)

91

How Manifold Your Wisdom

Pentecost—C 　　　　　　　　　　　 7.6.8.6.D.
Lavon Bayler 　　　　　　　　　　　 Alford

How manifold your wisdom
And works through all the earth.
The sea and land are filled with life
To which your love gave birth.
All look to you to feed them
As seasons come and go.
Your bounteous grace meets every need
And sets our hearts aglow.

We sing our songs to praise you,
O God, whose heirs we are.
No more will we be slaves to sin
Who fear you from afar.
If we are called to suffer,
We'll look to Christ to find
The courage and the confidence
To leave our doubts behind.

Christ calls us to be loving,
To live as God commands,
To do much greater works and pray
That truth will sweep all lands.
Empowered by the Spirit,
Who teaches all we need,
We share the peace that we are given
While making love our creed.
Amen.

(Psalm 104:24–34, 35b, John 14:8–7, 25–27, Romans 8:14–17)

92

Creator God, We Praise

Trinity Sunday (First Sunday
after Pentecost)—C
Lavon Bayler

L.M.D. 8.8.8.8.D.
(Creation)

Creator God, we chant your praise,
Your majesty and glory raise.
We look into the heavens with awe;
The moon and stars proclaim your law.
How then can we deserve your care,
Mere people who so often err?
And yet you honor us with grace
And welcome us with warm embrace.

O Jesus Christ, we give you thanks
For joining in our human ranks.
You taught us how to live in peace
And from our sins find full release.
Your suffering helps us to endure;
Your character helps make us pure.
O Christ, we hope and trust in you;
Walk with us and our strength renew.

O Holy Spirit, wisdom bright,
Come every day to lend us light.
Guide us in truth so we may live
With faithfulness, our all to give.
So help us hear your call aright
That it may be our deep delight
To honor you by what we do,
O Trinity, forever true.
Amen.

(Psalm 8, Proverbs 8:1–4, 22–31, John 16:12–15, Romans 5:1–5)

Related Hymns

93

Choose for Today

Proper 4
Lavon Bayler

10.10.10.10.
(Ellers)

Choose for today the God whom you will serve.
Who can you follow now without reserve?
Some limp along with idols they create.
Some never stop to contemplate their fate.

Do things we own have power to satisfy?
Is wisdom there, on which we can rely?
Will our possessions hear us when we plead?
Will they respond and help in times of need?

Will human sources hasten to our aid,
When we are hurting, troubled, or afraid?
Can we depend on others to supply
Loving acceptance when we rage or cry?

Surely we need a greater God than these,
One we can praise at work or on our knees,
One who will hear and answer when we pray,
One who will help us each and every day.

Sing a new song to God who made us all.
Worship the one who holds all worlds in thrall.
Who judges, loves, forgives, and heals each one,
Raising us up, despite what we have done.

Choose for all time and worship God alone,
Knowing the things of earth are not your own.
Honor the one who offers grace and peace,
Whose watchful care and love will never cease.
Amen.

(1 Kings 18:20–39, Psalm 96, Luke 7:1–10, Galatians 1:1–12)

94

Reign, O God

Proper 5
Lavon Bayler

7.7.7.7.D.
(St. George's Windsor)

Reign, O God, from age to age.
Come among your people here.
Our attention now engage,
Lest we turn away in fear.
Show us peace, for which we grope
When your ways are yet unknown.
Be our helper and our hope,
For we trust in you alone.

Hear and heal your church, we pray.
Free us from the bonds of death.
Show your new and better way.
Raise us by your Spirit's breath,
That we may no longer weep
For the things we cannot change,
But may know a joy so deep
That no pain can rearrange.

We accept your gift of grace,
And your call to serve and speak.
May no task seem commonplace,
As discipleship we seek.
We would praise you day by day,
Witnessing to what is true,
Christ's compassion to portray,
Giving thanks in all we do.
Amen.

(1 Kings 17:8–24, Psalm 30 and 146, Luke 7:11–17, Galatians 1:11–24)

95

Not Justified by Works

Proper 6—C
Lavon Bayler

CMD 8.6.8.6.D.
(St. Leonard)

Not justified by works of law,
But faith in Jesus Christ,
We come, O God, in grateful awe,
By steadfast love enticed.
Our hearts are glad, lips shout for joy,
As happiness abounds,
For we are all in your employ,
As praise to you resounds.

In morning light or deepest night,
You hear our prayerful sighs.
We plead our case as you invite
Admission of our lies.
Deceit and falsehood you deplore,
Yet eagerly forgive,
When we return to you once more
And penitently live.

Instruct us now and teach your way
Of love for humankind.
May we respond, in work and play,
With heart and strength and mind.
No gift too fine to honor you,
And so we give our all.
In every way, we would be true,
In answer to your call.
Amen.

(1 Kings 21:1–21a, Psalm 5:1–8, Luke 7:36–8:3, Galatians 2:15–21)

96

Thirsty Seekers

Proper 7—C
Lavon Bayler

8.7.8.7.
(Ringe Recht)

Thirsty, cast down souls will seek you,
Troubled ones will call your name.
God, we summon you for rescue;
Come among us, make your claim.

In the silence, you are speaking,
As we wait for you in prayer.
When your families are seeking
Common ground, we find you there.

When we live with fears, you claim us.
When our doubts exceed our trust,
You are present with your counsel;
You are faithful, you are just.

With your steadfast love, you claim us
When we dare to stand alone.
With the baptized saints, you name us,
Calling us to be your own.

God, our helper, hear our praises
When your Spirit sets us free.
Listen as your church now raises
Tributes to your sovereignty.
Amen.

(1 Kings 19:1–15a, Psalms 42 and 43, Luke 8:26–39, Galatians 3:23–29)

97

We Cry Aloud

Proper 8—C
Lavon Bayler

6.7.6.7.6.6.6.6.
(Nun Danket Alle Gott)

We cry aloud to God,
Through days of weary seeking.
Our troubled souls refuse
The comfort of God's speaking.
We call to mind the deeds
And wonders we've observed,
And then we meditate
On favors undeserved.

O Holy God, your ways
Are far beyond our knowing.
The wonders you've displayed
Are still among us flowing.
The people you redeem
Become your faithful flock.
Oh, lead us day by day,
Your myst'ry to unlock.

May we appreciate
The prophet's humble calling,
As we participate
In gratefully recalling:
Elisha's prayer request,
Elijah's gifts to know,
By being doubly blest;
Thus, we, too, seek to grow.
Amen.

(1 Kings 2:1–2, 6–14, Psalm 77:1–2, 11–20)

98

Called to Be Free

Proper 8—C
Lavon Bayler

11.10.11.10.10.
(Peeck)

Called to be free, as followers of Jesus,
Called to be faithful in discipleship,
We are to love our neighbors with compassion,
And recognize God's gracious ownership
Over the earth and all its leadership.

Live by the Spirit, not by fleeting impulse;
Do not devour another with your greed.
Put away quarrels, factions, and dissensions,
That you may sense another's crying need,
Doing your best, their cries for help to heed.

Love, joy, and peace reflect the Spirit's presence.
Patience and kindness, generosity,
Mark us as gentle, self-controlled disciples,
Living our faith with warm simplicity,
Open and caring, for the world to see.

Hand to the plow, we have one central purpose,
Living within God's now and future realm.
Let no distractions turn us from that purpose,
No quarrels, strife, or envy overwhelm.
Christ is our guide, whose hand is at the helm.
Amen.

(Luke 9:51–62, Galatians 5:1, 13–25)

99

We Cry for Help

Proper 9—C
Lavon Bayler

L.M.8.8.8.8.
(Deus Tuorum Militum)

We cry for help, O God, this day.
We seek your cleansing, healing way,
For we are broken, incomplete,
Without your love to guide our feet.

We sing your praise, for we receive
From you assurance to believe
That we can be your messengers,
And meet with grace all challengers.

You bid us meet with gentleness
The ones who mock you and transgress
The ways you teach us all to go.
O help us, Jesus Christ, to grow.

We see the burdens others bear,
Resolve their heavy loads to share,
And look to you, O God of peace,
To ease their pain and grant surcease.

You send us out to sow good seeds,
To listen to our sisters' needs,
To help our brothers in distress,
To harvest fruits of righteousness.

You test our work and stem our pride.
We look to you to lead and guide.
We praise you that your realm is near.
God, speak your Word for us to hear.
Amen.

(2 Kings 5:1–14, Psalm 30, Luke 10:1–11, 16–20,
Galatians 6:1–1–16, 7–16)

Hymns for Pentecost and the Season Following

100

Our God Judges

Proper 10—C
Lavon Bayler

10.10.10.4.
(Overlook Park)

Our God, whose plumb line judges one and all,
Give justice to the poor and weak, we pray.
Help us respond in answer to your call,
Without delay.

You fill our lives with hope and call us saints,
Accepting what we seek to offer you,
And listen when we utter our complaints,
'Though none are due.

We sense your grace has summoned us to share
Your steadfast love and truth without deceit.
Your peace is meant to strengthen us to care
For all we meet.

You offer us eternal life and joy
As your commands we promise to obey.
The law of love no power can destroy
Is ours today.

We love you, God, with heart and soul and mind,
Our strength devoted first to pleasing you,
Then loving neighbor, all of humankind,
With purpose true.
Amen.

(Psalm 82, Amos 7:7–17, Luke 10:25–37, Colossians 1:1–14)

101

O God of Truth

Proper 11—C
Lavon Bayler

L.M.8.8.8.8.
(Rockingham Old)

O God of truth and power and right,
Who judges our hypocrisy,
Turn us from greed and bigotry,
That we may be what you invite.

You meet us where we work and live,
Inviting us to put you first.
You give your Word to quench our thirst,
That blest, we also learn to give.

Help us to choose the better part,
Reflecting on your gracious care
And letting Christ our souls repair,
May serve with mind and strength and heart.

We worship, too, through those we aid,
Oppressed and needy, poor and lost.
O may we give, despite the cost,
That all may labor unafraid.

You call your church to act above
The standards of an anxious world,
That through our faith may be unfurled
A witness to your steadfast love.
Amen.

(Amos 8:1–12, Psalm 52, Luke 10:38–42, Colossians 1:15–28)

102

Teach Us to Pray

Proper 12—C
Lavon Bayler

S.M. with Refrain
(Marion)

Christ, teach us how to pray,
And help us to discern
How we should act, what we should say,
For we are slow to learn.
God loves, God cares
For all of humankind.

Just ask; you will receive.
Just search and you will find.
Just have the courage to believe
With heart and soul and mind.
God loves, God cares
For all of humankind.

Know God as Parent true;
Pray "hallowed be your name."
Cry out for bread each day anew;
Make food for all your aim.
God loves, God cares
For all of humankind.

We seek God's coming reign,
And reach for it today.
We want to live in God's domain,
For you, Christ, point the way.
God loves, God cares
For all of humankind.
Amen.

(Psalm 138, Luke 11:1–13)

103

Give Thanks to God

Proper 13—C
Lavon Bayler

C.M. 8.6.8.6.
(Grafenberg [Nun Danket Al])

Give thanks to God whose steadfast love
Protects, redeems, and heals.
God lifts us up in caring arms
When we make our appeals.

Cry out to God in troubled times,
When thirsty, faint, or lost.
God's kindly presence grants us hope
That fears cannot exhaust.

God teaches us to walk with Christ
In paths where we are freed
From anger, wrath, and lying ways,
From selfishness and greed.

We are renewed and blessed each day
By gifts that show God's care.
But they are not for us to store;
This bounty we must share.

Live, then, as people rich toward God,
Who answer when God calls.
Share Christ's compassion with the world,
Give praise whate'er befalls.
Amen.

(Psalm 107:1–9, 43, Hosea 11:1–11, Luke 12:13–21, Colossians 3:1–11)

104

Hear the Word

Proper 14—C
Lavon Bayler

8.7.8.7.D.
(Hyfreydol)

Hear the Word of God, O people.
Listen to what God will teach.
Worship not with empty gestures:
Stretch your hands, your God to reach.
Let your prayers be teamed with actions
Seeking justice for the poor.
Stand against the world's oppression;
Work for good that will endure.

Wash yourselves and turn from evil;
Seek the cleansing God provides.
Sins of scarlet are forgiven
By the one who leads and guides.
Doing good becomes our passion
When we live in covenant,
When the rebel sword is yielded,
Willing and obedient.

Share the bounty God has granted,
Giving thanks and doing good.
Honor God through deeds of kindness
In this earthly neighborhood.
Reaching ever for the heavens,
Where God reigns in righteousness,
We rejoice in our salvation
And the ways that God will bless.
Amen.

(Psalm 50:1–8, 22–23, Isaiah 1:10–20)

105

Fulfilled and Blessed

Proper 14—C   8.6.8.8.6.
Lavon Bayler   (Rest [Elton])

Fulfilled and blessed are those who wait,
Expectant and prepared.
Whose lamps are lit to celebrate
When Jesus knocks, ere soon or late,
And asks if we have cared.

The alms we share in thankfulness,
For all God gives in trust,
Provide a channel to express,
Through helping neighbors in distress,
Our zeal for causes just.

Where we invest our treasure now,
Our hearts will follow soon.
When selfishness we disavow,
Before God's will to humbly bow,
We may with God commune.

The realm of God through time and space
Is offered as a gift.
Fear not its promise to embrace
Until its hope seems commonplace
And all of life uplifts.
Amen.

(Luke 12:32–40)

A hymn based on Hebrews 11:1–3, 8–16 may be found in *Refreshing Rains of the Living Word,*
p. 223.

106

Stir and Save Us

Proper 15—C
Lavon Bayler

6.5.6.5.D.
(Lyndhurst)

Stir your might to save us,
God of strength and power.
We have been unfaithful,
And our fruits are sour.
In your lovely vineyard,
Briars and thorns have grown.
Weeds have choked your planting;
Come, reclaim your own.

May our roots grow deeply
In good soil: your Word.
Nourish us together,
Living all we've heard.
As we look to Jesus,
Link us with your saints,
Who, through grievous suffering,
Served without complaints.

Help us run with patience;
Help us persevere
When the race is painful
And the goal unclear.
Set your fires among us;
Warm us with the flames
That ignite compassion
And enflesh our aims.
Amen.

(Psalm 80:1–2, 8–19, Isaiah 5:1–7, Luke 12:49–56, Hebrews 11:29–12:2)

107

God Is Our Hope

Proper 16—C
Lavon Bayler

10.10.10.10.
(Field)

God is our hope, our refuge, and our guide.
We will rejoice in all God has supplied.
From early childhood to this present day,
We have been loved and helped along our way.

When we are frightened, threatened, or betrayed,
God has commanded: "Do not be afraid!"
When all the world seems cruel and unjust,
We dare to voice our faith: "In God we trust!"

Yet when God speaks with trumpet and with fire,
Seeking our highest motives to inspire,
We are in awe and tremble at the thought:
We have a greater role than we have sought.

We represent the reign of God on earth
As, in the church, we celebrate the worth
Of all God's people, lifting them above
All lesser loyalties to learn God's love.

With healing grace, our God has set us free
From crippling burdens for our destiny.
We have been called to praise our God always
In every word and deed, through all our days.
Amen.

(Psalm 71:1–6, Jeremiah 1:4–10, Luke 13:10–17, Hebrews 12:18–29)

108

Hear Now the Word

Proper 17—C
Lavon Bayler

6.6.4.6.6.6.4.
(Cutting)

Hear now the word of God;
Follow where Christ has trod,
Giving your best.
Let none suppress your joy;
Let none your faith destroy,
Living in God's employ,
Strengthened and blessed.

Let your rich heritage
Hallow your pilgrimage
With gratitude.
Led through the wilderness
And times of deep distress,
We will new trust confess:
God is our food.

Melt now our stubborn hearts
As prideful will departs
Before your throne.
Humbly we sing your praise,
Seeking to learn your ways.
You set our hearts ablaze;
Come, claim your own.
Amen.

(Psalm 81:1, 10–16, Jeremiah 2:4–13, Luke 14:1, 7–14,
Hebrews 13:1–8, 15–16)

109

You Have Known Us

Proper 18—C
Lavon Bayler

12.10.12.10
(Sweet Story)

You have known us, O God; we are clay in your hands.
You have shaped us according to your Word.
You have helped us to reach toward the gospel's demands;
By your Spirit our hearts are warmed and stirred.

We will praise you, O God, for the wonderful way
We are formed by the faith that makes us whole.
Your resources are with us to help us each day;
To be faithful in all things is our goal.

We receive grace and peace as a wonderful gift,
And we pass it along whene'er we can.
You refresh lives today as our prayers we uplift;
You were with us before our lives began.

We will grow as disciples who carry the cross,
As an emblem of love for humankind.
We have counted the cost: our possessions, no loss,
For the joy in God's service we will find.
Amen.

(Psalm 139:1–6, 13–18, Jeremiah 18:1–11, Luke 14:25–33, Philemon 1–21)

110

Winds of Judgment

Proper 19—C
Lavon Bayler

7.7.7.7.7.7.
(Toplady)

Winds of judgment, hot and strong,
Blow upon our waste and wrong.
God remembers fruitful lands,
Brought to deserts by our hands.
Humankind has gone astray,
Turned aside, and lost God's way.

In their hearts the fools have said,
"There's no God; your God is dead."
They consume the poor as bread,
Those whom God has loved and fed.
Yet, from anger, God will turn,
Seeking those who want to learn.

God forgives and brings relief
From our sin and unbelief.
Grace and love will overflow
Into lives that seek to grow.
Then God's mercy overcomes
All that fractures and benumbs.

Saints and sinners, come to eat,
Brought together at Christ's feet.
God rejoices when we're found,
And our lives with joy are crowned
When we answer and repent,
Heeding calls that God has sent.
Amen.

(Psalm 14, Jeremiah 4:11–12, 22–28, Luke 15:1–10, 1 Timothy 1:12–17)

A hymn based on Luke 15:1–10 and 1 Timothy 1:12–17 appears in *Refreshing Rains of the Living Word*, p. 229.

111

No Slave Can Serve

Proper 20—C
Lavon Bayler

8.8.8.8.L.M.
(Duke Street)

No slave can serve both God and wealth;
Those who are faithful turn from greed.
In Jesus Christ, we find true health,
Giving ourselves for those in need.

Faithful in little, we would be,
Giving attention every day
To smaller details we can see,
Learning to follow Jesus' way.

Honest in all we do and say,
We seek to serve where we are sent.
Faithful when challenge comes our way,
May every day for Christ be spent.

While we commit, we also pray,
Thanking our God and seeking aid
For people struggling in dismay:
God, help the people you have made.

Link us together, help us stand
For all that leads to godliness.
Send waves of knowledge through our land,
That we may learn true peacefulness.
Amen.

(Psalm 79:1–9, Jeremiah 8:18–9:1, Luke 16:1–13, 1 Timothy 2:1–7)

112

Sons and Daughters

Proper 21—C
Lavon Bayler

11.11.11.11.11.11.
(was 6.5.6.5.D. with refrain)
(St. Gertrude)

Caring sons and daughters may we always be,
God of our salvation, whom we serve with glee.
You have granted riches meant for us to share.
Gladly we would give them, showing forth your care.
Thank you for the bounty we can give away.
Thank you for your Spirit, with us every day.

Godly sons and daughters, we would be today,
Seeking now a presence who will guide our way.
You have promised refuge 'mid our daily toil,
Haven and deliverance when life's foes despoil.
Fearless in our witness, sheltered by your wings,
May we live for Jesus, not for love of things.

Faithful sons and daughters, let us be always,
Building for the future, giving you the praise.
Tempted not by riches, drawn to righteousness,
Greeting all your children with inclusiveness,
We will trust your mercy, and your love declare,
Finding life eternal here and everywhere.
Amen.

(Psalm 9:1–6, 14–16, 1 Timothy 6:6–19)

113

Worship God with Gratitude

Proper 22—C
Lavon Bayler

7.8.7.8.7.7.
(Grosser Gott Wir Loben Dich)

Worship God with gratitude;
Lift your prayers with joy and gladness.
With your faith and hope renewed,
Turn away from sin and sadness.
Grace in Christ is ours today;
Learn to follow and obey.

By the will of God we stand,
Unashamed to tell the story
Of a Savior near at hand,
Who imparts to us God's glory.
We will trust and work and pray,
All God's goodness to display.

All are gifted, called, and blessed,
By the God we praise and worship.
We would serve and give our best
Without fearing risk or hardship,
Disciplined in aim and thought,
Holding fast to all Christ taught.

May the love of God empower
Every act and all our witness.
May we seize this present hour
As the time to share forgiveness.
Led by faith to reach beyond
Claim or duty, we respond.
Amen.

(Luke 17:5–10, 2 Timothy 1:1–14)

114

Our Praise and Thanks

Proper 23—C　　　　　　　　　　　7.6.7.6.D.
Lavon Bayler　　　　　　　　　　　(St. Theodolph)

Our praise and thanks we bring you,
O God, of awesome deeds.
You know and bless your people
And meet us in our needs.
When we cry out for mercy,
You know the pain we feel.
When spirits falter, hopeless,
Your hands reach out to heal.

You hear the prayers we offer.
You test our faithfulness.
You help us grow through challenge.
You sense our weariness.
O God, when we are faithless,
Your faithfulness remains,
And we can trust your promise
That stretches and sustains.

Please help us, God, to listen
For cries that others make,
That we may ease their burdens,
Not look for their mistake.
So, when we make our witness
And share the truth we know,
God, keep us humbly open
To follow ways you show.
Amen.

(2 Kings 5:1–3,7–15c, Psalm 66:1–12; 111, Jeremiah 29:1, 4–7,
Luke 17:11–19, 2 Timothy 2:8–15)

115

The Days Will Come

Proper 24—C
Lavon Bayler

6.6.6.8.8.8.
(Rhosymedre)

The days will surely come
When we will build and plant,
For God has called us all
To join in covenant.
God's law is written on our hearts.
We'll turn in prayer as each day starts,
And then we'll share what God imparts.

O how we love God's law,
On which we meditate.
It helps us understand
God's realm for which we wait.
It turns our feet from evil's way
And guides us through each passing day
To know the one whom we obey.

The Word of God inspires
What we believe and teach,
Informing all we do,
Instructing those we reach.
Yet itching ears among us lurk,
Inviting us God's truth to shirk.
O Christ, equip us for our work.
Amen.

(Jeremiah 31:27–34, Psalm 119:97–104, 2 Timothy 3:14–4:5)

116

We Praise and Thank You

Proper 25—C
Lavon Bayler

9.8.9.8.
(St. Clement)

We praise and thank you, God of power;
Your wondrous deeds we know today.
Your presence brings our faith to flower,
And visions point your glorious way.

With glad rejoicing, we surrender
Our anxious boasts and proud pretense
To you, O God, our strong defender,
The one in whom our lives make sense.

You hear confessions that we offer;
You know how we transgress your law.
You tame the proud and wake the scoffer;
You fill the penitent with awe.

The humble you exalt and honor
And teach them all your ways to know.
We turn from certitude to wonder
And look to you to help us grow.

You satisfy our needs with plenty;
The threshing floors are full of grain.
This great abundance gives us entry
To times of sharing as you reign.
Amen.

(Psalm 65, Joel 2:23–32, Luke 18:9–14)

117

Your Grace Be with Us

Proper 26—C
Lavon Bayler

8.7.8.7.8.8.7.
(Mit Freuden Zart)

We cry for help; O God, how long
Will you yet fail to listen,
When all around is strife and wrong
And sins of grave omission?
Reveal your truth among us here;
Let love and justice now appear.
Your grace, O God, be with us.

Destruction reigns on every hand,
And violence distresses.
Your people fail to understand
The truth your law addresses.
We watch and listen for your word;
Let now your righteous will be heard.
Your grace, O God, be with us.

Set spirits right, remove false pride,
And grant us clearer vision.
Let us delight as Christ our guide
Inspires each wise decision.
Accept our love and thanks each day;
Help us fulfill your call, we pray.
Your grace, O God, be with us.
Amen.

(Habakkuk 1:1–4, 2:1–4, Psalm 119:137–144,
2 Thessalonians 1:1–4, 11–12)

118

Gather Friends at Table

Proper 26—C
Lavon Bayler

11.11.11.11.11.(6.5.6.5.D. Ref.)
(St. Gertrude)

Gather friends at table, welcoming as guest
Jesus Christ our Savior, by whom we are blest.
Sinners are invited to a common meal;
Lost and wandering people, come that Christ may heal.
Gather friends at table, welcoming as guest
Jesus Christ our Savior, by whom we are blest.

Let no pretense blind us to God's full intent
To include all seekers in love's covenant.
No one is excluded, no one is denied.
Faithfulness is never cause for foolish pride.
Gather friends at table, welcoming as guest
Jesus Christ our Savior, by whom we are blest.

May our prayers and worship give us strength to face
Emptiness within us, idols we embrace.
Loyalties have focused on the things we own,
Wasting precious moments meant for God alone.
Gather friends at table, welcoming as guest
Jesus Christ our Savior, by whom we are blest.

Listen as God teaches ways that we should go.
Sins that once were scarlet, God makes clean as snow.
Hear the call to justice; heed the call to share.
Where we battle evil, God is with us there.
Gather friends at table, welcoming as guest
Jesus Christ our Savior, by whom we are blest.
Amen.

(Psalm 32:1–7, Isaiah 1:10–18, Luke 19:1–10)

119

Look for God's Reign

All Saints' Day—C
Lavon Bayler

6.6.8.6.D. (S.M.D.)
(Diademata)

Look for the reign of God
In vision and in truth.
Seek in the ways that Jesus trod
The energies of youth,
To follow where Christ leads,
To do what God commands,
Becoming in your words and deeds
Your Savior's voice and hands.

Blessed are the humble poor,
Who live within God's rule,
And blessed are those who dwell secure,
Set free from hungers cruel.
God blesses those who weep,
Rewards the ones defamed;
With joy and laughter, they will leap,
Fulfilled and unashamed.

Praise God without restraints;
Give thanks in all you do.
Express your love toward all the saints
As God, in Christ, loves you.
Let even enemies
Receive your love and care.
Seek first our God Most High to please
In all your work and prayer.
Amen.

(Psalm 149, Daniel 7:1–3, 15–28, Luke 6:20–31, Ephesians 1:11–23)

120

We Will Extol You

Proper 27—C
Lavon Bayler

10.10.10.10.10.
(Old 124th)

We will extol you, God, and bless your name.
Rising to life each day, we will proclaim:
"Great is our God and greatly to be praised."
By all God's mighty works we are amazed.
We will extol you, God, and bless your name.

You, God, are just and kind in all your ways.
Each generation joins in songs of praise,
Lauding your actions and your majesty,
Praising your glorious splendor, bright and free.
You, God, are just and kind in all your ways.

Our mouths will speak your praise each day we live,
For we are awed by all the care you give.
When we in truth approach you, you are near.
Whene'er we call, we know that you will hear.
Our mouths will speak your praise each day we live.
Amen.

(Psalm 145:1–5, 17–21)

121

We Must Give Thanks

Proper 27—C   7.7.7.7.
Lavon Bayler   (Innocents)

We must always give you thanks,
God, who chose us from earth's ranks,
To be saved and sanctified,
In your glory to abide.

Thanks to all who share good news,
Helping us your way to choose.
May your truth sustain and bless
All who faith in you profess.

Standing firm in what we know,
Help us in your love to grow.
By your grace, grant hope each day;
Comfort broken hearts, we pray.

May our words express your care
To your people everywhere.
Strengthen us in all we do,
As our deeds give praise to you.
Amen.

(2 Thessalonians 2:13–17)

122

Be Glad, Rejoice

Proper 28—C
Lavon Bayler

8.6.8.6.D. (CMD)
(Ellacombe)

Be glad, rejoice, for God creates
New heavens and new earth.
May joy forever permeate
And fill our hearts with mirth.
We find delight in reaching out
To people in distress.
God helps us overcome our doubt
To act in ways that bless.

We plant and eat as God provides;
We build as God directs.
We know God hears our prayers, and guides
In ways that love expects.
We know we labor not in vain,
Though outcomes seem unsure.
In peace and justice, God will reign;
God's blessings will endure.

The wolf and lamb together feed
As partners in God's realm,
And differences of race and creed
No longer overwhelm.
God's saints will see a larger view
Than conflicts that destroy.
The work God gives us all to do
Will all our gifts employ.
Amen.

(Isaiah 65:17–25)

123

Come Now to Reign

Proper 28—C
Lavon Bayler

11.10.11.10.
(Welwyn)

Come now to reign among us, Christ, our Savior.
Come to inspire our love and faithfulness.
In God we trust, with you, O Christ, as mentor,
Strengthening lives that faint from weariness.

Help us to stand amid the storms of hatred.
Help us to testify in word and deed
To you, O Christ, whose love was unabated
Through days of trial and hours of grievous need.

Turn us away from idleness and worry.
Question our busyness that does no good.
Confront us in our aimless, frantic hurry,
Lest your intent may be misunderstood.

Grant us your wisdom as we try to serve you.
May we work quietly for truth and right,
While seeking first to do what you would value,
Praising and thanking God through day and night.
Amen.

(Isaiah 12, Luke 21:5–19, 2 Thessalonians 3:6–13)

124

God of Tender Mercy

Proper 29—C
Lavon Bayler

8.7.8.7.8.6.8.7.
(Vesper Hymn)

God of tender mercy, hear us,
People of the covenant.
With your blessings ever near us,
Help us to be confidant.
Praise and honor to the Ruler,
Jesus Christ our Savior!
Grant your light to guide and cheer us;
Hear each faithful supplicant.

Send us shepherds who will listen;
Send us leaders who will care.
To your realm we seek admission,
In your righteousness to share.
Praise and honor to the Ruler,
Jesus Christ our Savior!
We would join you in your mission,
Seeking to be just and fair.

We have heard the proclamation
That in Christ you're pleased to dwell.
Jesus, first in all creation,
You have sent to make us well.
Praise and honor to the Ruler,
Jesus Christ our Savior!
We, the church, give adoration,
As the story we retell.
Amen.

(Jeremiah 23:1−6, Luke 1:68−79, Colossians 1:11−20)

125

Christ Jesus We Adore

Proper 29—C
Lavon Bayler

6.6.6.6.8.8.
(Crofts 136th)

Christ Jesus we adore,
The one whose reign is sure,
Who rescues us from death,
And makes us strong and pure.
When he was tortured, he forgave,
Intent, by love, our lives to save.

In Christ, God's fullness dwelt,
And love became the sign
Of heaven come to earth,
Of life by God's design.
We share with all the saints in light;
God rescues us from powers of night.

The church, with Christ as head,
Now seeks to reconcile
All peoples of the earth,
From mountaintop to isle.
No race or creed will God exclude,
But all are welcomed and renewed.

Be strong in Christ, whose strength
Will help us to endure,
With patience and with joy,
The trials that are sure
To come to all who risk and lead,
Who go with Christ to those in need.
Amen.

(Jeremiah 23:1–6, Luke 1:68–79, 23:33–43, Colossians 1:11–20)

SPECIAL DAYS

126

As You Receive

Thanksgiving Day—C
Lavon Bayler

10.4.10.4.10.10.
(Sandon)

As you receive life's bounty day by day,
Give thanks to God.
As you discover meaning on your way,
Give thanks to God.
Offer first fruits of all that you possess,
Remembering God's gracious faithfulness.

Trace through your life the leading of God's hand.
Give thanks to God.
With joy and gladness, celebrate this land.
Give thanks to God.
We have survived through losses and distress
Because our God was always there to bless.

Worship with gladness; make a joyful noise.
Give thanks to God.
Join in the hearty singing God enjoys.
Give thanks to God.
For God is good, and we are here to praise
The one whose steadfast love surrounds our days.
Amen.

(Deuteronomy 26:1–11, Psalm 100)

127

God, We Rejoice

Thanksgiving Day—C
Lavon Bayler

11.10.11.10.
(Russian Hymn)

God, we rejoice in you! Receive our worship,
For we would thank you for life-giving bread.
You have implanted a gentleness in us;
And by your nearness, we are saved from dread.

Our prayers we offer with grateful thanksgiving,
And supplication to hear our requests.
Your peace surpasses our human discernment,
Guarding our hearts and minds for all life's tests.

In Jesus Christ, we know all that is true and
Just, pure and pleasing and honorable.
If there is anything worthy of praising,
May all our thinking be commendable.

Doing the works of God, seeking and trusting
One who was faithful and rose from the dead.
We will give thanks in our daily devotion,
Drinking pure water, eating heaven's bread.

We would continue to do all you teach us,
All we receive through our ears and our eyes.
Come, God of peace, to be with us and help us
Answer with justice all your peoples' cries.
Amen.

(John 6:25–35, Philippians 4:4–9)

128

You Call Us, God

God's Call—Installation
Lavon Bayler

SMD 6.6.8.6.d.
(Leominster)

You call us, God, to come
To worship you each day.
You bid us grow 'til we become
Disciples of Christ's way.
You lead us through all strife,
A presence ever near.
Your Word becomes our way of life,
A hope that conquers fear.

You call us, God, to hear
The voices of our world
To answer cries and bear the sneers
'Mid violence unfurled.
We seek to learn of needs,
Respond to calls for aid,
Repairing, through our words and deeds,
The good earth you have made.

You call us, God, to teach
The way of faithfulness.
You lead us to extend our reach,
The skeptics to address.
Help us to understand
Your Word in all its power,
That we may rise to your command
And do what you empower.

You call us to equip
New leaders for our day.
You call us to apostleship
That will your love display.
We ask that you will bless
Your people as they try
Your loving nurture to express,
By grace that you supply.
Amen.

Adapted from a hymn written for the inauguration of Charles Knicker as president of Eden
Theological Seminary.

Indexes

Appear to Us, O Christ	35	God, Our Beginning	19
As You Receive	126	God Our Refuge	31
Be Glad and Sing	86	God Provides for Us	38
Be Glad, O Righteous	57	God, the Heavens Proclaim	29
Be Glad, Rejoice	122	God, We Rejoice	127
Behold God's Servant	64	God Who Made Us	25
Behold the Mystery	24	Hear Now the Word	108
Blessed Are the Righteous	36	Hear the Word	104
Bring Your Promise	51	Hear Your Thirsty People	55
Called to Be Free	98	Heaven and Earth	84
Choose for Today	93	Heavens Proclaim	12
Christ Jesus We Adore	125	Here We Come	43
Christians Turn the World	39	How Manifold Your Wisdom	91
Come Now to Reign	123	If We Speak	32
Come, Spirit of God	90	In Your Holy Temple	34
Come to God's Glory	23	Join the Celebration	63
Come to the Temple	3	Join Us Daily	78
Come to This Level Place	37	Let All the Earth	16
Covenant Word	45	Let Heavens Be Glad	10
Creator God, We Praise	92	Let Our Joyous Song	75
Creator of Wisdom	67	Let Us Rejoice	8
Disciples We Are Called	42	Lift Up Your Voice	48
Faithful and Loving God	56	Listen for Good News	14
Far from Home	58	Live with Expectation	26
Few Are the Days	73	Lo, a Mystery	41
Fountain of Life	27	Look for God's Reign	119
From Bleak Gethsemane	72	Morning by Morning	62
Fulfilled and Blessed	105	No Slave Can Serve	111
Gather Friends at Table	118	Not Justified by Works	95
Gather Us, Your Children	54	Now, by God's Mercy	13
Gathered as Witnesses	87	O Christ, We Seek to Be	30
Gathered at Your Throne	81	O God of Hosts	7
Give Thanks, Our Savior Lives	76	O God of Truth	101
Give Thanks to God	103	O Holy Spirit, Send	28
Gladness and Joy	77	O Suffering God	74
Glory to God	11	O Word of Light	15
God Is Our Hope	107	On This Day	21
God of Peace	5	Our God Judges	100
God of Tender Mercy	124	Our Light and Our Salvation	53

Our Praise and Thanks	114	The People Tremble	47
Praise Our God	59	The Realm of God Is Near	2
Praises, Praises, Praises	79	Thirsty Seekers	96
Press toward the Call	60	'Tis the Season	18
Receive Our Treasures	50	To Martha's Table	65
Reign, O God	94	To You, O God	66
Rejoice, People of Light	9	Wake from Sleep	46
Remembering the Supper	69	We Cry Aloud	97
Reveal to Us, Jesus	33	We Cry for Help	99
Shepherd and Judge	20	We Live in Covenant	71
Sing Aloud!	4	We Must Give Thanks	121
Sons and Daughters	112	We Praise and Thank You	116
Spirit, You Offer	85	We Seek Your Word	44
Stir and Save Us	106	We Sing with Gladness	22
Teach Us to Pray	102	We Who Have Trusted	70
Thank God	17	We Will Extol You	120
Thank You for Jesus	89	When Christ Appears	82
Thanks Be to You	40	When John the Baptist	6
Thanksgiving and Glory	83	Whoever Clings to God	52
The Cross	68	Winds of Judgment	110
The Days Are Coming	1	With All Your Heart	49
The Days Will Come	115	Worship God with Gratitude	113
The Doors Were Shut	80	You Call Us, God	128
The Grace of God	88	You Have Known Us	109
The Mind of Jesus	61	Your Grace Be with Us	117

TOPICAL INDEX OF HYMNS

(by hymn number)

Adoration and Praise

As You Receive	126
Be Glad and Sing	86
Be Glad, O Righteous	57
Be Glad, Rejoice	122
Choose for Today	93
Christ Jesus We Adore	125
Come Now to Reign	123
Come to God's Glory	23
Come to the Temple	3
Creator God, We Praise	92
Gathered as Witnesses	87
Gathered at Your Throne	81
Give Thanks to God	103
God Is Our Hope	107
God of Peace	5
God of Tender Mercy	124
God, Our Beginning	19
God Our Refuge	31
God, the Heavens Proclaim	29
God Who Made Us	25
Hear Now the Word	108
Hear Your Thirsty People	55
Heaven and Earth	84
Here We Come	43
How Manifold Your Wisdom	91
In Your Holy Temple	34
Let All the Earth	16
Let Heavens Be Glad	10
Listen for Good News	14
Look for God's Reign	119
Not Justified by Works	95
On This Day	21
Our Praise and Thanks	114
Praise Our God	59
Praises, Praises, Praises	79
Receive Our Treasures	50
Reign, O God	94
Sing Aloud!	4

Thanks Be to You	40
The Days Are Coming	1
The Grace of God	88
Thirsty Seekers	96
To You, O God	66
We Cry for Help	99
We Must Give Thanks	121
We Praise and Thank You	116
We Will Extol You	120
Worship God with Gratitude	113

Advent

Come to the Temple	3
God of Peace	5
Let Us Rejoice	8
O God of Hosts	7
Sing Aloud!	4
The Days Are Coming	1
The Realm of God Is Near	2
When John the Baptist	6

Anger

Be Glad and Sing	86
Give Thanks to God	103
The Cross	68
Winds of Judgment	110

Anxiety

As You Receive	126
Come Now to Reign	123
God of Peace	5
O God of Truth	101

Awe and Wonder

Behold the Mystery	24
Covenant Word	45
Creator God, We Praise	92
Glory to God	11
God Is Our Hope	107

God, the Heavens Proclaim   29

Here We Come   43

In Your Holy Temple   34

Not Justified by Works   95

Now, by God's Mercy   13

On This Day   21

Press toward the Call   60

The Mind of Jesus   61

We Praise and Thank You   116

We Will Extol You   120

Baptism

Be Glad and Sing   86

God Who Made Us   25

Live with Expectation   26

O Christ, We Seek to Be   30

Thirty Seekers   96

When John the Baptist   6

Bless (-ed, -ing)

As You Receive   126

Be Glad, Rejoice   122

Blessed Are the Righteous   36

Bring Your Promise   51

Come to This Level Place   37

Far from Home   58

Fountain of Life   27

Fulfilled and Blessed   105

Gathered at Your Throne   81

Give Thanks to God   103

God of Tender Mercy   124

God Provides for Us   38

Hear Now the Word   108

Hear the Word   104

Let Heavens Be Glad   10

Listen for Good News   14

Live with Expectation   26

Look for God's Reign   119

O Holy Spirit, Send   28

On This Day   21

Our Light and Our Salvation   53

Our Praise and Thanks   114

Praises, Praises, Praises   79

Sing Aloud!   4

We Must Give Thanks   121

We Sing with Gladness   22

Worship God with Gratitude   113

Christmas

Glory to God   11

Heavens Proclaim   12

Let All the Earth   16

Let Heavens Be Glad   10

Listen for Good News   14

Now, by God's Mercy   13

O Word of Light   15

Rejoice, People of Light   9

Thank God   17

We Sing with Gladness   22

Church

Behold the Mystery   24

Christ Jesus We Adore   125

Gathered as Witnesses   87

God Is Our Hope   107

God of Tender Mercy   124

Let All the Earth   16

O Christ, We Seek to Be   30

O God of Truth   101

Reign, O God   94

Rejoice, People of Light   9

Thirsty Seekers   96

Comfort

Come to the Temple   3

Listen for Good News   14

We Cry Aloud   97

Communion

Gather Friends at Table   118

Gathered at Your Throne   81

Join Us Daily   78

Morning by Morning   62

Receive Our Treasures   50

Remembering the Supper   69

Thanksgiving and Glory   83

Community

Behold the Mystery   24

Christ Jesus We Adore   125

Christians Turn the World	39
Come, Spirit of God	90
God Who Made Us	25
Lift Up Your Voice	48
No Slave Can Serve	111
Sing Aloud!	4
Sons and Daughters	112

Confession

Be Glad, O Righteous	57
Faithful and Loving God	56
Heaven and Earth	84
In Your Holy Temple	34
Live with Expectation	26
Morning by Morning	62
O Holy Spirit, Send	28
Praises, Praises, Praises	79
Stir and Save Us	106
Thank You for Jesus	89
We Live in Covenant	71
We Praise and Thank You	116
With All Your Heart	49

Consecration, Dedication

God of Peace	5
No Slave Can Serve	111
Stir and Save Us	106
Whoever Clings to God	52

Courage

God Provides for Us	38
How Manifold Your Wisdom	91
Let Us Rejoice	8
O Word of Light	15
Shepherd and Judge	20
Teach Us to Pray	102
The Mind of Jesus	61

Covenant

Behold God's Servant	64
Come to the Temple	3
Covenant Word	45
Gather Friends at Table	118
God of Tender Mercy	124
Hear the Word	104

Hear Your Thirsty People	55
Here We Come	43
Remembering the Supper	69
The Days Are Coming	1
The Days Will Come	115
The People Tremble	47
We Live in Covenant	71

Cross

Creator of Wisdom	67
From Bleak Gethsemane	72
Morning by Morning	62
Press toward the Call	60
The Cross	68
You Have Known Us	109

Death

Blessed Are the Righteous	36
Christ Jesus We Adore	125
Creator of Wisdom	67
Few Are the Days	73
From Bleak Gethsemane	72
God, Our Beginning	19
God Provides for Us	38
Lo, a Mystery	41
Morning by Morning	62
O Suffering God	74
Reign, O God	94
The Cross	68
The Doors Were Shut	80
The Mind of Jesus	61
'Tis the Season	18
To Martha's Table	65

Discipleship

Appear to Us, O Christ	35
Called to Be Free	98
Choose for Today	93
Come to This Level Place	37
Disciples We Are Called	42
Live with Expectation	26
O Christ, We Seek to Be	30
O Suffering God	74
Our Light and Our Salvation	53
Reign, O God	94

Remembering the Supper 69
Spirit, You Offer 85
Thanksgiving and Glory 83
The Doors Were Shut 80
We Live in Covenant 71
When Christ Appears 82
You Call Us, God 128
You Have Known Us 109

Doubt

Be Glad, Rejoice 122
Gather Us, Your Children 54
How Manifold Your Wisdom 91
Join Us Daily 78
Shepherd and Judge 20
The Doors Were Shut 80
Thirsty Seekers 96

Easter Season

Be Glad and Sing 86
Gathered as Witnesses 87
Gathered at Your Throne 81
Give Thanks, Our Savior Lives 76
Gladness and Joy 77
Heaven and Earth 84
Join Us Daily 78
Let Our Joyous Song 75
Praises, Praises, Praises 79
Spirit, You Offer 85
Thank You for Jesus 89
Thanksgiving and Glory 83
The Doors Were Shut 80
The Grace of God 88
When Christ Appears 82

Epiphany Season

Appear to Us, O Christ 35
Behold the Mystery 24
Blessed Are the Righteous 36
Christians Turn the World 39
Come to God's Glory 23
Come to This Level Place 37
Covenant Word 45
Disciples We Are Called 42
Fountain of Life 27

God Our Refuge 31
God Provides for Us 38
God, the Heavens Proclaim 29
God Who Made Us 25
Here We Come 43
If We Speak 32
In Your Holy Temple 34
Live with Expectation 26
Lo, a Mystery 41
O Christ, We Seek to Be 30
O Holy Spirit, Send 28
Reveal to Us, Jesus 33
Thanks Be to You 40
The People Tremble 47
Wake from Sleep 46
We Seek Your Word 44

Equality

Come to God's Glory 23
We Sing with Gladness 22

Eternal Life

Few Are the Days 73
Our God Judges 100
Sons and Daughters 112
'Tis the Season 18

Evil

Come to This Level Place 37
Gather Friends at Table 118
Gladness and Joy 77
Hear the Word 104
Hear Your Thirsty People 55
If We Speak 32
Let Heavens Be Glad 10
Our Light and Our Salvation 53
Sing Aloud! 4
The Days Will Come 115
We Live in Covenant 71
We Seek Your Word 44
We Who Have Trusted 70

Faith and Aspiration

Behold God's Servant 64
Blessed Are the Righteous 36

Called to Be Free   98
Come to God's Glory   23
Gathered as Witnesses   87
Gathered at Your Throne   81
God, the Heavens Proclaim   29
Hear Now the Word   108
If We Speak   32
In Your Holy Temple   34
Join the Celebration   63
Let Us Rejoice   8
Live with Expectation   26
Not Justified by Works   95
O God of Truth   101
Press toward the Call   60
Spirit, You Offer   85
The Mind of Jesus   61
The People Tremble   47
We Live in Covenant   71
We Must Give Thanks   121
We Seek Your Word   44
When Christ Appears   82
Worship God with Gratitude   113
You Have Known Us   109

Faithfulness

As You Receive   126
Come Now to Reign   123
Creator God, We Praise   92
Faithful and Loving God   56
Few Are the Days   73
Gather Friends at Table   118
Gathered as Witnesses   87
Give Thanks, Our Savior Lives   76
God of Tender Mercy   124
God Provides for Us   38
Heaven and Earth   84
No Slave Can Serve   111
Not Justified by Works   95
O Word of Light   15
Our Praise and Thanks   114
Reveal to Us, Jesus   33
Shepherd and Judge   20
Sons and Daughters   112
Thanks Be to You   40

The Days Are Coming   1
The Grace of God   88
The Mind of Jesus   61
Thirsty Seekers   96
We Cry Aloud   97
We Who Have Trusted   70
Worship God with Gratitude   113
You Call Us, God   128
You Have Known Us   109

Fear

Appear to Us, O Christ   35
Choose for Today   93
Come to God's Glory   23
Far from Home   58
From Bleak Gethsemane   72
Give Thanks to God   103
Glory to God   11
God Is Our Hope   107
God Who Made Us   25
How Manifold Your Wisdom   91
Let Heavens Be Glad   10
Morning by Morning   62
O God of Hosts   7
O Suffering God   74
On This Day   21
Our Light and Our Salvation   53
Press toward the Call   60
Reign, O God   94
Remembering the Supper   69
Thank You for Jesus   89
The Days Are Coming   1
The Doors Were Shut   80
The People Tremble   47
Thirsty Seekers   96
To You, O God   66
Whoever Clings to God   52
Worship God with Gratitude   113
You Call Us, God   128

Forgiveness

Choose for Today   93
Christ Jesus We Adore   125
Christians Turn the World   39

Come, Spirit of God	90	**God, Glory of**		
Covenant Word	45	Bring Your Promise	51
Faithful and Loving God	56	Come to God's Glory	23
Far from Home	58	Creator God, We Praise	92
Few Are the Days	73	Fountain of Life	27
Fountain of Life	27	Glory to God	11
Give Thanks, Our Savior Lives	76	God, Our Beginning	19
Hear the Word	104	God, the Heavens Proclaim	29
In Your Holy Temple	34	God Who Made Us	25
Let All the Earth	16	Hear Your Thirsty People	55
Morning by Morning	62	Heavens Proclaim	12
Not Justified by Works	95	Here We Come	43
O Holy Spirit, Send	28	In Your Holy Temple	34
Thank God	17	Let Heavens Be Glad	10
The Cross	68	Now, by God's Mercy	13
The Doors Were Shut	80	Praises, Praises, Praises	79
We Live in Covenant	71	Spirit, You Offer	85
Winds of Judgment	110	Wake from Sleep	46
Worship God with Gratitude	113	We Must Give Thanks	121
		We Seek Your Word	44
		Worship God with Gratitude	113

Free(-dom)

		God, Guidance of		
Behold God's Servant	64	As You Receive	126
Bring Your Promise	51	Be Glad, Rejoice	122
Called to Be Free	98	Bring Your Promise	51
Christians Turn the World	39	Come to the Temple	3
Come to This Level Place	37	God of Peace	5
Give Thanks, Our Savior Lives	76	God of Tender Mercy	124
Glory to God	11	God Our Refuge	31
God Is Our Hope	107	God Provides for Us	38
Live with Expectation	26	God, the Heavens Proclaim	29
Look for God's Reign	119	Hear the Word	104
Morning by Morning	62	Lift Up Your Voice	48
O Christ, We Seek to Be	30	Live with Expectation	26
O Word of Light	15	O Christ, We Seek to Be	30
On This Day	21	On This Day	21
Praise Our God	59	Rejoice, People of Light	9
Praises, Praises, Praises	79	Sons and Daughters	112
Shepherd and Judge	20	Thanksgiving and Glory	83
Spirit, You Offer	85	We Cry for Help	99
Thank You for Jesus	89	Your Grace Be with Us	117
Thirsty Seekers	96		
To Martha's Table	65	**God, Love of**		
Wake from Sleep	46	Be Glad and Sing	86
We Seek Your Word	44	Be Glad, O Righteous	57

Behold the Mystery	24
Choose for Today	93
Christ Jesus We Adore	125
Come to God's Glory	23
Faithful and Loving God	56
Few Are the Days	73
Gladness and Joy	77
Glory to God	11
God Is Our Hope	107
God, Our Beginning	19
God, the Heavens Proclaim	29
God Who Made Us	25
Heaven and Earth	84
How Manifold Your Wisdom	91
If We Speak	32
In Your Holy Temple	34
Listen for Good News	14
Look for God's Reign	119
Morning by Morning	62
On This Day	21
Praise Our God	59
Praises, Praises, Praises	79
Remembering the Supper	69
Sons and Daughters	112
Spirit, You Offer	85
Teach Us to Pray	102
Thank You for Jesus	89
Thanks Be to You	40
The Cross	68
We Cry for Help	99
We Must Give Thanks	121
We Who Have Trusted	70
When Christ Appears	82
When John the Baptist	6
Whoever Clings to God	52
Winds of Judgment	110
With All Your Heart	49
Worship God with Gratitude	113
You Call Us, God	128

God, Majesty of

Creator God, We Praise	92
God, Our Beginning	19
God, the Heavens Proclaim	29
God Who Made Us	25

Here We Come	43
Let Heavens Be Glad	10
We Will Extol You	120

God, Promises of

Behold the Mystery	24
Bring Your Promise	51
Christians Turn the World	39
Covenant Word	45
Gathered as Witnesses	87
Join the Celebration	63
Let Our Joyous Song	75
Let Us Rejoice	8
O God of Hosts	7
Our Praise and Thanks	114
Sons and Daughters	112
The Days Are Coming	1
We Sing with Gladness	22

God, Providence of

As You Receive	126
Be Glad, Rejoice	122
Gladness and Joy	77
God of Peace	5
God Provides for Us	38
Our Praise and Thanks	114
The Grace of God	88
We Praise and Thank You	116
We Sing with Gladness	22

God, Realm of, Reign of, Rule of

Be Glad, Rejoice	122
Come Now to Reign	123
Come to This Level Place	37
Fountain of Life	27
Fulfilled and Blessed	105
God Is Our Hope	107
God of Tender Mercy	124
God Our Refuge	31
God Provides for Us	38
Hear the Word	104
Let All the Earth	16
Let Heavens Be Glad	10
Lo, a Mystery	41

Look for God's Reign 119
Reign, O God 94
Rejoice, People of Light 9
Shepherd and Judge 20
Teach Us to Pray 102
The Days Will Come 115
The People Tremble 47
The Realm of God Is Near 2
We Cry for Help 99
We Praise and Thank You 116
We Seek Your Word 44

God, Ways, Will of

Christ Jesus We Adore 125
Christians Turn the World 39
Come to the Temple 3
Fountain of Life 27
Fulfilled and Blessed 105
Gather Friends at Table 118
God of Peace 5
God, the Heavens Proclaim 29
Hear Now the Word 108
Hear Your Thirsty People 55
Let All the Earth 16
Let Our Joyous Song 75
Let Us Rejoice 8
Morning by Morning 62
O Holy Spirit, Send 28
O Suffering God 74
On This Day 21
Praise Our God 59
Reign, O God 94
'Tis the Season 18
We Cry Aloud 97
We Live in Covenant 71
Worship God with Gratitude 113

God, Works of

Glory to God 11
God, We Rejoice 127
How Manifold Your Wisdom 91
Join Us Daily 78
Listen for Good News 14
Morning by Morning 62
On This Day 21

Our Praise and Thanks 114
Receive Our Treasures 50
We Cry Aloud 97
We Will Extol You 120

Good Friday

Behold God's Servant 64
Creator of Wisdom 67
From Bleak Gethsemane 72
Morning by Morning 62
O Suffering God 74
Press toward the Call 60
The Cross 68
We Live in Covenant 71
We Who Have Trusted 70

Gospel

Be Glad and Sing 86
Give Thanks, Our Savior Lives 76
Listen for Good News 14
We Seek Your Word 44
When Christ Appears 82
You Have Known Us 109

Grace

Appear to Us, O Christ 35
Be Glad, O Righteous 57
Behold the Mystery 24
Choose for Today 93
Creator God, We Praise 92
Glory to God 11
God Is Our Hope 107
God of Peace 5
God Provides for Us 38
Heavens Proclaim 12
Here We Come 43
How Manifold Your Wisdom 91
Join the Celebration 63
Let All the Earth 16
O Word of Light 15
On This Day 21
Our God Judges 100
Praises, Praises, Praises 79
Reign, O God 94
The Days Are Coming 1

The Grace of God 88
We Live in Covenant 71
We Must Give Thanks 121
We Seek Your Word 44
We Sing with Gladness 22
Winds of Judgment 110
With All Your Heart 49
Worship God with Gratitude 113
You Call Us, God 128
You Have Known Us 109
Your Grace Be with Us 117

Healing, Health, Wholeness

Choose for Today 93
Gather Friends at Table 118
Gathered at Your Throne 81
Give Thanks, Our Savior Lives 76
Give Thanks to God 103
Glory to God 11
God of Peace 5
God of Tender Mercy 124
O Christ, We Seek to Be 30
O Holy Spirit, Send 28
O Word of Light 15
Our Praise and Thanks 114
Reign, O God 94
Reveal to Us, Jesus 33
Thank You for Jesus 89
The Mind of Jesus 61
The People Tremble 47
We Cry for Help 99
We Seek Your Word 44
We Sing with Gladness 22
We Who Have Trusted 70
When John the Baptist 6
You Have Known Us 109

Holy Spirit

Appear to Us, O Christ 35
Be Glad and Sing 86
Behold God's Servant 64
Called to Be Free 98
Come, Spirit of God 90
Creator God, We Praise 92
God, Our Beginning 19

Heaven and Earth 84
How Manifold Your Wisdom 91
Live with Expectation 26
O Christ, We Seek to Be 30
O Holy Spirit, Send 28
O Suffering God 74
Reign, O God 94
Sons and Daughters 112
Spirit, You Offer 85
The Doors Were Shut 80
The Grace of God 88
Thirsty Seekers 96
When John the Baptist 6
You Have Known Us 109

Holy Week

Behold God's Servant 64
Creator of Wisdom 67
Few Are the Days 73
From Bleak Gethsemane 72
O Suffering God 74
Remembering the Supper 69
The Cross 68
To Martha's Table 65
To You, O God 66
We Live in Covenant 71
We Who Have Trusted 70

Hope

Blessed Are the Righteous 36
Covenant Word 45
Creator God, We Praise 92
Few Are the Days 73
Fulfilled and Blessed 105
Gathered as Witnesses 87
Give Thanks to God 103
Glory to God 11
God Is Our Hope 107
God Our Refuge 31
Heavens Proclaim 12
If We Speak 32
Let Our Joyous Song 75
Our God Judges 100
Reign, O God 94

Thank God 17
To Martha's Table 65
To You, O God 66
Wake from Sleep 46
We Live in Covenant 71
We Must Give Thanks 121
Whoever Clings to God 52
Worship God with Gratitude 113
You Call Us, God 128

Hospitality
Lift Up Your Voice 48
To Martha's Table 65

Jesus Christ
Appear to Us, O Christ 35
Be Glad and Sing 86
Behold God's Servant 64
Behold the Mystery 24
Called to Be Free 98
Christ Jesus We Adore 125
Come Now to Reign 123
Come to God's Glory 23
Come to the Temple 3
Creator God, We Praise 92
Creator of Wisdom 67
From Bleak Gethsemane 72
Gather Friends at Table 118
Gather Us, Your Children 54
Gathered as Witnesses 87
Gathered at Your Throne 81
Gladness and Joy 77
Glory to God 11
God of Peace 5
God of Tender Mercy 124
God, We Rejoice 127
Hear Now the Word 108
How Manifold Your Wisdom 91
Join Us Daily 78
Let Our Joyous Song 75
Let Us Rejoice 8
Listen for Good News 14
Live with Expectation 26
Look for God's Reign 119

Morning by Morning 62
Not Justified by Works 95
Now, by God's Mercy 13
O Holy Spirit, Send 28
Praises, Praises, Praises 79
Remembering the Supper 69
Reveal to Us, Jesus 33
Shepherd and Judge 20
Sons and Daughters 112
Stir and Save Us 106
Thanksgiving and Glory 83
The Cross 68
The Doors Were Shut 80
The Mind of Jesus 61
To Martha's Table 65
We Live in Covenant 71
We Sing with Gladness 22
When Christ Appears 82
Worship God with Gratitude 113

Joy, Rejoice
As You Receive 126
Be Glad and Sing 86
Be Glad, O Righteous 57
Bring Your Promise 51
Called to Be Free 98
Christ Jesus We Adore 125
Come to the Temple 3
Come to This Level Place 37
Gather Us, Your Children 54
Gathered as Witnesses 87
Gathered at Your Throne 81
Give Thanks, Our Savior Lives 76
Gladness and Joy 77
Glory to God 11
God, the Heavens Proclaim 29
Hear Now the Word 108
Hear Your Thirsty People 55
Heaven and Earth 84
Heavens Proclaim 12
Here We Come 43
Join the Celebration 63
Join Us Daily 78
Let Heavens Be Glad 10
Let Our Joyous Song 75

Let Us Rejoice 8
Listen for Good News 14
Look for God's Reign 119
Not Justified by Works 95
O Christ, We Seek to Be 30
O Word of Light 15
Our God Judges 100
Praise Our God 59
Receive Our Treasures 50
Reign, O God 94
Rejoice, People of Light 9
Sing Aloud! 4
Thanks Be to You 40
The Cross 68
The Grace of God 88
'Tis the Season 18
To You, O God 66
We Sing with Gladness 22
Winds of Judgment 110
With All Your Heart 49
Worship God with Gratitude 113
You Have Known Us 109

Judgment

Be Glad, O Righteous 57
Choose for Today 93
Fountain of Life 27
Gathered as Witnesses 87
Give Thanks, Our Savior Lives 76
God, Our Beginning 19
Let Heavens Be Glad 10
O God of Truth 101
O Suffering God 74
Our God Judges 100
Shepherd and Judge 20
Sing Aloud! 4
Spirit, You Offer 85
Thank You for Jesus 89
Winds of Judgment 110

Justice

Be Glad, Rejoice 122
Covenant Word 45

Gather Friends at Table 118
God of Tender Mercy 124
God, We Rejoice 127
Hear the Word 104
Lift Up Your Voice 48
Our God Judges 100
Rejoice, People of Light 9
Thank You for Jesus 89
The People Tremble 47
We Will Extol You 120

Lenten Season

Be Glad, O Righteous 57
Behold God's Servant 64
Bring Your Promise 51
Creator of Wisdom 67
Faithful and Loving God 56
Far from Home 58
Few Are the Days 73
From Bleak Gethsemane 72
Gather Us, Your Children 54
Hear Your Thirsty People 55
Join the Celebration 63
Lift Up Your Voice 48
Morning by Morning 62
O Suffering God 74
Our Light and Our Salvation 53
Praise Our God 59
Press toward the Call 60
Receive Our Treasures 50
Remembering the Supper 69
The Cross 68
The Mind of Jesus 61
To Martha's Table 65
To You, O God 66
We Live in Covenant 71
We Who Have Trusted 70
Whoever Clings to God 52
With All Your Heart 49

Light

Be Glad and Sing 86
Behold God's Servant 64
Christ Jesus We Adore 125

Come to God's Glory 23
Creator God, We Praise 92
Creator of Wisdom 67
Few Are the Days 73
Fountain of Life 27
Gathered at Your Throne 81
God of Tender Mercy 124
Heavens Proclaim 12
Lift Up Your Voice 48
Not Justified by Works 95
Now, by God's Mercy 13
O Suffering God 74
O Word of Light 15
Our Light and Our Salvation 53
Rejoice, People of Light 9
Remembering the Supper 69
Thank You for Jesus 89
The Grace of God 88
The People Tremble 47
To You, O God 66
We Sing with Gladness 22
When Christ Appears 82

Love of God and Neighbor
Called to Be Free 98
Christians Turn the World 39
Come Now to Reign 123
Come, Spirit of God 90
From Bleak Gethsemane 72
Here We Come 43
How Manifold Your Wisdom 91
If We Speak 32
Join Us Daily 78
Let Heavens Be Glad 10
O Suffering God 74
Our God Judges 100
Reveal to Us, Jesus 33
Shepherd and Judge 20
Spirit, You Offer 85
Thank God 17
Thank You for Jesus 89
Thanksgiving and Glory 83
The Grace of God 88
The Mind of Jesus 61

To Martha's Table 65
We Live in Covenant 71
Whoever Clings to God 52
You Have Known Us 109
Your Grace Be with Us 117

Mercy
Bring Your Promise 51
Christians Turn the World 39
God of Tender Mercy 124
Heavens Proclaim 12
Now, by God's Mercy 13
Our Praise and Thanks 114
Sons and Daughters 112
Thanksgiving and Glory 83
The Days Are Coming 1
The People Tremble 47
Wake from Sleep 46
We Live in Covenant 71
Winds of Judgment 110

Ministry and Mission
Behold God's Servant 64
Come, Spirit of God 90
Disciples We Are Called 42
God of Tender Mercy 124
Now, by God's Mercy 13
O Christ, We Seek to Be 30
Thanks Be to You 40
The Mind of Jesus 61
The People Tremble 47
Wake from Sleep 46

Neighbors
Called to Be Free 98
Disciples We Are Called 42
Fulfilled and Blessed 105
Let All the Earth 16
O God of Hosts 7
Our God Judges 100
'Tis the Season 18

Peace
Be Glad and Sing 86
Be Glad, Rejoice 122

Called to Be Free 98
Choose for Today 93
Come to God's Glory 23
Creator God, We Praise 92
Give Thanks, Our Savior Lives 76
Glory to God 11
God of Peace 5
God, Our Beginning 19
God, We Rejoice 127
God Who Made Us 25
Here We Come 43
How Manifold Your Wisdom 91
Join the Celebration 63
Let All the Earth 16
Listen for Good News 14
No Slave Can Serve 111
On This Day 21
Our God Judges 100
Praises, Praises, Praises 79
Reign, O God 94
Rejoice, People of Light 9
Thanks Be to You 40
The Doors Were Shut 80
The Grace of God 88
To Martha's Table 65
We Cry for Help 99
We Seek Your Word 44
You Have Known Us 109

Penitence

Appear to Us, O Christ 35
Gathered as Witnesses 87
In Your Holy Temple 34
Not Justified by Works 95
Stir and Save Us 106
Thank You for Jesus 89
We Praise and Thank You 116
When John the Baptist 6
Winds of Judgment 110
With All Your Heart 49

Pentecost Season

As You Receive 126
Be Glad, Rejoice 122
Called to Be Free 98

Choose for Today 93
Christ Jesus We Adore 125
Come Now to Reign 123
Come, Spirit of God 90
Creator God, We Praise 92
Fulfilled and Blessed 105
Gather Friends at Table 118
Give Thanks to God 103
God Is Our Hope 107
God of Tender Mercy 124
God, We Rejoice 127
Hear Now the Word 108
Hear the Word 104
How Manifold Your Wisdom 91
Look for God's Reign 119
No Slave Can Serve 111
Not Justified by Works 95
O God of Truth 101
Our God Judges 100
Our Praise and Thanks 114
Reign, O God 94
Sons and Daughters 112
Stir and Save Us 106
Teach Us to Pray 102
The Days Will Come 115
Thirsty Seekers 96
We Cry Aloud 97
We Cry for Help 99
We Must Give Thanks 121
We Praise and Thank You 116
We Will Extol You 120
Winds of Judgment 110
Worship God with Gratitude 113
You Call Us, God 128
You Have Known Us 109
Your Grace Be with Us 117

Prayer

Be Glad, Rejoice 122
Choose for Today 93
Christians Turn the World 39
Come Now to Reign 123
Come to the Temple 3
Covenant Word 45
Faithful and Loving God 56

From Bleak Gethsemane 72
Gather Friends at Table 118
God of Peace 5
God, the Heavens Proclaim 29
Hear the Word 104
How Manifold Your Wisdom 91
Let All the Earth 16
Let Our Joyous Song 75
Live with Expectation 26
No Slave Can Serve 111
O God of Hosts 7
O Suffering God 74
Our God Judges 100
Our Light and Our Salvation 53
Our Praise and Thanks 114
Receive Our Treasures 50
Shepherd and Judge 20
Spirit, You Offer 85
Teach Us to Pray 102
Thank God 17
Thank You for Jesus 89
The Days Will Come 115
Thirsty Seekers 96
We Seek Your Word 44
We Who Have Trusted 70
Worship God with Gratitude 113
You Have Known Us 109

Reconciliation
Christians Turn the World 39
With All Your Heart 49

Resurrection
Appear to Us, O Christ 35
Gladness and Joy 77
God Provides for Us 38
God, We Rejoice 127
Join Us Daily 78
Let Our Joyous Song 75
Praises, Praises, Praises 79
The Doors Were Shut 80

Risk-Taking
Christ Jesus We Adore 125
Let Us Rejoice 8

O Suffering God 74
Thank God 17
The Mind of Jesus 61
Thirsty Seekers 96

Salvation
Bring Your Promise 51
Christ Jesus We Adore 125
Fountain of Life 27
Gather Us, Your Children 54
Gladness and Joy 77
Glory to God 11
God Our Refuge 31
God Provides for Us 38
Hear the Word 104
Hear Your Thirsty People 55
Heavens Proclaim 12
Here We Come 43
Join the Celebration 63
Let Heavens Be Glad 10
Let Our Joyous Song 75
Listen for Good News 14
Our Light and Our Salvation 53
Sing Aloud! 4
Sons and Daughters 112
The Cross 68
The Days Are Coming 1
To You, O God 66
We Must Give Thanks 121
We Sing with Gladness 22
We Who Have Trusted 70
When John the Baptist 6
With All Your Heart 49

Service (Servant)
Behold God's Servant 64
Bring Your Promise 51
Choose for Today 93
Come Now to Reign 123
Creator of Wisdom 67
Give Thanks, Our Savior Lives 76
Join the Celebration 63
Join Us Daily 78
Let Us Rejoice 8
No Slave Can Serve 111

O Holy Spirit, Send 28
On This Day 21
Our Light and Our Salvation 53
Press toward the Call 60
Reign, O God 94
Shepherd and Judge 20
Stir and Save Us 106
Thank God 17
The Grace of God 88
The Mind of Jesus 61
We Who Have Trusted 70
When John the Baptist 6
With All Your Heart 49
Worship God with Gratitude 113
You Have Known Us 109

Sharing
Bring Your Promise 51
Fulfilled and Blessed 105
Glory to God 11
Let Us Rejoice 8
Sons and Daughters 112
We Sing with Gladness 22

Sin, Sinners
Appear to Us, O Christ 35
Be Glad, O Righteous 57
Behold God's Servant 64
Creator God, We Praise 92
Far from Home 58
Few Are the Days 73
Gather Friends at Table 118
Gathered as Witnesses 87
God Our Refuge 31
God Provides for Us 38
How Manifold Your Wisdom 91
Lift Up Your Voice 48
Live with Expectation 26
Morning by Morning 62
O Suffering God 74
Praises, Praises, Praises 79
Receive Our Treasures 50
Rejoice, People of Light 9
Shepherd and Judge 20
Thank You for Jesus 89

The Cross 68
The Days Are Coming 1
The People Tremble 47
We Live in Covenant 71
We Seek Your Word 44
We Who Have Trusted 70
Winds of Judgment 110
With All Your Heart 49
Worship God with Gratitude 113
Your Grace Be with Us 117

Steadfast Love
As You Receive 126
Be Glad, O Righteous 57
Behold God's Servant 64
Few Are the Days 73
Fountain of Life 27
Give Thanks to God 103
Hear Your Thirsty People 55
Not Justified by Works 95
O God of Truth 101
Our God Judges 100
Praises, Praises, Praises 79
The Days Are Coming 1
Thirsty Seekers 96
To You, O God 66

Stewardship
Behold the Mystery 24
Called to Be Free 98
Fulfilled and Blessed 105
Give Thanks to God 103
God, Our Beginning 19
Join the Celebration 63
Let Us Rejoice 8
No Slave Can Serve 111
O God of Truth 101
Receive Our Treasures 50
To Martha's Table 65
Winds of Judgment 110
You Call Us, God 128

Teaching
Appear to Us, O Christ 35
Be Glad, O Righteous 57

Gathered as Witnesses	87
Give Thanks to God	103
God, We Rejoice	127
Hear the Word	104
How Manifold Your Wisdom	91
Join the Celebration	63
Let All the Earth	16
Not Justified by Works	95
Reveal to Us, Jesus	33
Teach Us to Pray	102
The Days Will Come	115
The Doors Were Shut	80
The People Tremble	47
We Cry for Help	99
We Praise and Thank You	116
Worship God with Gratitude	113
You Call Us, God	128

Thanksgiving, Thankfulness

As You Receive	126
Be Glad and Sing	86
Be Glad, O Righteous	57
Come to the Temple	3
Creator God, We Praise	92
Fulfilled and Blessed	105
Give Thanks to God	103
God of Peace	5
God, We Rejoice	127
Hear Now the Word	108
Hear the Word	104
Hear Your Thirsty People	55
Heavens Proclaim	12
Let All the Earth	16
Let Our Joyous Song	75
Listen for Good News	14
Look for God's Reign	119
No Slave Can Serve	111
Not Justified by Works	95
Praises, Praises, Praises	79
Reign, O God	94
Sing Aloud!	4
Sons and Daughters	112
Thank God	17
Thank You for Jesus	89
Thanks Be to You	40

Thanksgiving and Glory	83
The Grace of God	88
We Must Give Thanks	121
We Praise and Thank You	116

Trust

Be Glad, O Righteous	57
Blessed Are the Righteous	36
Come Now to Reign	123
Creator God, We Praise	92
Few Are the Days	73
Fountain of Life	27
God Is Our Hope	107
God, Our Beginning	19
God Our Refuge	31
God Provides for Us	38
God, We Rejoice	127
Hear Now the Word	108
Let Our Joyous Song	75
Let Us Rejoice	8
Our Praise and Thanks	114
Reign, O God	94
Reveal to Us, Jesus	33
Sing Aloud!	4
Thank God	17
Thank You for Jesus	89
The Days Are Coming	1
The Doors Were Shut	80
Thirsty Seekers	96
'Tis the Season	18
To You, O God	66
We Who Have Trusted	70
Worship God with Gratitude	113

Truth

Appear to Us, O Christ	35
Be Glad and Sing	86
Come Now to Reign	123
Covenant Word	45
Creator God, We Praise	92
From Bleak Gethsemane	72
Give Thanks, Our Savior Lives	76
Gladness and Joy	77
Glory to God	11
God of Peace	5

God, Our Beginning 19
God Provides for Us 38
God, the Heavens Proclaim 29
How Manifold Your wisdom 91
Join Us Daily 78
Let Heavens Be Glad 10
Look for God's Reign 119
O God of Truth 101
O Word of Light 15
Our God Judges 100
Our Praise and Thanks 114
Receive Our Treasures 50
Reveal to Us, Jesus 33
The Days Are Coming 1
The Days Will Come 115
The Doors Were Shut 80
The People Tremble 47
We Must Give Thanks 121
We Sing with Gladness 22
Your Grace Be with Us 117

Unity

Come, Spirit of God 90
Come to This Level Place 37
Let All the Earth 16
Let Heavens Be Glad 10
O Christ, We Seek to Be 30
Thank You for Jesus 89
When Christ Appears 82

Vision

Come, Spirit of God 90
God, Our Beginning 19
Heaven and Earth 84
If We Speak 32
Join Us Daily 78
Look for God's Reign 119
Spirit, You Offer 85
When Christ Appears 82
When John the Baptist 6
Your Grace Be with Us 117

Witness

Come Now to Reign 123
Creator of Wisdom 67

Gathered as Witnesses 87
Give Thanks, Our Savior Lives 76
Glory to God 11
Join Us Daily 78
Let All the Earth 16
Live with Expectation 26
Now, by God's Mercy 13
O God of Truth 101
Our Praise and Thanks 114
Praises, Praises, Praises 79
Reign, O God 94
The Doors Were Shut 80
We Sing with Gladness 22

Worship

As You Receive 126
Choose for Today 93
Come to God's Glory 23
Fountain of Life 27
Gather Friends at Table 118
Gather Us, Your Children 54
Gathered at Your Throne 81
God, the Heavens Proclaim 29
God, We Rejoice 127
God Who Made Us 25
Hear the Word 104
Here We Come 43
Let Heavens Be Glad 10
O God of Truth 101
Press toward the Call 60
Reveal to Us, Jesus 33
Thank God 17
Thanksgiving and Glory 83
Worship God with Gratitude 113
You Call Us, God 128

Zeal

Fulfilled and Blessed 105
Glory to God 11
Press toward the Call 60
Rejoice, People of Light 9

INDEX OF SCRIPTURE READINGS

(The italicized scriptures indicate the alternate series of readings
for the Sundays following Pentecost.)

Old Testament

Genesis
11:1–9 . . . . .Pentecost
15:1–6 . . . . .Proper 14
15:1–12, 17–18 . . . . .Lent 2
18:1–10a. . . . . .Proper 11
18:20–32 . . . . .Proper 12
32:22–31 . . . . .Proper 24
45:3–11, 15 . . . . .Epiphany 7

Exodus
12:1–14 . . . . .Maundy
. . . . .Thursday
32:7–14 . . . . .Proper 19
34:29–35 . . . . .Epiphany Last,
. . . . .Transfiguration

Numbers
6:22–27 . . . . .Holy Name
21:4b–9 . . . . .Holy Cross

Deuteronomy
26:1–11 . . . . .Lent 1
26:1–11 . . . . .Thanksgiving
30:9–14 . . . . .Proper 10
30:15–20 . . . . .Proper 18

Joshua
5:9–12 . . . . .Lent 4

1 Samuel
2:1–10 . . . . .Visitation
2:18–20, 26 . . . . .After Christmas 1

2 Samuel
11:26–12:15. . . . . . .Proper 6

1 Kings
8:22–23, 41–43 . . . . .Epiphany 9
8:22–23, 41–43 . . . .Proper 4
17:8–24 . . . . .Proper 5
17:17–24 . . . . .Proper 5
18:20–39 . . . . .Proper 4
19:1–15a. . . . . .Proper 7
19:15–16, 19–21 Proper 8
21:1–21a. . . . . .Proper 6

2 Kings
2:1–2, 6–14 . . . . .Proper 8
5:1–3, 7–15c . . . . .Proper 23
5:1–14 . . . . .Proper 9

Nehemiah
8:1–3, 5–6, 8–10. . . . .Epiphany 3

Job
14:1–14 . . . . .Holy Saturday
19:23–27a. . . . . . . .Proper 27

Psalms
1 . . . . .Epiphany 6
1 . . . . .Proper 18
5:1–8 . . . . .Proper 6
8 . . . . .Trinity Sunday
8 . . . . .New Year's Day
14 . . . . .Proper 19
15 . . . . .Proper 11
16 . . . . .Proper 8
17:1–9 . . . . .Proper 27
19 . . . . .Epiphany 3
22 . . . . .Good Friday
22:19–28 . . . . .Proper 7
23 . . . . .Easter 4
24:7–10 . . . . .Presentation
25:1–10 . . . . .Advent 1

25:1–10 . . . . .Proper 10

27 . . . . .Lent 2

29 . . . . .Epiphany 1,
Baptism of Jesus

30 . . . . .Easter 3

30 . . . . .Proper 9

30 . . . . .Proper 5

31:1–4, 15–16 . . . . . .Holy Saturday

31:9–16 . . . . .Lent 6, Passion
Sunday

32 . . . . .Lent 4

32 . . . . .Proper 6

32:1–7 . . . . .Proper 26

33:12–22 . . . . .Proper 14

36:5–10 . . . . .Epiphany 2

36:5–11 . . . . .Monday in Holy
Week

37:1–9 . . . . .Proper 22

37:1–11, 39–40 . . . . .Epiphany 7

40:5–10 . . . . .Annunciation

42 and 43 . . . . .Proper 7

45 . . . . .Annunciation

46 . . . . .Proper 29

47 . . . . .Ascension

49:1–12 . . . . .Proper 13

50:1–8, 22–23 . . . . . .Proper 14

51:1–10 . . . . .Proper 19

51:1–17 . . . . .Ash Wednesday

52 . . . . .Proper 11

63:1–8 . . . . .Lent 3

65 . . . . .Proper 25

66:1–9 . . . . .Proper 9

66:1–12 . . . . .Proper 23

67 . . . . .Easter 6

70 . . . . .Wednesday in
Holy Week

71:1–6 . . . . .Epiphany 4

71:1–6 . . . . .Proper 16

71:1–14 . . . . .Tuesday in Holy
Week

72:1–7, 10–14 . . . . . .Epiphany

77:1–2, 11–20 . . . . . .Proper 8

78:1–2, 34–38 . . . . . .Holy Cross

79:1–9 . . . . .Proper 20

80:1–7 . . . . .Advent 4

80:1–2, 8–19 . . . . . . .Proper 15

81:1, 10–16 . . . . .Proper 17

82 . . . . .Proper 10

82 . . . . .Proper 15

84 . . . . .Presentation

84:1–7 . . . . .Proper 25

85 . . . . .Proper 12

91:1–2, 9–16 . . . . . . .Lent 1

91:1–6, 14–16 . . . . . .Proper 21

92:1–4, 12–15 . . . . . .Epiphany 8

96 . . . . .Christmas Day 1

96 . . . . .Proper 4

96:1–9 . . . . .Epiphany 9

96:1–9 . . . . .Proper 4

97 . . . . .Christmas Day 2

97 . . . . .Easter 7

98 . . . . .Christmas Day 3

98 . . . . .Proper 27

98 . . . . .Proper 28

98:1–5 . . . . .Holy Cross

99 . . . . .Epiphany Last,
Transfiguration

100 . . . . .Thanksgiving

103:1–8 . . . . .Proper 16

104:24–34, 35b . . . . .Pentecost

107:1–9, 43 . . . . .Proper 13

110 . . . . .Ascension

111 . . . . .Proper 23

112 . . . . .Proper 17

113 . . . . .Visitation

113 . . . . .Proper 20

114 . . . . .Easter Evening

116:1–2, 12–19 . . . . .Holy Thursday

118:1–2, 14–24 . . . . .Easter

118:1–2, 19–29 . . . . .Palm Sunday

118:14–29 . . . . .Easter 2

119:97–104 . . . . .Proper 24

119:137–144 . . . . . . .Proper 26

121 . . . . .Proper 24

126 . . . . .Lent 5

137 . . . . .Proper 22

138 . . . . .Epiphany 5

138 . . . . .Proper 12

139:1–6, 13–18 . . . . .Proper 18

145:1–5, 17–21 . . . . .Proper 27

146 . . . . .Proper 5
146 . . . . .Proper 21
147:12–20 . . . . .After Christmas 2
148 . . . . .After Christmas 1
148 . . . . .Easter 5
149 . . . . .All Saints' Day
150 . . . . .Easter 2

Proverbs
8:1–4, 22–31 . . . . .Trinity Sunday
25:6–7 . . . . .Proper 17

Ecclesiastes
1:2, 12–14,
2:18–23 . . . . .Proper 13
3:1–13 . . . . .New Year's Day

Isaiah
1:1, 10–20 . . . . .Proper 14
1:10–18 . . . . .Proper 26
5:1–7 . . . . .Proper 15
6:1–8(9–13) . . . . .Epiphany 5
7:10–14 . . . . .Annunciation
9:2–7 . . . . .Christmas Day 1
12 . . . . .Proper 28
12:2–6 . . . . .Advent 3
25:6–9 . . . . .Easter Evening
42:1–9 . . . . .Monday in Holy
Week
43:1–7 . . . . .Epiphany 1,
Baptism of Jesus
43:16–21 . . . . .Lent 5
49:1–7 . . . . .Tuesday in Holy
Week
50:4–9a. . . . . .Lent 6, Passion/
Palm Sunday
50:4–9a. . . . . .Wednesday in
Holy Week
52:7–10 . . . . .Christmas Day 3
52:13–53:12 . . . . .Good Friday
55:1–9 . . . . .Lent 3
55:10–13 . . . . .Epiphany 8
58:1–12 . . . . .Ash Wednesday

58:9b–14 . . . . .Proper 16
60:1–6 . . . . .Epiphany
62:1–5 . . . . .Epiphany 2
62:6–12 . . . . .Christmas Day 2
65:1–9 . . . . .Proper 7
65:17–25 . . . . .Proper 28
65:17–25 . . . . .Easter
66:10–14 . . . . .Proper 9

Jeremiah
1:4–10 . . . . .Epiphany 4
1:4–10 . . . . .Proper 16
2:4–13 . . . . .Proper 17
4:11–12, 22–28 . . . . . .Proper 19
8:18–9:1. . . . . .Proper 20
14:7–10, 19–22 . . . .Proper 25
17:5–10 . . . . .Epiphany 6
18:1–11 . . . . .Proper 18
23:1–6 . . . . .Proper 29,
Christ the Ruler
23:23–29 . . . . .Proper 15
29:1, 4–7 . . . . .Proper 23
31:7–14 . . . . .After Christmas 2
31:27–34 . . . . .Proper 24
32:1–3a, 6–15 . . . . . . .Proper 21
33:14–16 . . . . .Advent 1

Lamentations
1:1–6 . . . . .Proper 22
3:1–9, 19–24 . . . . .Holy Saturday
3:19–26 . . . . .Proper 22

Daniel
7:1–3, 15–18 . . . . .All Saints' Day

Hosea
1:2–10 . . . . .Proper 12
11:1–11 . . . . .Proper 13

Joel
2:1–2, 12–17 . . . . .Ash Wednesday
2:23–32 . . . . .Proper 25

Amos

6:1a, 4–7 . . . . .Proper 21
7:7–17 . . . . .Proper 10
8:1–12 . . . . .Proper 11
8:4–7 . . . . .Proper 20

Micah

5:2–5a. . . . . .Advent 4

Habakkuk

1:1–4, 2:1–4 . . . . .Proper 22
1:1–4, 2:1–4 . . . . . . .Proper 26

Zephaniah

3:14–20 . . . . .Advent 3

Haggai

1:15b–2:9. . . . . .Proper 27

Malachi

3:1–4 . . . . .Presentation
3:1–4 . . . . .Advent 2
4:1–2a. . . . . .Proper 28

New Testament

Matthew

2:1–12 . . . . .Epiphany
6:1–6, 16–21 . . . . . . .Ash Wednesday
25:31–46 . . . . .New Year's Day
27:57–66 . . . . .Holy Saturday

Luke

1:26–38 . . . . .Annunciation
1:39–55 . . . . .Advent 4
1:39–57 . . . . .Visitation
1:47–55 . . . . .Advent 4
1:68–79 . . . . .Advent 2
1:68–79 . . . . .Proper 29,
                          Christ the Ruler
2:1–14 . . . . .Christmas Day 1
2:8–20 . . . . .Christmas Day 2
2:15–21 . . . . .Holy Name
2:22–40 . . . . .Presentation
2:41–52 . . . . .After Christmas 1

3:1–6 . . . . .Advent 2
3:7–18 . . . . .Advent 3
3:15–17, 21–22 . . . . .Epiphany 1,
                          Baptism of Jesus
4:1–13 . . . . .Lent 1
4:14–21 . . . . .Epiphany 3
4:21–30 . . . . .Epiphany 4
5:1–11 . . . . .Epiphany 5
6:17–26 . . . . .Epiphany 6
6:20–31 . . . . .All Saints' Day
6:27–38 . . . . .Epiphany 7
6:39–49 . . . . .Epiphany 8
7:1–10 . . . . .Epiphany 9
7:1–10 . . . . .Proper 4
7:11–17 . . . . .Proper 5
7:36–8:3 . . . . .Proper 6
8:26–39 . . . . .Proper 7
9:28–36 . . . . .Lent 2
9:28–43 . . . . .Epiphany Last,
                          Transfiguration
9:51–62 . . . . .Proper 8
10:1–11, 16–20 . . . . .Proper 9
10:25–37 . . . . .Proper 10
10:38–42 . . . . .Proper 11
11:1–13 . . . . .Proper 12
12:13–21 . . . . .Proper 13
12:32–40 . . . . .Proper 14
12:49–56 . . . . .Proper 15
13:1–9 . . . . .Lent 3
13:10–17 . . . . .Proper 16
13:31–35 . . . . .Lent 2
14:1, 7–14 . . . . .Proper 17
14:25–33 . . . . .Proper 18
15:1–3, 11b–32 . . . . .Lent 4
15:1–10 . . . . .Proper 19
16:1–13 . . . . .Proper 20
16:19–31 . . . . .Proper 21
17:5–10 . . . . .Proper 22
17:11–19 . . . . .Proper 23
18:1–8 . . . . .Proper 24
18:9–14 . . . . .Proper 25
19:1–10 . . . . .Proper 26
19:28–40 . . . . .Palm Sunday
20:27–38 . . . . .Proper 27
21:5–19 . . . . .Proper 28

21:25–36 . . . . .Advent 1
22:14–23:56 . . . . .Lent 6, Passion
                Sunday
23:33–43 . . . . .Proper 29,
                Christ the Ruler
24:1–12 . . . . .Easter
24:13–49 . . . . .Easter Evening
24:44–53 . . . . .Ascension Day

John
1:1–14 . . . . .Christmas Day 3
1:10–18 . . . . .Christmas Day 2
2:1–11 . . . . .Epiphany 2
3:13–17 . . . . .Holy Cross
5:1–9 . . . . .Easter 6
6:25–35 . . . . .Thanksgiving
10:22–30 . . . . .Easter 4
12:1–8 . . . . .Lent 5
12:1–11 . . . . .Monday in Holy
                Week
12:20–36 . . . . .Tuesday in Holy
                Week
13:1–17, 31b–35 . . . .Maundy
                Thursday
13:21–32 . . . . .Wednesday in
                Holy week
13:31–35 . . . . .Easter 5
14:8–17, (25–27) . . . .Pentecost
14:23–29 . . . . .Easter 6
16:12–15 . . . . .Trinity Sunday
17:20–26 . . . . .Easter 7
18:1–19:42 . . . . .Good Friday
19:38–42 . . . . .Holy Saturday
20:1–18 . . . . .Easter
20:19–31 . . . . .Easter 2
21:1–19 . . . . .Easter 3

Acts
1:1–11 . . . . .Ascension Day
2:1–21 . . . . .Pentecost
5:27–32 . . . . .Easter 2
8:14–17 . . . . .Epiphany 1,
                Baptism of Jesus
9:1–20 . . . . .Easter 3
9:36–43 . . . . .Easter 4

10:34–43 . . . . .Easter
11:1–18 . . . . .Easter 5
16:9–15 . . . . .Easter 6
16:16–34 . . . . .Easter 7

Romans
5:1–5 . . . . .Trinity Sunday
8:14–17 . . . . .Pentecost
10:8b–13 . . . . .Lent 1
12:9–16b . . . . .Visitation

1 Corinthians
1:18–24 . . . . .Holy Cross
1:18–31 . . . . .Tuesday in Holy
                Week
5:6b–8 . . . . .Easter Evening
10:1–13 . . . . .Lent 3
11:23–26 . . . . .Maundy
                Thursday
12:1–11 . . . . .Epiphany 2
12:12–31a . . . . .Epiphany 3
13:1–13 . . . . .Epiphany 4
15:1–11 . . . . .Epiphany 5
15:12–20 . . . . .Epiphany 6
15:19–26 . . . . .Easter
15:35–38, 42–50 . . . . .Epiphany 7
15:51–58 . . . . .Epiphany 8

2 Corinthians
3:12–4:2 . . . . .Epiphany Last,
                Transfiguration
5:16–21 . . . . .Lent 4
5:20b–6:10 . . . . .Ash Wednesday

Galatians
1:1–12 . . . . .Epiphany 9
1:1–12 . . . . .Proper 4
1:11–24 . . . . .Proper 5
2:15–21 . . . . .Proper 6
3:23–29 . . . . .Proper 7
4:4–7 . . . . .Holy Name
5:1, 13–25 . . . . .Proper 8
6:1–16 . . . . .Proper 9

Ephesians

1:3–14 . . . . After Christmas 2
1:11–23 . . . . All Saints' Day
1:15–23 . . . . Ascension Day
3:1–12 . . . . Epiphany

Philippians

1:3–11 . . . . Advent 2
2:5–11 . . . . Holy Name
2:5–11 . . . . Lent 6, Passion/
  Palm Sunday
3:4b–14 . . . . Lent 5
3:17–4:1 . . . . Lent 2
4:4–7 . . . . Advent 3
4:4–9 . . . . Thanksgiving

Colossians

1:1–14 . . . . Proper 10
1:11–20 . . . . Proper 29,
  Christ the Ruler
1:15–28 . . . . Proper 11
2:6–19 . . . . Proper 12
3:1–11 . . . . Proper 13
3:12–17 . . . . After Christmas 1

1 Thessalonians

3:9–13 . . . . Advent 1

2 Thessalonians

1:1–4, 11–12 . . . . Proper 26
2:1–5, 13–17 . . . . Proper 27
3:6–13 . . . . Proper 28

1 Timothy

1:12–17 . . . . Proper 19
2:1–7 . . . . Proper 20
6:6–19 . . . . Proper 21

2 Timothy

1:1–14 . . . . Proper 22
2:8–15 . . . . Proper 23

3:14–4:5 . . . . Proper 24
4:6–8, 16–18 . . . . Proper 25

Titus

2:11–14 . . . . Christmas Day 1
3:4–7 . . . . Christmas Day 2

Philemon

1:21 . . . . Proper 18

Hebrews

1:1–12 . . . . Christmas Day 3
2:14–18 . . . . Presentation
4:14–16, 5:7–9 . . . . . . Good Friday
9:11–15 . . . . Monday in Holy
  Week
10:4–10 . . . . Annunciation
10:5–10 . . . . Advent 4
10:16–25 . . . . Good Friday
11:1–3, 8–16 . . . . Proper 14
11:29–12:2 . . . . Proper 15
12:1–3 . . . . Wednesday in
  Holy Week
12:18–29 . . . . Proper 16
13:1–8, 15–16 . . . . . . Proper 17

1 Peter

4:1–8 . . . . Holy Saturday

Revelation

1:4–8 . . . . Easter 2
5:11–14 . . . . Easter 3
7:9–17 . . . . Easter 4
21:1–6a . . . . New Year's Day
21:1–6 . . . . Easter 5
21:10, 22–22:5 . . . . . . Easter 6
22:12–14, 16–17,
  20–21 . . . . Easter 7

Abundance
Advent 3
Christmas Season 2
Epiphany 2
Monday of Holy Week
Proper 8

Advent
Advent 1, 2, 3, 4

Ambassador(s)
Lent 4

Anxiety
Advent 3
Lent 2

Assurance
Proper 6

Awe and Wonder
Epiphany 5, Last
Easter Evening
Trinity Sunday
Proper 11, 16, 23, 25

Banquet
Proper 17

Baptism
Advent 2, 3
Epiphany 1

Beginning
Advent 1
New Year's Day
Easter 2

Birth
Christmas Eve/Day, Proper 1

Bless(ing)
Christmas Season 1, 2
New Year's Day
January 1 (Jesus and Mary)
Epiphany 1, 6
Lent 3, 6 (Passion and Palm
Sunday)
Easter 3, 4, 6
Proper 17, 21, 25, 26, 27

Bounty
Thanksgiving Day

Bread
Lent 1
Thanksgiving Day

Call(s)
Lent 1, 5
Easter 6
Pentecost
Proper 14, 17, 28

Caring
Advent 3
Epiphany 2, 3, 5
Tuesday of Holy Week
Easter 4
Trinity Sunday
Proper 8, 10, 20, 21, 24

Challenge
Proper 5, 10

Change
Christmas Season 2

Epiphany 4, 8
Ash Wednesday
Easter 6

Child(ren)
January 1 (Jesus and Mary)
Christmas Season 2

Chosen
Lent 5
Easter Sunday

Church
Epiphany
Epiphany 3
Ascension Day
Easter 7
Proper 20, 28, 29
Thanksgiving Day

Comfort
Easter 4

Command(ments)
Proper 9, 17, 18, 20, 24

Commitment
Epiphany Last
Proper 8, 18, 22

Communion
Maundy Thursday

Community
Epiphany 3

Compassion
Christmas Season 1
Lent 4
Proper 5
Thanksgiving Day

Confidence
Proper 7

Conscience
Proper 22

Courage
Epiphany 4
Wednesday of Holy Week
Proper 27

Covenant
Advent 1, 2
Epiphany 9
Lent 2, 3
Monday of Holy Week
Maundy Thursday
Good Friday
Proper 7, 14, 23, 24

Creation
Trinity Sunday
Proper 4, 28

Cross
Lent 6 (Passion Sunday)
Good Friday
Holy Saturday

Death
Good Friday
Holy Saturday
Easter Sunday

Deceit
Proper 15

Deeds
Easter 2
Thanksgiving Day

Deliverance
Lent 1
Wednesday of Holy Week

Denial
Good Friday

Desolation
Epiphany 2

Devotion
Proper 18

Dimness
Holy Saturday

Discipleship
Advent 2
Epiphany 4, 5
Wednesday of Holy Week
Maundy Thursday
Good Friday
Holy Saturday
Easter Sunday

Discipline(s)
Ash Wednesday
Holy Saturday
Proper 22

Distress
Lent 6 (Passion Sunday)

Doubt
Easter Sunday
Easter 4

Empowerment
Epiphany 9
Maundy Thursday

Endurance
Epiphany 4
Trinity Sunday

Enemies
Epiphany 7

Envy
Epiphany 7

Eternity
Proper 21

Evil
Christmas Eve/Day, Proper 2
Proper 10, 12, 25, 26

Excellence
Advent 2
Proper 29

Exile(s)
Proper 22

Failure
Epiphany Last

Faith
Epiphany
Epiphany 3, 4, 6, 9
Lent 1, 6 (Passion and Palm
    Sunday)
Easter 2, 4, 7
Trinity Sunday
Proper 4, 5, 6, 7, 11, 14, 15, 21,
    22, 23, 26, 27
All Saints' Day

Faithfulness
Christmas Eve/Day, Proper 3
Christmas Season 1
Epiphany 5, 8
Lent 3, 4, 6 (Palm Sunday)
Monday of Holy Week
Tuesday of Holy Week
Easter 3, 5, 6
Ascension Day
Proper 5, 7, 8, 10, 11, 12, 14,
    15, 18, 20, 22, 23, 24, 28
Thanksgiving Day

Fasting
Ash Wednesday

Fear(s)
Advent 3
January 1 (Jesus and Mary)
Epiphany 4, Last
Lent 2
Good Friday
Holy Saturday
Easter 2
Proper 17, 19, 23

Fire
Advent 2, 3
Epiphany 1
Pentecost
Proper 4, 15

First Fruits
Thanksgiving Day

Food
Thanksgiving Day

Forgiveness
Christmas Eve/Day, Proper 3
Christmas Season 1
Epiphany 5, 7, 9
Lent 1, 4, 6 (Passion Sunday)
Easter Sunday
Easter Evening
Easter 6, 7
Ascension Day
Proper 4, 6, 11, 12, 25
Fortress
Tuesday of Holy Week

Freedom
Lent 1
Proper 8, 16

Fruit
Advent 3
Epiphany 6, 8
Lent 1, 3
Proper 15
Thanksgiving Day

Future
New Year's Day

Generosity
Advent 3
Ash Wednesday
Proper 21

Gladness
Lent 4
Proper 4, 25, 28

Glory of God
Advent 2
Christmas Eve/Day, Proper 1, 2
January 1 (Jesus and Mary)
Epiphany
Epiphany 9, Last
Trinity Sunday
Proper 4, 27, 28

Gift(s)
New Year's Day
January 1 (Jesus and Mary)
Epiphany 2, 3, 8, 9, Last
Lent 1, 3
Easter 2, 3
Proper 12, 16, 22

Giving
Epiphany 7
Ash Wednesday
Wednesday of Holy Week

Goal(s)
Lent 5

Golden Rule
Epiphany 7

Good Fight
Proper 25

Good News
Advent 3, 4

Christmas Eve/Day, Proper 1
Epiphany 3, 5
Easter Sunday
Easter Evening
Easter 3, 4
Ascension Day
Proper 5, 6, 27

Goodness
Christmas Eve/Day, Proper 2
Christmas Season 2
Epiphany 8
Easter 4
Proper 12, 16

Gospel
Advent 2
Epiphany
Epiphany 9
Proper 5, 11, 22
All Saints' Day

Grace
Christmas Eve/Day, Proper 1,
    2, 3
Christmas Season 2
Epiphany
Epiphany 5
Ash Wednesday
Easter 2, 7
Trinity Sunday
Proper 5, 6, 10, 15, 19, 22, 26
All Saints' Day

Grain
Proper 25

Gratitude
Easter 6

Greed
Proper 13
Grief
Good Friday
Proper 22

Growth
Christmas Season 1
Epiphany 8
Ash Wednesday

Guidance
Epiphany
Trinity Sunday

Guilt
Lent 6 (Passion Sunday)

Healing
Epiphany 2, 4, 6, 9
Easter Sunday
Easter 3, 6
Proper 7, 9, 16, 20, 21, 23, 28

Hearing
Easter 3, 6
Proper 24

Hearts
Advent 2
Epiphany 3, 8
Ash Wednesday
Lent 2
Proper 10, 12, 14, 24, 26

Help(er)
Epiphany 3
Wednesday of Holy Week
Proper 7, 9, 15, 16, 17, 21, 22,
    24

Holy, Holiness
Proper 5

Holy Spirit
Christmas Season 2
Easter 4
Ascension Day
Pentecost
Trinity Sunday

Proper 8, 22
All Saints' Day

Hope
Christmas Season 2
Epiphany 4, 6
Good Friday
Holy Saturday
Proper 7, 11, 25, 27
All Saints' Day

Hospitality
Proper 9

Humility
Lent 6 (Passion and Palm Sunday)
Proper 25
All Saints' Day

Hunger
Advent 4
Epiphany 6
Proper 13

Hypocrisy
Ash Wednesday

Identity
Proper 15

Idolatry
Proper 18, 20

Image
Epiphany 7

Inspiration
Epiphany 2

Jealousy
Epiphany 7

Jesus Christ
Advent 1, 2, 4
Christmas Eve/Day, Proper 3

Christmas Season 1, 2
January 1 (Jesus and Mary
Epiphany
Epiphany 5, 6
Lent 2, 4, 5, 6
Palm Sunday
Tuesday of Holy Week
Wednesday of Holy Week
Maundy Thursday
Good Friday
Holy Saturday
Easter Sunday
Easter Evening
Easter 2, 3, 5
Ascension Day
Trinity Sunday
Proper 4, 5, 8, 9, 10, 13, 15, 18,
    22, 24, 28, 29
All Saints' Day

Joy
Advent 2, 4
Christmas Eve/Day, Proper 1, 3
Christmas Season 2
January 1 (Jesus and Mary)
Epiphany
Epiphany 2, 3, 6, 8
Lent 2, 3, 4, 5, 6
Palm Sunday
Wednesday of Holy Week
Maundy Thursday
Proper 6, 9, 19, 20, 25, 27
All Saints' Day
Thanksgiving Day

Joyful Noise
Proper 23
Thanksgiving Day

Judgment
Christmas Eve/Day, Proper 3
Proper 10, 19
Justice
Advent 1, 3
Epiphany

Monday of Holy Week
Proper 14, 15, 26

Kindness
Christmas Season 1
Proper 27

Law
Epiphany 3, 6
Proper 24

Lies
Proper 15

Life
Christmas Eve/Day, Proper 1
Epiphany 8, 9
Lent 6 (Palm Sunday)
Tuesday of Holy Week
Easter Sunday
Easter 4
Ascension Day
Pentecost
Trinity Sunday
Proper 15, 16, 17, 21, 22
Thanksgiving Day

Light(s)
Christmas Eve/Day, Proper 1, 3
Christmas Season 2
Epiphany
Epiphany 2
Monday of Holy Week
Tuesday of Holy Week
Easter 6
Proper 4, 9

Listen
Epiphany 8, Last
Proper 7, 17, 24, 26

Loss, Lost
Easter Evening
Proper 19, 26

Love
Advent 2
Christmas Season 1
Epiphany 3, 4, 6, 7, 8
Ash Wednesday
Lent 1, 2, 4, 6 (Passion and Palm
    Sunday)
Wednesday of Holy Week
Maundy Thursday
Good Friday
Easter 2, 3, 4, 5, 6,7
Pentecost
Trinity Sunday
Proper 5, 8, 10, 16, 18, 19, 21,
    22, 26, 27, 28 29

Majesty
January 1 (Jesus and Mary
Epiphany 5
Trinity Sunday
Proper 6

Mercy
Advent 1, 4
Christmas Eve/Day, Proper 2
Epiphany 7
Ash Wednesday
Lent 3
Easter 4
Proper 10, 16, 19, 21, 22, 29

Message, Messengers
Advent 2

Ministry and Mission
New Year's Day
Epiphany Last
Easter 3
Ascension Day
Proper 24

Miracle(s)
Epiphany 2

Name(s)
January 1 (Jesus and Mary)
Easter 7
Proper 9, 15, 28

Need(s)
Lent 4
Easter 5
Proper 11, 26

Newness
Advent 1
Christmas Eve/Day, Proper 2
New Year's Day
Epiphany 6
Ash Wednesday
Lent 1, 4, 5
Easter Sunday
Easter 5
Proper 5, 27, 28

Obedience, Obey
January 1 (Jesus and Mary)
Easter 2
Proper 14, 18

Open Eyes
Lent 6 (Passion Sunday)
Monday of Holy Week
Easter 2

Pain
Good Friday
Proper 20

Partnership
Advent 2

Path
Proper 27

Patience
Christmas Season 1

Peace
Advent 3
Christmas Eve/Day, Proper 1, 3
Christmas Season 1
Epiphany 1, 9
Easter 2, 6, 7
Pentecost
Proper 6, 9, 12, 14, 15, 20, 29

Piety
Ash Wednesday

Poor
Proper 11

Power
Epiphany 5
Easter Evening
Easter 3
Pentecost
Proper 10, 11, 16, 22
All Saints' Day

Praise
Christmas Eve/Day, Proper 1, 2
Christmas Season 1
January 1 (Jesus and Mary)
Epiphany 4, 5
Easter 2, 3, 4, 5, 6
Proper 5, 16, 23, 25, 27, 28
All Saints' Day

Prayer
Christmas Season 1
Epiphany 7
Lent 4, 6 (Passion Sunday)
Easter 3, 6
Proper 4, 24, 25, 26

Preparation
Advent 1, 2

Presence
Christmas Eve/Day, Proper 3
Epiphany 5, 6

Lent 1
Easter Sunday
Easter Evening
Easter 2, 3, 5
Proper 17, 24, 26, 28

Promises
Advent 1
January 1 (Jesus and Mary)
Epiphany 8
Easter 5
Easter Sunday
Easter Evening
Proper 14

Prophets
Epiphany 4
Proper 8

Protection
Proper 21

Purification
Advent 2

Purposes of God
Epiphany 3, 5, 8

Radiance
Epiphany

Realm
Epiphany 6
Proper 6, 8, 9, 10, 14, 21, 29

Reconciliation
Ash Wednesday
Lent 4

Refuge
Epiphany 7
Monday of Holy Week
Tuesday of Holy Week
Holy Saturday

Reign
Easter 3, 6
All Saints' Day
Proper 28

Rejoice
Advent 2
Christmas Eve/Day, Proper 1
Lent 4, 6 (Palm Sunday)
Proper 6, 25, 28

Relationships
Advent 2
Proper 12, 14

Remembrance
Maundy Thursday

Renewal
Epiphany 8
Proper 13, 28

Resources
Proper 20

Responsibility
January 1 (Jesus and Mary)
Thanksgiving Day

Resurrection
Epiphany 6
Lent 5
Easter Sunday

Revelation
Epiphany
Epiphany Last
Ascension Day
Proper 5
All Saints' Day

Riches
Epiphany 3
Thanksgiving Day

Righteousness
Advent 1
Christmas Eve/Day, Proper 2
Easter 7

Rock
Epiphany 3
Tuesday of Holy Week
Holy Saturday

Sacrifice
Good Friday
Easter Evening
Thanksgiving Day

Saints
Easter 7
All Saints' Day

Salvation
Advent 1, 2, 3
Christmas Eve/Day, Proper 1, 2
Epiphany 2
Lent 1, 6 (Palm Sunday)
Tuesday of Holy Week
Wednesday of Holy Week
Good Friday
Easter Sunday
Easter Evening
Easter 2, 4
Proper 6, 12, 20, 24, 25, 26, 28
All Saints' Day

Seek(ing)
Advent 2
Easter 7
Proper 19, 26

Self-Examination
Ash Wednesday
Good Friday

Send
Epiphany 5

Servants, Service
New Year's Day
Epiphany 2, 3, 9
Lent 2, 6 (Passion and Palm
  Sunday)
Monday of Holy Week
Tuesday of Holy Week
Maundy Thursday
Good Friday
Easter 6
Proper 14, 19, 20, 24

Shadows
Christmas Eve/Day, Proper 1, 2

Sharing
Advent 3
Proper 17, 21
Thanksgiving Day

Shepherd
Easter 4
Proper 19
Thanksgiving Day

Sight
Easter 3

Silence, Stillness
Proper 29

Sin(ners)
Wednesday of Holy Week
Proper 19, 24

Song
Advent 3
Epiphany 9
Proper 7, 28

Sorrow
Advent 2
Good Friday

Spiritual Needs
Christmas Season 2
All Saints' Day
Thanksgiving Day

Star(s)
Epiphany

Steadfast Love
Advent 1
Christmas Eve/Day, Proper 3
Epiphany 2, 5, 8
Ash Wednesday
Lent 3, 6 (Palm Sunday)
Monday of Holy Week
Holy Saturday
Easter 2
Proper 6, 12, 13, 16

Stewardship
Epiphany
Thanksgiving Day

Strength
Advent 3
Epiphany 1, 3
Lent 3
Tuesday of Holy Week
Proper 25, 27, 28, 29
Suffering
Lent 6 (Passion Sunday)
Proper 10

Table
Maundy Thursday

Teach(er)
Epiphany 8
Lent 4, 6 (Palm Sunday)
Wednesday of Holy Week
Easter 2, 6
Proper 11, 24

Temptation
Lent 3
Wednesday of Holy Week

Thanks(giving)
Christmas Season 1
Epiphany 9
Maundy Thursday
Easter 3, 4
Trinity Sunday
Proper 5, 9, 15, 16, 21, 28
Thanksgiving Day

Thirst
Lent 3
Easter 7
Proper 13

Thorns
Epiphany 8

Thoughts
Thanksgiving Day

Treasures
Ash Wednesday
Proper 14

Trembling
Epiphany 9
Easter Evening

Troubles
Easter 6

Trust(worthy)
Advent 1, 3
Epiphany 4, 6, 7
Lent 6 (Passion Sunday)
Good Friday
Easter Sunday
Proper 4, 5, 6, 11, 20, 21, 22,
24, 28
All Saints' Day

Truth(ful)(ness)
Advent 2
Christmas Eve/Day, Proper 3
Christmas Season 2
Epiphany 3, 9
Lent 1
Good Friday
Easter Evening
Trinity Sunday
Proper 20, 23, 26, 29
All Saints' Day

Understanding
Proper 24

Unity
Lent 5
Easter 7

Values
Easter 4
All Saints' Day
Proper 26

Violence
Proper 22

Vision
Pentecost
Proper 25

Walk
Easter 4
Proper 8, 13

Water
Easter 4, 5
Proper 17

Way(s)
Advent 1
Lent 2
Easter 7
Pentecost

Proper 20, 29

Wealth
Proper 20

Welfare
Proper 23

Weariness
Wednesday of Holy Week

Welcome
Proper 26

Wholeness
Good Friday

Will of God
Christmas Season 2
Lent 6 (Passion Sunday)
Holy Saturday
Proper 17

Wisdom
Christmas Season 1
Tuesday of Holy Week
Easter 3
Trinity Sunday
Proper 29

Witness
Christmas Eve/Day, Proper 3
Christmas Season 2
Epiphany 9
Lent 2, 6 (Palm Sunday)
Easter 2
Ascension Day
Proper 9, 25, 27

Word
Christmas Eve/Day, Proper 3
Christmas Season 2
Epiphany 3, 4, 6
Lent 6 (Passion Sunday)
Easter 6
Proper 6, 9, 15, 16, 17, 23, 24, 26

Work(s)
Advent 2
Epiphany 5, 8, 9
Lent 6 (Palm Sunday)
Easter 4, 5
Pentecost
Proper 4, 13, 18, 23, 26, 27, 28

World
Easter 2, 4, 6

Pentecost
Proper 18, 20, 25, 26

Worship
Epiphany
Epiphany 9, Last
Easter 7
Proper 6, 9, 11, 12, 29
Thanksgiving Day

About the Author

Lavon (Burrichter) Bayler is no stranger to worship planners, having authored four previous book of lectionary-based resources: *Fresh Winds of the Spirit* (1986), *Whispers of God* (1987), *Refreshing Rains of the Living Word* (1988), and *Fresh Winds of the Spirit, Book 2* (1992). Revisions in the *Common Lectionary* have prompted this new volume.

Since her last book, Lavon and her husband, Bob, have become grandparents to Sarah Elizabeth Bayler, in whose honor this book is dedicated. Lavon's busy schedule as minister of the Fox Valley Association, Illinois Conference, United Church of Christ, and Bob's as senior vice president for religion and health for UCC-related EHS Health Care keep them from "spoiling" this first representative of a new generation but not from carrying a full portfolio of pictures they're eager to show.

Ms. Bayler spent twenty years in parish ministry before joining the conference staff fifteen years ago. She resources and counsels pastors and congregations, assists pastoral search committees, and administers her association of fifty-two churches, often appearing in one of their pulpits on Sunday morning or on other special occasions. She has led numerous retreats, workshops, and seminars on a variety of topics.

The Baylers have three adult sons and a daughter-in-law in addition to their granddaughter.